How to Attract
INVESTORS

Customers

Right
Business
Model

Investment
Opportunity

Superior
Product

Good
Management

How to Attract
INVESTORS
a personal guide to understanding
their mindset and requirements

Uffe Bundgaard-Jørgensen

CRC Press
Taylor & Francis Group
Boca Raton London New York

CRC Press is an imprint of the
Taylor & Francis Group, an **informa** business

How to Attract Investors: A Personal Guide to Understanding Their
Mindset and Requirements

First published 2017 by Pan Stanford Publishing Pte. Ltd.

Published 2023 by CRC Press
Taylor & Francis Group
6000 Broken Sound Parkway NW, Suite 300
Boca Raton, FL 33487-2742

ISBN 13: 978-981-4745-20-8 (hbk)

This book contains information obtained from authentic and highly regarded sources. Reasonable efforts have been made to publish reliable data and information, but the author and publisher cannot assume responsibility for the validity of all materials or the consequences of their use. The authors and publishers have attempted to trace the copyright holders of all material reproduced in this publication and apologize to copyright holders if permission to publish in this form has not been obtained. If any copyright material has not been acknowledged please write and let us know so we may rectify in any future reprint.

Visit the Taylor & Francis Web site at
http://www.taylorandfrancis.com

and the CRC Press Web site at
http://www.crcpress.com

British Library Cataloguing-in-Publication Data
A catalogue record for this book is available from the British Library.

Contents

Preface

Some great musicians cannot read music sheets, and reading music sheets do not make you a great musician. The same goes for entrepreneurs and investors; formal knowledge about business theory and money does not automatically lead to success, but it might help.

More and more entrepreneurs believe that the route to success is blocked unless they get a bit of help from investor money. They often forget that money does not make the success; only an excellent business case does, sometimes in combination with investor money.

Attracting investors and living with them as co-owners is a big challenge. Getting investors "on board" is like a marriage with a pre-defined divorce (investors' exit). Remember that the shareholders' agreement is both a "marriage certificate" and a "divorce agreement".

This book addresses many of the challenges connected to investor search and negotiation, but nothing can replace practical experience.

Why This Book?

Investors are often looked upon as a homogeneous group of people with money to invest. However, they are very diverse in their investment capacity and preferences, just like car owners. The only common denominator for car owner preferences is that a car needs an engine, wheels, speeder, brakes, seats and that it can be driven when started. Which car they end up buying, however, depends on personal preferences, needs and money available. The common denominator for investor preferences is a good business case. The "engine, wheels, speeder, brakes and seats" together make the comprehensive business plan. The elements of a comprehensive business plan are discussed in Chapter 2. However, which business case the investors prefer in the end depends on their personal preferences and financial capacity. Who the investors are and the difference in their preferences are discussed in Chapter 1. The challenges connected to negotiating with investors are discussed in Chapter 3, and Chapter 4 deals with the challenges faced in living with investors as co-owners. Each chapter can be read separately.

I started writing this book a few years ago because I had experienced that attracting investors and keeping them interested posed an insurmountable challenge for many entrepreneurs and managers of young growth enterprises. Some of the big hurdles seem to be the extreme difficulty in understanding the mindset and terminology of investors.

Investor "lingo" serves the same purpose as the doctor's lingo. The purpose is to be precise and international, not to confuse. An elbow is an elbow, even if it is *caput radii* in doctor's lingo and not *albue, coude* or *łokieć*. This is practical because *caput radii* have the same meaning for a Danish, French or Polish doctor. If doctors did not have a common professional language, they would need a dictionary every time they communicated about diseases and patients. Investor lingo serves the same purpose, and by converting many of the terms into formulas, communication becomes more operational also across countries. Today you do not need a thick "guide to investor terminology" like former times; now you just "Google it". However, not all explanations found via Google on Wikipedia are easy to understand. Hopefully, this book will help you understand how investor terms are used in practice.

With respect to investors' mindset and preferences, it is simple; they want to invest in exciting projects which they can understand and which can become a success and secure a high return on their investment. However, investors always have access to alternative investment opportunities. Any business proposition, therefore, needs not only to be good but also to be much better than any other investment opportunity available.

We all know that

A success is always easy to spot after it has become a success.

This applies in the investment world, but it also applies outside the traditional investment and entrepreneurial world. When in 1995 a lonely mother submitted her first manuscript for publishing, many publishing houses turned down the offer. In the end, Bloomsbury gave her the green light. The book was published in 1997 and became a famous series of seven books which have now been read by millions of kids, youngsters and families from all over the world. The author was J. K. Rowling, who is a very wealthy woman today! The title of the manuscript was "Harry Potter and the wise stones". Was Bloomsbury's decision based on wisdom or luck? A well-known Danish publishing house turned down the offer to publish a Danish version of the international bestseller *The Da Vinci Code* by Dan Brown. They did not see a Danish market for the book, and the book did not fit their publishing profile. Another Danish publisher made money on the book.

Publishers have their own criteria for making the "yes" or "no" decision. Some criteria are common among all publishers, while others differ. Those criteria might sometimes lead to the wrong decision, and sometimes they give the right answer. The same applies to investors, who are very different but most often apply the same criteria in different ways. Therefore, if a business proposal is turned down by one investor, it does not necessarily mean that another investor will not invest. Many years back, the venture fund I managed and many of my venture capital (VC) colleagues turned down a unique investment opportunity; we did not believe they could make money! The investment opportunity was SKYPE.

All investors look for signs for a potential success, both for the business and for themselves, and if they do not see the potential success, they will not invest. The success for an investor is a potential high capital gain. In this book, we will both present some of the many criteria and checks which investors apply, and we will probe into the differences between different type of investors and their mindsets.

The New Version of *How to Attract Investors*

A short first version of this book (60 pages) was realised in 2007 as part of the EU-funded InvestorNet project. At that time, I coordinated a European network of high-tech VC funds. The current totally revised and expanded version provides a more elaborate guide into the mindset of investors who have an interest in investing in new or young growth companies. It also provides tips and advice as to what should be presented to investors in order to create interest and meet their requirements. You will, therefore, find relevant tips to tell and inputs for writing a convincing story, which needs to include a strong business model and a convincing strategy. I hope that the book will make you understand the importance of value chain analysis of a well-defined intellectual property rights strategy, the need for a strong management team and many other relevant issues. Last but not least, the book also includes a "survival guide" for investor negotiations and a life with investors.

So many good business proposals fail in getting funded for a number of reasons. The proposal is presented to the wrong investors or the presentation and business plan lacks a compelling story or reflects lack of insight into what investors need to know in order to make a positive investment decision. The business plan may also be too weak to convince the investors that they can make money from an investment. The management may fail in convincing investors that they can turn their vision into reality, simply because of lack of charisma when presenting. Last but not least, too many projects do not get funded because of an unrealistic (overoptimistic) perception of the development stage and the growth potential, when assessed from a commercial point of view.

The book is an attempt to encapsulate 10 years of personal experiences as CEO of a large Danish early-stage technology VC fund and 15 years of experiences as coach and advisor, working with investors and entrepreneurs from all over Europe. The feedback and bewilderment of entrepreneurs when they get a "no" from investors stirred my interest to write this book. The findings and conclusions have been confirmed through close contacts with international investor colleagues, while working with them as co-investors, or during the period I served as a member of the Board of the European Venture Capital Association in the 1990s. In 2014 these findings were used while advising the European Commission on application guidelines and evaluation criteria for the new Horizon 2020 SME Instrument. This new EU grant scheme financially supports the commercial exploitation of innovation results from European small and medium enterprises (SMEs). My findings during the 2 years I served as chairman of the Horizon 2020 SME Innovation Advisory Committee for the European Commission have also been used.

From practical experience, it has been demonstrated that the findings and conclusions are relevant across a broad range of technologies and industry sectors. They have, in practice, been applied in a large number of cases from different business sectors and technologies, such as food technology, transport technology, tourism, energy (both conventional and renewable), nanotechnology and photonics, ICT (in the very broad sense), medical devices, biotechnology (including drug development), publishing, elder care and social services.

The common concerns and needs of all these business cases were funding. The common hope was to attract investors or other similar type of funding. The common denominator for an approach which has yielded results has always been:

- An easy-to-understand presentation of the problem which was being solved by the solution
- A clear description why and how the solution could create value for the customers
- An easy-to-understand explanation why the chosen business model was the right one
- Good understanding of market and market conditions
- A convincing team behind the business case
- The right choice of potential investors to whom the case would appeal
- Highlighting why and how the investor could make money from the investment

In principle, it is straightforward and easy to catch investor interest. To do so you just need to have a good business case, understand the mindset of investors and their preferences and find the right investor, and last but not least, you need to be a good storyteller.

General Disclaimer

Some of the examples used to illustrate concrete problems and challenges are taken from "real life" cases. In order not to violate confidential information given to me, these cases have been modified so that individual persons or companies are not recognisable.

Acknowledgement

Some sections of this book have been written and edited as part of the EU-funded Social Innovation for the Elder sector (SiForAGE) project during 2014 and 2015. However, the bulk of the writing process took place over many years while putting bits of pieces of the "Investor Readiness Puzzle" together. The book also reflects direct input from discussions with participants in more than 125 master classes on "How to Attract Investors" that I have conducted throughout Europe since 2010. The input and reaction received from the many participants have helped in sharpening the message.

I would also like to send special thanks for constructive and inspiring input to colleagues and partners from the many EU-funded projects in which I have been involved. While finalising the manuscript, I happened to meet Dr. Aisté Dirzytè, head of Psychological Well Being Research Laboratory in Vilnus, Lithauania. Thanks to her comments which helped sharpen the final version of Chapter 4.

The book would never have been realised had it not been from the inspiration and strong effort of my co-authors and colleagues from InvestorNet-Gate2Growth, Louise Pierrel Mikkelsen, Rasmus Egvad and Carmen Bianca Socaciu, who helped to steer the book through the many pitfalls of the writing and the editorial process. Also my two sons Rune Sonne Bundgaard-Jørgensen and Esben von Bundgaard-Jørgensen Selvig have inspired me and voiced concerns and criticism when needed. My wife Lise Børresen has been the comforting and supportive witness to the long writing process.

I would also like to thank Pan Stanford Publishing for the encouragement and support during the entire editing process. However, the final responsibility for the findings, conclusions and selection of issues, cases and examples is entirely mine.

Uffe Bundgaard-Jørgensen
InvestorNet-Gate2Growth, Denmark
Fall 2016

Introduction

Many TV channels have seen a great opportunity in making a good business out of the hype connected to the funding of innovation by making "negotiations" between wealthy businesspersons and entrepreneurs hungry for funding into great TV shows. TV shows such as the "Dragon's Den" and others have attracted hundred thousands, if not millions, of viewers. They are all great shows, but the format risks giving a wrong impression of how investors in reality address the challenge of selecting investments. The shows also give a biased view of entrepreneurs and their seriousness and effort to match investor expectations. The format of a TV show cannot illustrate that attracting investors or making the right investment decisions is hard work, combined with luck. Showing this is not the objective of TV shows; the objective is entertainment and profit for the TV channel. In real life, finding and convincing investors to invest is hard work for entrepreneurs, combined with a good insight in the way investors act and think, helped with a bit of luck. In this book, we focus on the "hard work". To push for luck is up to the reader, but with better preparation, it is easier to push the luck button.

The focus of this book is on investors[1] seen as "customers" who will buy a share of the business the entrepreneur wants to sell to the investors. If you want to sell any product to a customer, you need to understand who your customer is and what his or her preferences and needs are. This golden rule also applies if you want to sell a share of your business to an investor. However, Chapter 2 on the "business plan puzzle" can also be a useful guide for any other commercial endeavour not needing investor money, or if the planned funding

---

[1]This book focuses on the preferences and behavior of investors, who make active investments in SMEs.

route is public grants such as the SBIR,[2] H2020 SME instrument[3] or similar national support schemes with business innovation objectives.

The book is also about storytelling, not fairy tales or fiction, but about telling a convincing story to investors or public grant providers about the business idea and concept.

The task to convince investors is simple, provided that

- The business case is exiting,
- It is an interesting deal offered to the investor and a good match with his or her preferences,
- The assumptions behind the business idea and vision about the future are realistic and told in a convincing way.

If you can tick √ for each of these three points, investors will listen if you can find them.

Storytelling is about convincing potential investors that a business case is an interesting investment opportunity that they cannot miss. Any good storyteller needs to know and understand his or her "audience" and understand what makes them listen and smile. He or she needs to appear trustworthy and be able to answer all types of questions about the story.

This book is also about how to find who the right investors are and how to meet with them and negotiate a fair and balanced deal. If you have already experienced that it is difficult to find and convince investors, in particular Chapters 1 and 3 have relevance.

If reading the book has not helped, or you are still uncertain about how to address the funding challenge, my advice is to find a good and trusted advisor who can help. However, be careful, not all advisors are good advisors, even if the bronze plate on the door

---

[2]The Small Business Innovation Research (SBIR) programme is a US Government programme intended to help certain small businesses conduct research and development (R&D). Funding takes the form of contracts or grants. The objective is to provide funding for some of the best early-stage innovation ideas that are, however promising, still too high risk for private investors, including venture capital firms. The recipient projects must, therefore, have the potential for commercialisation and must meet specific US Government R&D needs.

[3]Introduced in 2014, H2020 SME Instrument is a new grant scheme targeting SMEs within the European Union.

is carefully polished. Some advisors are more interested in the fee being paid than in the advice given or in finding investors. Some might find the money but not necessary the right investor for your case. The importance of finding the right investor is, in particular, discussed in Chapters 3 and 4.

When dealing with investors, two fundamentals should be understood and remembered:

1. Investors always have access to alternative investment opportunities.

2. The business proposition offered to them needs not only to be good but also much better than any other investment opportunity the investor has access to.

This reasoning also applies to most grants. In very few business-oriented grant programmes, projects which have passed a quality threshold scoring automatically get funded. The successful applications are those which are better than the other qualified applications fighting for a slice of the same limited grant budget.

Irrespective of the funding received, all projects are confronted with at least two types of risks:

1. **Controllable risks** (CR), which can be addressed to some extent through planning and knowledge.

2. **Uncontrollable risks** (U-CR), which come from the "outside world" and cannot be removed or reduced via planning. Good contingency plans may reduce the impact.

The investors will always require that the **"risk-adjusted" return on investment** (ROI)[4] is attractive.

---

[4]The ROI (or multiple) can tell "how many times you get your money back". It does not take into account the time dimension. Euro 100 today has a higher value to you than 100€ in 5 years' time. Also the term internal rate of return (IRR) is often used as a yardstick. However, IRR and ROI are directly connected. An ROI of 5 calculated on "money back/multiple" in 5 years equals an IRR close to 40%. See more about financial terms and calculations in Annexure 4.

In Chapters 1 and 3 you will find a presentation of the challenges connected to estimate both risks and the "risk adjusted return of investment".

When we talk about risk, it is not only the business or technology risk which has to be taken into account. A successful growth company can also run into life-threatening troubles from pure liquidity problems or when a needed "next round of funding" does not materialise as expected. Many "successful" companies have been lost alone due to liquidity or funding problems, and consequently the early investors also suffer a loss!

In daily life, investors do not make formal risk analysis or have access to advanced risk models. They are not sitting with a calculator making this type of probability calculation. First of all they do not know the risk factor percentage exactly, and they know that the budget based on which they try to make the ROI calculation is also connected to uncertainty. However, the risk-adjusted ROI conceptually illustrates the way they are reasoning (although subconsciously). This also means that their final decision is always influenced by the perceived risk factors.

Only if the investors believe that the risk-adjusted ROI is higher than any alternative investment opportunities available to them, they will be tempted to invest. They know that their estimation of the risk-adjusted ROI is highly subjective. It is heavily influenced by what they know about the technology and the business sector. Their final perception is also influenced by the way the "story" is told. Therefore, most investors, after being satisfied with all the formal analysis and calculations, will "lean back" and consider "after all, do I like and believe in this team and their project?" and if yes, they might make the investment.

The entire book is focused on giving an insight in the way different types of investors make decisions, and what they need to know before making this decision. It also provides guidance in how to prepare and present a business opportunity in a convincing way and prepare for the probing investor questions.

Investors will probe into all the other elements behind the budgets. They will look into the assumptions about cost, revenues and the chosen business model and many more issues, not to forget the conditions offered to them for the investment. Their decision will also be influenced by the way the case is being told, and how the probing questions are being answered. Combined together, it gives the investors an impression of you and your team. They want to quickly understand if they are facing a fool, a leader or an imposter.

The four chapters in this book provide a good basis for telling a convincing business story and to secure a good background for answering the many probing questions. It also provides tips for negotiating a fair and balanced deal.

Readers' Guide

A book like *How to Attract Investors* can be read from start to end, but it is probably more relevant to jump to the sections or chapters of the book which are most relevant to you right now and then later read the other parts. For making the book readable in this manner, some subjects have been covered more than once in the text. The book is divided into four chapters, with each chapter further divided into a number of sections. The chapters and different sections are briefly introduced as follows:

Chapter 1: Investors and Funding

This chapter provides an introduction to who investors are and what processes are normally used for assessing business opportunities. The focus is on venture capital funds and business angels. The last part also deals with the potential importance of public grants.

- **The deal funnel and investors** introduce the reader to the complicated world of investors and the background for some of the challenges entrepreneurs face when trying to attract money from investors.
- **How it all started and venture capital and business angels** focus on the different types of investors. These sections illustrate some of the challenges and risks facing investors and some of the differences between venture capital funds and business angels. They also address issues related to "willingness to take risk".
- **Risk** discusses how risks, whether real or perceived, influence investment decisions and behaviour.
- **How difficult can it be? and attracting investors** focus on some

of the challenges an entrepreneur faces during the search for funding and during negotiations with investors. They also deal with tips about what should be included in the first presentation to investors.

- **Investors, funding and grants** introduce and explain some of the different funding instruments, including public grants, their structure and requirements. They also include a discussion on the benefits of combining public grants and private investments.

Chapter 2: Business or Just a Dream: The Business Plan Puzzle

The second chapter deals with all the elements which should be considered while compiling materials to be presented before investors. The "business plan puzzle", which is used to guide you through all these elements, summarises findings from manuals and guide books on many investor websites. If you end up "ticking off" all these elements, you have a rather complete business plan, but this does not automatically imply that the business plan is good; it is only complete!

- **The 3 circles, market, sales and marketing** is a first introduction to how market assumption and customer reaction play a role in convincing investors about the soundness of a business plan.
- **Management and team** touches upon the importance or strong management teams and how difficult it is, in reality, to judge if a team is good or inadequate.
- The different sections in **business plan puzzle** provide, in greater details, an overview of the information investors normally expect to find covered in a business plan and associated material. They also touch upon the qualifications investors expect to find represented in the management team and provide guidance to tools and methods to achieve the desired levels.
- **Value chains and business models** focus on the special challenges connected to value chain analysis and business model development.
- **Competition and competitors** provide a short introduction to the type of considerations related to competitors which should be

present in the material and ready to be presented and discussed with investors.

- **IPR** or "can a patent make you rich?" discusses the various issues to be taken into consideration when making a strategy for IPR protection.
- **Regulatory issues and certification** provide observation points about these two often overlooked issues.

Chapter 3: Ready to Meet with Investors and Accept Their Investments and Conditions?

The third chapter uses a number of real-life examples to illustrate many of the issues connected to finding and negotiating with investors, which cannot be put in "formulas" or schematic forms. The many examples should, hopefully, illustrate that all cases are different, and even the best textbook cannot replace "real-life experience".

- **Funding and liquidity and investor exits** is about budgets, liquidity and ways of calculating the "pre-money" valuation.
- **Contacting investors and investor negotiations** takes you through the funding process from the realisation of capital needs until the financing has taken place. It outlines critical and important issues to consider when proceeding from one stage to the next in a process which is largely sequential rather than concurrent.
- **Terms of investment** touches upon the formal agreements and their role and various pitfalls often encountered.
- **The risk of dilution** deals with one of the important problems connected to securing funding of a business growth through a series of sequential funding rounds.
- **Management and the board** provides a few practical tips related to both management and board composition.
- **Do it yourself (DIY) or get help from an advisor** is about the role an experienced advisor can play when supporting the entrepreneur in the investor search and negotiation process.

Chapter 4: Life with Investors

The last chapter digs into aspects of the mindset of investors, which is often difficult to understand. It also, via examples, illustrates the importance of building the required mutual trust which will be needed when a crisis occurs—not "if" but "when". All companies will sooner or later be facing unforeseen challenges, and it is the ability to tackle unforeseen challenges or real crisis which makes the difference between success and failure.

- **Decisions—rational or not** deals with some of the fundamental problems connected to understand and explain investor decisions and reactions.
- **Relationship with investors and negotiation** is an anecdotal introduction to some of the many challenges which the entrepreneur might face after the investment has been made. It deals with the mindset of investors, and how it influences investment decisions, and decisions after the investment has been made.
- **Negotiations** and **exit** are the final sections which deal with the challenges of living with investors and potential solutions for avoiding conflicts.

Chapter 1

Investors and Funding

> This chapter provides an introduction to investors and the processes normally used for assessing business opportunities. The focus of the chapter is on venture capital funds and business angels. The last section deals with the potential importance of public grants.

In reality, investors can be considered as discriminating customers who might want to buy shares in your company. If you want to sell something to someone, the golden rule from any manual in the art of selling is: **get to know your customers and their preferences**. Chapter 1 intends to give a "behind the curtain" view on who investors are and probe a little into part of their mindset. It also provides an insight into how to attract their attention and understand their preferences.

1.1 Introduction

In the "good old days" when life appeared simpler, even fundraising for new enterprises was simpler. For example, in 1968 Bob Noyce's business plan for INTEL was a one pager, which still excited investors. He did his own typewriting and noted that "he had little feeling about

How to Attract Investors: A Personal Guide to Understanding Their Mindset and Requirements
Uffe Bundgaard-Jørgensen
Copyright © 2017 Pan Stanford Publishing Pte. Ltd.
ISBN 978-981-4745-20-8 (Hardcover), 978-981-4745-21-5 (eBook)
www.panstanford.com

how detailed it should be". However, he got funded despite typing errors (Fig. 1.1).

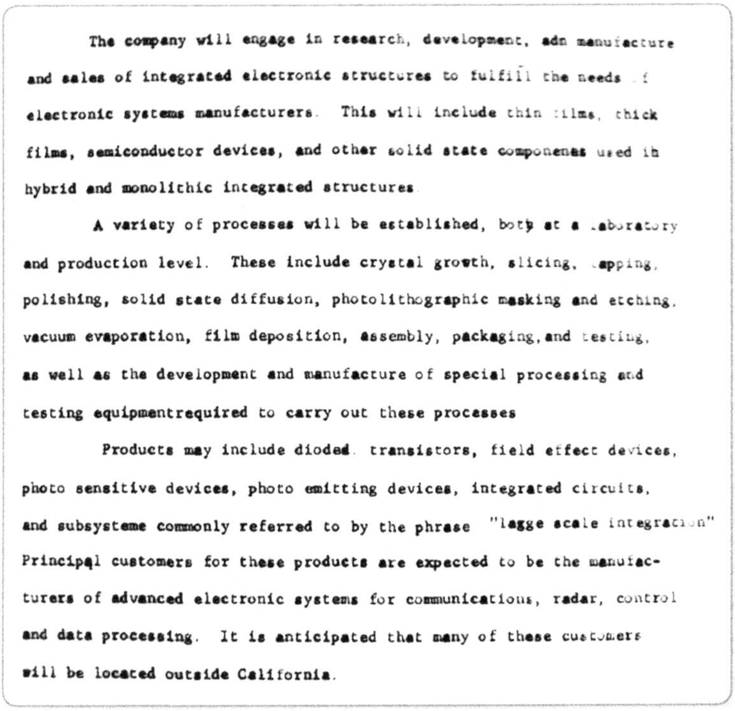

The company will engage in research, development, adn manufacture and sales of integrated electronic structures to fulfill the needs of electronic systems manufacturers. This will include thin films, thick films, semiconductor devices, and other solid state componenss used in hybrid and monolithic integrated structures.

A variety of processes will be established, both at a laboratory and production level. These include crystal growth, slicing, lapping, polishing, solid state diffusion, photolithographic masking and etching, vacuum evaporation, film deposition, assembly, packaging, and testing, as well as the development and manufacture of special processing and testing equipmentrequired to carry out these processes.

Products may include dioded, transistors, field effect devices, photo sensitive devices, photo emitting devices, integrated circuits, and subsysteme commonly referred to by the phrase "lagge scale integracion" Principal customers for these products are expected to be the manufacturers of advanced electronic systems for communications, radar, control and data processing. It is anticipated that many of these customers will be located outside California.

Figure 1.1 Bob Noyce's business plan (INTEL – 1968).[1]

Today life is more complicated, and the competition for funding is much harder. Many people do not recognise the different nature of bank financing and private equity financing.[2] Nor do they recognise, from an investor perspective, how complicated it is for an investor to invest in private equity, compared to invest in assets traded in the public market. Investors who are looking for investment opportunities in new or young companies are not a homogeneous

---

[1]Private photo of business plan taken at IT museum/USA
[2]In Section 1.12, the fundamental difference between bank and equity funding is discussed.

group.[3] Some invest "other people's money" and are often organised as a "venture capital (VC)" fund or "private equity" company. Others invest their own money and are typically called "business angels". The common denominator for all investors is an interest to make money from the investment. However, their investment preferences, risk willingness and negotiation skills and choice of investment processes vary.

A new emerging source of funding now is "crowdfunding",[4] which is the practice of funding a project or venture by raising monetary contributions from a large number of people, including potential future customers, typically via the Internet. As the motives behind crowdfunding vary between genuine interests in the output from a concrete project (e.g. a new record or design product) to pure financial objectives, this subject is outside the scope of this book.

Compared to the days of Bob Noyce, the competition for private equity funding has increased. Bank financing, as the only source of financing, is available for very few small and medium enterprises (SMEs) with a good growth potential. Therefore, today thousands of unsolicited business plans are sent to investors every year. Each business plan competes with all the other for the investors' time and money.

A bank, with its large organisation, can easily process many loan applications at the same time. However, individual investors will only allocate time for a thorough analysis and examination of a few selected projects and will eventually select even fewer for investment. The investors simply have limited processing capacity. A business angel is normally a "one-man shop", and even the VC teams are most often very small. The majority of the investment proposals received would, therefore, be screened very quickly. For the investors, time is a very scarce resource, which needs to be allocated only on potentially best deals.

---

[3]See Section 1.12 for more information about the different types of investors.
[4]The crowdfunding model is fuelled by three types of actors: the project initiator with a project to be funded, individuals or groups who support the idea and a moderating organization (the platform) bringing the parties together to launch the idea. Typical types: donation crowdfunding, reward crowdfunding, loan crowdfunding and equity crowdfunding. In 2013, this industry grew to over $5.1 billion worldwide.

Today a business plan is not typed on a traditional typewriter like Bob Noyce did. It is often composed with all the "bells and whistles" of modern computer and layout technology. Many business plans are written, while drawing on the advice from hundreds of books about business plan writing. But many entrepreneurs and their advisors seem to have little feeling for what should be included, what should be left out and how detailed it should be, and what should be send to the investors, and when, in order to catch their attention. Also identifying the right investors to approach is often left to luck. "Better more than less" characterises often the material presented to an investor. Some even e-mail the entire material in multi-colours, not only to one but to many potential investors.

The book does not intend to be a manual on how to write a business plan. There exist hundreds of good and average books on that subject. The focus is to provide a guideline to what should be included and what not when approaching investors. The proposed selection of items to be included is an attempt to reflect the mindset of investors, how they think, what they want to see, how they decide and why. It is also based on the "selection of the fittest" philosophy. Only the business proposals which have the highest quality and the best fit to the individual investors' preferences survive the investors' selection process, as illustrated in Fig. 1.2.

1.2 The Deal Funnel: Survival of the Fittest

The left part (A) of the "deal funnel" illustrates how many unsolicited investment proposals are processed in a typical VC fund (Fig. 1.2).[5] The small team of the VC fund simply has very limited time to read all the materials it receives. Hence, very short time (minutes, not hours!) is used to decide "this fits our interest or not" (see right part (C) of the "deal funnel"). However, deals presented from advisors, friends or colleagues, who know the investors' real investment preferences and risk willingness, have a greater chance of getting full attention (= B solicited deals).

---

[5]The numbers reflect my own experience from running a large Danish VC fund for many years.

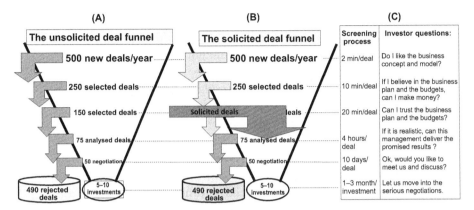

Figure 1.2 (A) The unsolicited "deal funnel"and (B) the solicited "deal funnel".

Even among those who get full attention, only a few investment proposals are selected for close examination, due diligence and investment. Therefore, it is important to structure the approach to investors in such a way that it is your proposal which continues to surface among the most interesting deals all the way through to the final investment decision.

Experienced entrepreneurs know about the "deal funnel". Therefore, they secure, via own search or with help from advisors, to identify the most relevant investors to approach. Often a direct phone contact is made with the investors before the material is send. This is done in order to secure that the investors have a prior interest in this particular investment proposal. If the pitch is right, they might even be looking forward to receive it. Even this approach does not secure an investment, but at least "full investor attention". If the investors like a proposal, but for some reasons do not want to invest, many investors provide courtesy guidance on what can be improved, or even an introduction to an investor colleague, who might be better suited for this particular case.

One could ask why so many unsolicited deals are sent to the many VC funds? The answer is simple: This type of investors are easy to find. They have their own websites, and most of the thousands of VC funds around the globe are also members of a national or an international VC fund associations (such as BVCA, EVCA and NVCA). A click on the websites of these associations and a full list of VC funds emerges with an URL to their websites!

The tens of thousands of "business angels"[6] are much more difficult to find. Most are private persons with a very selective taste for investments. Most of them do not want to advertise their wealth or investment appetite. Neither do they want to search for investment opportunities among unsolicited proposals. They are interested either in pre-screened deals which fit their preferences, or referrals from trusted friends. Many are member of national or regional business angels networks, which again often are member of international associations of business angels.[7] In particular, the regional or very local business angel network managers often provide a pre-screening function, and only those few successful deals which meet the network selection criteria are invited to present at the regular network meetings.

Irrespective of which type of investors the entrepreneur is looking for, he or she will be met with a selection and screening process not unlike the one illustrated in Fig. 1.2.

How do investors, in practice, cope with all the investment proposals they receive on an annual basis? Do they study them all, or is there a secret trick? In most cases, it is rather simple. Investors are only interested in spending time on quality projects which fit their preferences. In many cases, only four quick questions need to be answered before the investors can decide if they would commit time to a thorough examination of the business plan, commence discussion with an entrepreneur or start the "due diligence" process:

Investors need to be convinced that they:

- Like and understand the business concept and the business model.
  - » Tips to the entrepreneur:
    - ◊ Only approach investors who will understand your project and like your business model.
    - ◊ Make it easy to understand which problem(s) is solved, and the value created for the customers.

---

[6]Alone in the UK, there are more than 4000 registered business angels and more than 90 business angel networks.
[7]For example, European Business Angel Network (EBAN).

- Can make money on this investment, if they take all the information presented at "face value".
  - » Tips to the entrepreneur:
    - ◊ Make your own calculations about the investment case seen through the eyes or the investor.
- Can trust all the information in the investment summary and the business plan.
  - » Tips to the entrepreneur:
    - ◊ Make it easy to understand the value created for customers through the solution/opportunity your business concept provides.
    - ◊ Make it easy to identify and verify the assumptions on which the business concept is build.
- Can trust that the entrepreneur or the management team can deliver the expected results.
  - » Tips to the entrepreneur:
    - ◊ If possible, include good CVs and references.
    - ◊ Secure that all required competences in the management team is present and described or will be added.

If the investors have put a big "√" on each of the aforementioned issues, then it is likely that they would start a closer examination of the entire business plan, and if they are pleased with what they read and have funds available for investment right now, they might invite for a first meeting.

This first meeting might be very difficult because investors and entrepreneurs look at the investment opportunity in different ways, and often also do not "speak the same language". The entrepreneur is looking for money, and once the funding transaction has been successfully completed, the entrepreneur is relieved of seeing money flowing into his company. The investors, however, are looking for return on investment (ROI). Therefore, immediately after the transaction is completed, the investors are concerned about how to realise their ROI, i.e. when can they exit[8] from the investment and how much can they possibly gain? These different ways of looking at the transaction are why VC might be "Manna from Heaven" for

---

[8]Exit is another word for selling their shares in the company.

some companies, while other companies should be looking for other sources of financing.

During the many master classes on "How to attract investors" I have conducted around Europe, I have often asked the participants why they have come to the master class. The answer is often "because I need money". This might be the right reason, but investors do not "provide money" to people "who need money". Investors are looking for investment opportunities and want to "buy shares", if they are cheap enough and expected to increase in value! When posing the same question at similar seminars in the USA, the answer is often "because I want to learn how to impress the VCs". In Europe, you never hear the formulation: "I am here because I want to learn the best way to present this unique investment opportunity to investors." The "I need money" attitude partly explains why the dialogue between investors and entrepreneurs is so difficult in most parts of the old continent.

Many politicians and entrepreneurs actually believe that the big problem about funding of new enterprises is "lack of money". Often the favoured solution is: "If more money is provided, all will be fine", so why do the investors not just provide it?

If you look at the international capital market, money is not a scarce resource. Money is, in principle, always available if the required risk-adjusted ROI and liquidity criteria are met. So why is then funding of young growth enterprises so difficult? And if there is no "lack of capital", why do a lot of projects not get funded? This apparent paradox needs an explanation.

Some projects are unfortunately of low quality and do not deserve funding; hence it is not "lack of capital" but "bad projects" which are the cause of no funding. The real funding problem concerns business projects which seem excellent but are still not able to attract investors. However, also this paradox can be explained in many other ways than "lack of money":

- Market imperfections: The companies looking for funding and the investors who set out to finance them do not find each other.
- Investors and entrepreneurs "do not understand each other", even though they speak the same language.
- Different opinions related to the perception of "risk factors".

1.3 What Makes the Private Equity Sector so Difficult to Understand?

For an entrepreneur, the most well-known private equity source of funding is venture capital or "VC money". Although the VC funds can be easily found through various directories, getting their undivided attention is like "getting a camel through the eye of a needle", and the entrepreneur seldom understands why. The other natural source of finance is business angels. These investors, however, are often virtually invisible.

To make matters worse, the entrepreneur is often unfamiliar with the normal investor language, which is filled up with financial terms and lingo such as internal rate of return (IRR), ROI, initial public offering (IPO), net present value (NPV), preferred stock, anti-dilution clauses, β-values, exit conditions, syndication, term sheet, pre-money valuation, risk-adjusted calculations or Monte Carlo simulation. The entrepreneurs often also have problems understanding the difference between the stock market investment criteria and the special considerations to be taken by investors when investing in "private equity".

Both VC funds and business angels are professional investors who are active in the so-called "private equity" segment.[9] These professional investors, however, always have the alternative to invest in less risky and more liquid financial assets which offer the investor two-way prices. They can also invest in real estate, currencies, commodities and other fairly liquid assets. If they should choose to invest in private equity, which is less liquid, incurs higher risk and transaction costs and demands a time-consuming involvement in due diligence and other work, the investors must be compensated with a much higher expected return on the investment than can be found on the publicly traded markets.

In short, the difference between "private equity" and publicly traded assets is primarily:

- Lack of liquidity

---

[9]Private equity investment: Investing in unlisted stocks or other financial instruments for which there is no regulated market open to the public.

- High transaction cost, thus widening the spread and not offering two-way prices
- High risk and difficulties in assessing the risk/reward ratio

Higher risk goes hand in hand with the higher rewards that investors can be expected to demand for putting their capital at risk. It is generally recognised that the greater the uncertainty/risk, the higher potential ROI or IRR the investor will demand. The risk-adverse investors will invest conservatively and allocate most of their assets to investments that are considered low risk (e.g. short-term bonds of high credit quality, such as supra-nationals or government bonds denominated in the currency where they are residing). If the investors want to achieve a higher return than the low-risk offers, they need to take on more risk.

If we look at a private equity investment and focus on the early stage technology investments, the true value of a company is very difficult to assess, even after a long and costly due diligence process.

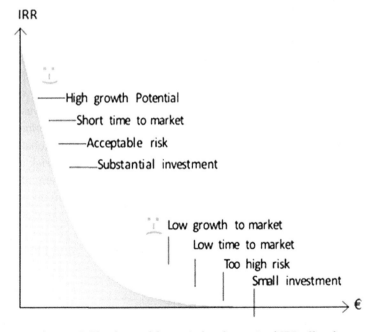

IRR

High growth Potential
Short time to market
Acceptable risk
Substantial investment

Low growth to market
Low time to market
Too high risk
Small investment

€

Figure 1.3 The demand for capital and perceived IRR offered.

We do, however, have some knowledge from empirical data. These findings suggest various relationships between cause and effect; e.g. we know that the "perceived" risk is higher the younger the company, and that the risk is consequently reduced the older and more successful the company is.

Along with increased "maturity" of a project, the expected reward expressed as the risk-adjusted ROI or IRR of a project also increases. The rational investors want to optimise the risk/reward ratio, i.e. when there is no more effect in terms of added reward being generated from taking on more risk. This holds true whether the investors are a VC fund or a business angel. Neither would invest in a project unless the expected risk-adjusted ROI of the offered investment opportunity is perceived better than any alternative investment opportunities offered by other private equity investment opportunities.

Assessing the risk or the potential realistic ROI or IRR is difficult, when it comes to investments in individual companies, especially investments in young companies with no track record or history. Risk cannot be reduced through analysis, as typically there is no data or history to analyse. Furthermore, once the investment is made, the investors are typically stuck with the investment for many years and cannot easily turn it into cash profitably. They must wait until exit, which depends entirely on past and perceived future success of further business development. Besides funding, the investors must allocate many human resources to their investment, not only when assessing the investment opportunity, but also after funding has taken place. Monitoring and developing the portfolio company until exit often prove not to be a straightforward process. These costs have to been taken into consideration as part of the overall costs of the transaction when making a private equity investment.

On the positive side, private equity investments typically offer the investors direct influence with their investment in terms of substantial voting rights in shareholder meetings, a board seat and direct contact with management. In other words, it gives power to influence decisions that have material effect on the outcome of their investment.

1.3.1 Influence of Risk on Investment Preferences

It is difficult for any outsider to understand the individual investor's different types of investment preferences. Some investors have experience and background within some sectors. Therefore, investment opportunities from these sectors are looked upon with greater interest than proposals from other sectors/technologies. Some investors have a longer time horizon for their investment than others, and the willingness to take risk also differs. There is, therefore, a need to have a basic understanding of the different types of private equity investors.

In order to illustrate the differences in investment behaviour, we will look at the major differences in attitude to risk between the two major sources for finance in the private equity market, VC funds and business angels, in Sections 1.5–1.8. These two types of investors may not react in the same way with respect to risk. However, they are both an important source of funding for new companies.

In the USA, business angels have, for many years, funded[10] 30–40 times more ventures annually than the venture capitalists. According to various sources, including the National Venture Capital Association (NVCA), USA, it is suggested that the business angel community invests about $100 billion in entrepreneurial firms, which represents between three and five times the size of the VC industry.[11] In the UK, it is estimated that business angels invest more than three times as much capital in small entrepreneurial firms than the formal VC markets. The number of firms that business angels fund in the UK may also be 30–40 times greater than the number supported by venture capitalists.

Even if the size of the European business angel market is less impressive than its US counterpart, "angel funding" represents a substantial part of the funding of entrepreneurial firms in Europe. Despite the current significant size, the potential scale of the business angel market is probably much greater than the current figures suggest. Some academics suggest that the actual size of the

---

[10]*Angel Investment: Matching Startup Funds with Startup Companies—The Guide for Entrepreneurs and Individual Investors*, Mark van Osnabrugge and Robert J. Robinson, John Wiley & Sons, 2000.
[11]See footnote no. 3.

business angel market potentially could grow into 10–20 fold the size of few years ago. However, since the millennium, the market for risk capital has undergone significant changes with more focus on risk than back in the late 1990s. Therefore, it is relevant to look at the investment pattern and differences in risk behaviour of these two major funding sources.

1.4 How It All Started

We can start by looking back in time and examining how the concepts of the modern times, "venture capital" and "business angel", developed. Let us take a look at how it became the important founding basis of many of today's successful technology firms not only in the USA, but also in Europe and now slowly also in other parts of the world. It is fair to say that the concepts of VC and business angel started in the USA a few decades after the Second World War. That it started in the USA may not come as a surprise, when looking at the American business culture. In the book *Fish Can't See Water*,[12] the authors Hammerich and Lewis argue that the American culture or the "frontier spirit" and the "American dream" make American corporate executives act boldly, show willingness to invest and aim at getting the biggest piece of the pie.

Hence, "once upon a time"—so all the good stories start—before the VC industry emerged as a special asset class of its own, groups of these successful executives regularly met over a lunch at the university faculty clubs at Berkeley, Princeton, Stanford, Harvard or MIT, actually also some British executives met in similar cosy places in Cambridge and Oxford, UK. Those who did not meet at the university faculty clubs probably met at "The 19th hole" of the local golf club. In order to please their professor friends, they began to do small private investments in business concepts of bright students. They were all successful businesspersons or former entrepreneurs themselves and could remember the difficulties experienced back in time when they started their own business. They were now attracted by the emerging and exciting new technologies of the 1960s and

---

[12]*Fish Can't See Water: How National Culture Can Make or Break Your Corporate Strategy*, Kai Hammerich and Richard D. Lewis, Wiley, 2013.

wanted not only "to be good" but also to make money. These early investors soon demonstrated that they were able to spot new technology and business concepts and they were also willing to take substantial risks.

The saying goes[13] that they often invited a young aspiring entrepreneur to join their lunch. The invited entrepreneur would, in most cases, have been recommended by some friendly professors of their acquaintance. The entrepreneur was invited to present his or her business idea. After the presentation, the entrepreneur was dismissed, while the lunching party discussed the proposal on their own. If an agreement to invest in the venture was made, and each member of the lunching group had decided for his or her personal size of participation, the entrepreneur was called back in and the terms of the investment were presented to him. If the entrepreneur agreed, a lawyer was called in to do the legal foot-work, and a few weeks later, the company was given initial funding and on its way to success, or failure. One of these investments was actually in Bob Noyce and in INTEL. It is also said that the birth of companies such as AOL, Amazon and Cisco and many other of today's household names came about in this way. Some benefited from investments from one single "angel", while others benefited from "lunch consortium" investments. Even Bill Gates started Microsoft from a business angel investment of $280.000 some 30 years ago; this turned out to be a very profitable investment!! SKYPE also got started based on angel investments.

Since then a number of non-tech but high-growth companies have benefited from similar type of private funding, such as Curves, QB (Quick Beauty) House, Starbucks and other rapidly growing "Blue Ocean"[14] companies, which are not tech companies, but sprung out of the service sector.

The success of many of these investments (the failure was not much spoken about) attracted other people with money to invest in high-risk and (potentially) high-reward projects. Many of these

---

[13]I have met a few of these persons and have the story "directly from the horse's own mouth".

[14]*Blue Ocean Strategy: How to Create Uncontested Market Space and Make the Competition Irrelevant*, W. Chan Kim and Renée Mauborgne, Harvard Business Review Press, 2005.

people did not want the direct involvement in the portfolio companies like these first "venture capitalists" or "business angels", as this special breed of investors is now called. However, they trusted these guys who were able to spot potential winners and willing to invest their own money along with the funds coming from their friends. These newcomers pooled their individual money into a fund from which a "fund manager" could invest, and the "venture fund" concept was born. Later professional asset managers actively began to raise formal funds for this type of investments. The capital requirements grew with the number and the size of portfolio companies. This, in turn, led to structured offers being made to financial institutions such as insurance companies, pension funds and mutual funds offering the opportunity to participate in these exciting new types of investments. The investors in the VC funds are often called "fund of funds" investors. Today they also include large corporations with substantial liquid assets.

Substantial capital gains were made through both trade sales[15] and exits via IPO at the then new electronic stock exchange NASDAQ. This again led to the emergence of still more VC funds. The biotech revolution with its substantial appetite for capital and the "new Internet economy" added fuel to the market. So over the years, a whole new financial industry and asset class, "the VC industry", was born, and the business angel segment continued to strive.

1.5 Venture Fund and Its Performance Challenge

The typical venture fund of today looks like Fig. 1.4. It is organised with a management company which invests in a number of portfolio companies through one or more "closed-end"[16] funds, each with a maturity of 10–15 years.[17]

The money in the fund from which the VC fund managers invest in the portfolio companies often comes from institutional investors (pension funds, mutual funds, fund of funds, saving institutions,

---

[15]Trade sales: the investor sells his or her shares in the company, e.g. to a larger corporation.
[16]A closed-end fund is a fund with pre-determined period until liquidation.
[17]If the fund still has money on the account, then after 10–15 years, the money would be paid back inclusive of eventual capital gains.

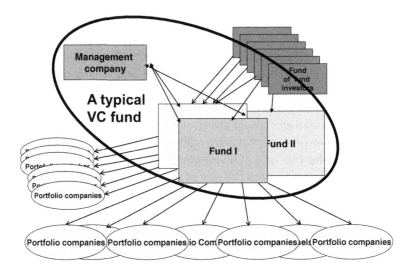

Figure 1.4 The typical structure of a VC fund.

insurance companies and industries). These institutional investors allocate a few percentage of their capital under management for investments in the VC asset class. But they also expect to see a return, which reflects not only the risk they are taking but also the liquidity constraint imposed by having their money locked for a period of 10–15 years.

The principle behind a closed-end fund is that it will be liquidated after a pre-determined period. This puts certain constraints on the investment strategy of the VC fund managers. They primarily make new investments when the fund is young, monitor and nurture the successful portfolio companies with follow-up investments later in the funds' lifetime, and the last part of the lifetime of the fund is a rush for exiting from the investments made. Many of these fund managers are more or less in a constant fundraising process, or considering it. In order to "stay in business", the management company should regularly address the financial market and raise new funds to replace those, which are getting closed and liquidated.

The following analysis of risk management strategies is primarily related to the behaviour of VC managers of closed-end funds, but it also applies to "evergreen" funds.[18,19] The financing of evergreen funds is normally provided by shareholders from the institutionalised finance industry. The predictability of fund performance and achieving "industry performance benchmarks" also plays an important role here.

Over the years and following the success and growth of the VC industry, the way business is conducted has slowly changed. Not only did VC teams with substantial funds under management begin to enter the later-stage market and engage in the lucrative management buy-out (MBO)/management buy-in (MBI) and pre-IPO market, but also the VC funds which were being faithful to the early stage concept had to adhere to the business objectives of the institutional investors and their requirement for meeting predefined investment return "hurdle rates".[20]

Over time, the classical VC funds, which were originally based on private as opposed to "institutional" money, got replaced by VC funds largely financed from institutional investors. The good thing about this development was that the capital available for investments grew. However, the conditions to get access to this capital, which was chasing high returns from the rather illiquid VC investments, also changed. In this new market, a precondition to raise a new fund quickly became based on "proven past performance" and an ability to demonstrate performance at least equal to the minimum hurdle rates. The institutional investors preferred to invest in funds managed by management teams, who had demonstrated a good track record.

This is, in principle, an absolutely reasonable investment strategy, but it has potentially severe implications. A VC management

---

[18]An "evergreen" fund is a fund which is not pre-destined to be liquidated. Such funds are often operated under a normal corporate structure; some are public listed, i.e. 3i.

[19]To complicate matters further, some closed-end funds are taken over by financial institutions, e.g. banks, and converted into evergreen funds, while maintaining a successful management team.

[20]"Hurdle rate" is a term used for the expected minimum return on investment the investors in a fund require to be satisfied. Often fund performance above the hurdle rate is divided between investors and the VC management team with a ratio of, e.g. 80/20.

team which is failing to achieve the hurdle rate is not greeted with great smiles from its investors, and the doors are closed for new fundraising! Many of the institutional investors became hesitant to invest in new funds, which were to be managed by young teams who had not yet demonstrated continuous fulfilment of the hurdle rate requirement. The requirement to produce such a track record of high performance has put enormous pressure on short-term performance of a fund and has, to some extent, led to an avoidance of taking unnecessary high risk. It is recognised that the real success of a fund cannot be properly demonstrated until the final proceeds from the VC operations are transferred to the investors after liquidation of a fund. However, spectacular exits early in the lifetime of a fund can provide a good starting point for fund managers in the process to raise a new VC fund.

There are many good reasons behind the performance requirements from the institutional investors. One of them is related to the behaviour of the normal reader of this book, who also wants a good return on private fund, e.g. life savings! Among investors in VC funds, we find pension funds and life insurance companies. If your savings are in a pension fund, you, dear reader, would also like the highest possible return. Therefore, you would normally choose the pension fund which demonstrates the best performance. Therefore, the quality of the managers of the institutional investors also becomes measured on benchmarks related to the industry.

In this game, a "balanced score card" does not exist. Over-performance of a benchmark or hurdle rate is not rewarded in a balanced way compared to the "punishment" for underperformance. This has an important influence on the way risk is managed by the individual VC fund managers. The managers of the institutional investors can hedge the risk by investing in a balanced basket of VC funds. The managers of the VC fund only have their own performance to rely on; hence they also need to hedge the risk. In their case, it is done by diversifying their investment into a number of portfolio companies.

It is also important to understand the principles behind the remuneration system in the entire capital "food chain". Therefore, you need to understand the reaction pattern of the individual agents in the different levels in this capital food chain.

If we consider the period from 1980s until now (2015), the VC industry has experienced a rapid growth. A substantial number of funds for investments have become available and with unprecedented amounts of money ready to be invested. However, a large part of the VC industry has also become "institutionalised" and increasingly focused on the "predictability of the performance of its portfolio". In order to attract more funds to the VC industry, the spokespersons of the organisations NVCA, British Venture Capital Association (BVCA) and European Venture Capital Association (EVCA) also began to promote the VC industry as an "asset class" and introduced "standard reporting criteria and accounting principles". This was a great achievement and made it possible to attract still more funds from institutional investors.

These efforts have greatly improved the quality of the statistics about fund performance and shed light on which type of VC investments are more likely to produce stable predictable returns. The result is an increased interest in allocating funding for the successful part of the VC industry by institutional investors. It has also created much more focus on the risk/return ratio related to investment in the different phases of business development, be it seed, early stage or later stage.

The positive results and good performance of the "later-stage" sector investments compared to the rather random excellent performance within the early stage sector are unfortunately shifting the interest of the institutional investors, including the large European Investment Fund.[21] The interest has moved from "classical venture capital funds", which are early stage tech investments, to the more mature segment of the VC industry. Most probably, this trend is caused by the overall better returns offered by these later-stage funds, combined with less risk for the investors.[22] This also means less risk for the asset manager of the institutional investors, who might otherwise risk losing his or her job for taking on investment

---

[21]The European Investment Fund supports Europe's micro, small and medium businesses by improving their access to finance through a wide range of selected financial intermediaries across Europe. (www.eif.org)

[22]Over both 10- and 30-year periods, the share of dollars invested, which go to losing deals, has been roughly 55%. Venture Capital Returns and Loss Rates, Bruce Booth, Pharma and Health Care, July 2012.

risks without being able to harvest the sufficient rewards in the form of high returns. In the end, it is always a question of risk–reward ratios.

However, despite an average low performance of early stage investments, there are clear examples of very high performances of certain very experienced early stage technology funds, but the variation between good performers and bad performers is greater in this segment than it is in the later-stage segment.

The explanation behind the high performance is partly a result of the ability to "pick the winners" and/or intelligent combination of seed funds and later-stage funds under same management[23] and partly a result of excellent monitoring and support to "star" portfolio companies. The good result is also derived from optimal timing of when to invest and when to exit, a few "lucky punch" and finally the ability of killing unsuccessful ventures early on (not throwing good money after bad money).

I once met the R&D manager of one of the largest German pharmaceutical companies. When I asked him what characterised an excellent R&D manager of a large corporation, he answered: "Not necessarily the ability to pick the good research results to promote, but to kill failures early on, but only obvious failures, which makes it dammed difficult!" The same principles apply to good VC fund managers.

1.6 Business Angels

It is said that the term "angel" originally came from Broadway theatre, where it was used to describe wealthy individuals who provided money for theatrical productions. In the 1980s, the term "angel" was used to describe the investors who supported young technology companies. Although the individual investors who gathered in at the

---

[23]At Atlas, across both Technology and Life Science franchises, we believe a seed-led, measured approach to investing can help us channel capital towards winners more effectively: we provide start-ups with small amounts of seed capital (<< \$1 M) to cherish their theses, and we watch for early "signal" around team, product/technology and market traction. We are expecting our post-A-round capital-weighted loss rate to be far less than historic industry averages. Venture Capital Returns and Loss Rates, Bruce Booth, Pharma and Health Care, July 2012.

19th hole or in the faculty clubs of the Ivy League universities hardly saw themselves as "angels", they guided their investment behaviour in order to make sound business investments and to support brilliant entrepreneurs on their way to fame and glory.

Today business angels are often retired entrepreneurs or executives who may be interested in investing for reasons that go beyond pure monetary return, but a financial return is still expected. Business angels are not sponsoring a venture in order to be mentioned in the annual report as benefactors. The motivation may include an interest to be kept abreast of current developments in a particular business arena, mentoring another generation of entrepreneurs or making use of their experience and networks on a less than full-time basis. Thus, in addition to funds, business angels can often provide valuable management advice and important contacts.

Around 2007, there were more than 200,000 active business angels in the USA and more than 4000 in the UK. The number of investments made per year matched these numbers. Both in the USA and Europe, business angels have started to coalesce into informal groups with the goal of sharing deal flow and due diligence work, and pooling their funds to make larger investments. These business angel networks are generally local organisations made up of 10–150 accredited investors interested in early stage investing.

The past few years, both in North America and Europe, have seen the emergence of networks of business angel networks, through which companies applying for funding with one group are then brought before other angel groups to raise additional capital.

Business angels typically invest their own money, unlike the venture capitalists who manage the pooled money of others in a professionally managed fund. For business angels, although typically reflecting the investment judgement of an individual, the actual entity which provides the funding may be a trust, a business, a limited liability company, investment fund or other vehicle.

A Harvard report[24] by William R. Kerr, Josh Lerner and Antoinette Schoar provides evidence that business angel-funded start-up companies have historically been less likely to fail than companies that rely on other forms of initial financing. The reason is probably

[24]The Consequences of Entrepreneurial Finance: A Regression Discontinuity Analysis, William R. Kerr, Josh Lerner and Antoinette Schoar, HBS Working Knowledge, Hbswk.hbs.edu, Retrieved 2012-12-01.

the strong personal involvement in the company by the business angel investor as non-executive director or mentor.

The business angel capital fills the gap in seed funding between FFF—family, friends and fools—and more robust early stage financing through formal VC. In general, there is no "set amount" for business angel investors, and the range can go anywhere from a few thousand to a few million euros.

In general, business angel investments bear extremely high risks and are usually subject to dilution[25] from future investment rounds. Because a large percentage of angel investments is also completely lost, when early stage companies fail, professional angel investors seek investments which have the potential to return at least 10 or more times their original investment within 5–7 years and through a defined exit strategy.

Current "best practices" suggest that business angels should set their sights even higher, looking for companies which will have at least the potential to provide a 20×–30× return over a 5- to 7-year holding period.

After taking into account the need to cover failed investments and the multi-year holding time for even the successful investments, however, the actual effective IRR[26] for a typical successful portfolio of angel investments is, in reality, typically as "low" as 20–30%, and not all business angels have a successful portfolio of deals. Because the investors need high rates of return on any given investment, it can make business angel financing an expensive source of funding, because you will need to give up a large part of the ownership in order to secure a high return for the investor.[27]

However, cheaper sources of capital, such as bank financing, are usually not available for most early stage ventures.

1.6.1 Other Relevant Investors with Alternative Investment Objectives

Both business angels and VC funds can be characterised as "financial investors" whose primary interest is to have a financial return from

---

[25]See Section 3.5 for dilution and other risks.
[26]Internal rate of return.
[27]See further discussion on this subject in Chapter 3.

the investment, primarily in the form of capital gains, but could also be in the form of dividends. In theory, they tend to compare the risk-adjusted ROI of any new investment opportunity with the potential return from all alternative ways of money placement. Also, in principle only, the farther away their knowledge is about the technology and business environment of the new investment opportunity, the higher is the perceived risk.

Therefore, there will be a tendency that these investors are very much focused on proven revenue streams and exceptional high growth potential. However, for many businesses with a more modest growth potential or ambition, there are other private equity investors around: particularly larger businesses from the same sector which could have a professional or business interest in securing that new products or services are provided, which their own business could also benefit from.

In a recent discussion with an inventor from Tunisia, the issue of Intellectual Property Rights (IPR) was brought up. He had developed a new and efficient eco-friendly way of protecting different horticultural products against pests and insects. Patent protection had been filed for Tunisia only, and the focus of his business concept was Tunisia. This means that the business growth potential, protected by this IPR, was not exceptionally high. As the perceived risk was still high because no international sales or market penetration could substantiate a high growth business case, an attractive investment case indicating double-digit growth rate could not be established. Would this mean that private equity funding would be excluded, as the standard benchmark returns could not be met? Not necessarily, because in this business sector, there were other big players, both large horticulture producers and larger export companies who could see larger business opportunities for themselves, if they could export "eco-certified" products.

Some of these companies could potentially become investors. Their ROI requirement would assumingly be lower than the requirement from the financial investors, partly because the perceived risk was lower (they know the market and themselves a potential customer), partly because they have a self-interest in getting this new bio-pesticide into the market, because that would enhance their own business.

This type or investors exist and can be identified through canvassing the larger players in your own business segment, and trying to find out who among the most important players are active also on the investment front. Many good companies have been funded this way, not with 100 million euros, but with enough money to secure that the worst barriers for growth can be removed. However, securing investment from this type of investors creates a new challenge, namely to secure that the shareholders' agreement to be signed does not block, in the future, the attraction of more direct financial investors if funding requirement suddenly becomes bigger, because unanticipated new business opportunities are opening up.

I have seen many corporate shareholders' agreements which have been formulated with a focus on only this type of investors. If the wordings in these agreements are not carefully formulated, such an investment could turn out to be very costly, in particular if the text in the shareholders' agreements does not anticipate that other types of investors need to be attracted, e.g. investors with a very strict focus on short-term financial return.

The case example in Chapter 3 (Section 3.4), where a grant-optimising strategy has been pursued, illustrates how important it is to secure that short-term funding solutions do not block the realisation of long-term solutions. The example illustrates how a short-term grant-optimising solution changed from being a blessing to a burden.

1.7 Management of Risk

The two types of private equity investors, business angels and VC funds, look upon investment risk in different ways. This has wide implications for the availability of funding for early stage technology companies. To illustrate this difference, we will in particular examine in this section the art of "management of risk". The examination is based on the assumption of general "rational behaviour" with respect to investment decisions, an assumption on which much economic theory is built. It is a relevant question to seek an answer for, if this assumption, in reality, applies to the individual investor. This assumption will be challenged later in this book. Although most investors will argue that they act in a fully rational way, and that their preferences are transparent and consistent, it is demonstrated in Daniel Kahneman's excellent book[28] *Thinking Fast and Slow* that this does not always reflect real-life decisions.

However, let us, as a starting point, take a look at how risk is managed by a fully rational management team of a closed-end VC fund and compare it to the similar "rational behaviour" of a business angel. As both types of investors are an important part of the source for funding of new businesses, it is relevant to try to get a deeper insight in their investment strategy. Are the more risk-adverse VC mangers "chickens", and are the risk-taking business angels just naive people who love to take risks? Or does it just make business angels "feel good" to help a new start-up? Or is there an apparent rational behaviour behind investing in start-up and early stage companies and incurring lots of risk, but potentially also high reward?

Ideally there should be no difference between the two types of investor attitude to risk, if the investment goal is financial reward and the investment capabilities are the same. However, there are strong indications that the behaviour is different. This is primarily due to the asymmetrical "reward" principles in the funding funnel of VC funds. In the monograph *Willingness to Take Risk*,[29] analysis has been done in two ways, partly as a numerical simulation exercise and partly by using mathematics derived from traditional economic theory. From this analysis, we can directly jump to the conclusion:

> Under *ceteris paribus* conditions, the rational behaving VC management team will take fewer and smaller risks than the rational behaving business angel.

This conclusion ought to have wide political implications as regards to the importance of supporting and encouraging more business angels to step into the early stage technology market.

Let us first review the "food chain" for the funding or capital fund. In general terms, all our savings are chasing the highest return, with due respect to risk and liquidity. In the long run, the risk-adjusted

---

[28]*Thinking Fast and Slow*, Daniel Kahneman, Penguin Books, 2011.
[29]*Willingness to Take Risk*, Uffe Bundgaard-Jørgensen and Rune Bundgaard-Jørgensen, Copenhagen, 2007.

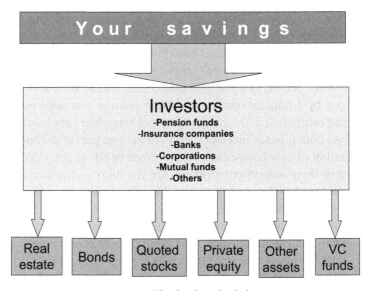

Figure 1.5 The funding food chain.

return from investing in the different market segments should balance. Economists can argue for a lifetime over which period such a calculation shall be made. So while waiting for a response, let us just, for the sake of argument, accept this assumption.

Figure 1.5 illustrates in an oversimplified way the "funding food chain". The total amount of money available for investments comes from all the savings made by individuals (including your own saving for your pension), companies and institutions. This money has a large number of investment options. In theory, at least, money will flow in the direction where the risk-adjusted return is the highest. Hence, money will not flow in the direction of VC as an asset class, if the expected return offered does not match alternative investment opportunities.

If we look at the capital flowing into the VC segment, we find that the institutional investors also have more choice between different types of VC funds. There exist many different types of venture funds and market segments, each with its particular risk and return profile. The reasoning about long-term "equal return" should also govern the investment policy here.

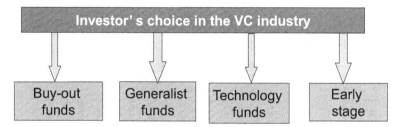

Figure 1.6 The venture capital segment.

However, a little depending on the period analysed, on average later-stage funds perform over the return from early stage funds. However, some fund of funds investors still hope for the "lucky punch" with early stage funds, and it is also evident from, e.g. the EVCA statistics that the performance of the upper quartile of early stage fund in some periods is a nice match to the return from later-stage funds. So despite the historical average lower performance of earlier stage funds, the capital is still flowing in the early stage VC direction. Admittedly, "the ticket" to be a successful player in the later-stage market is also much higher than "the ticket" to the early stage sector, as successful later-stage funds are generally much larger than early stage funds. This may also explain why some institutional investors invest a smaller amount in the early stage VC sector simply because the entry ticket is cheaper.

1.7.1 Venture Capital Risk Management

Let us now take a closer look at the individual VC fund (exemplified by "Fund 1" in Fig. 1.7). Let us examine its risk behaviour in a situation where the management team wants to stay in the market and be able to raise new funds, when the old ones get liquidated. The return to the fund investors (the institutional investors) from the individual VC funds managed by the team is generated through the capital gains achieved from the successful exits from its portfolio investments. Thus, over the lifespan of the individual VC fund, a large number of individual portfolio investments are made; some are successful, while others turn out to be failures. When the decision to invest is made, each portfolio company is believed to be the winner; however,

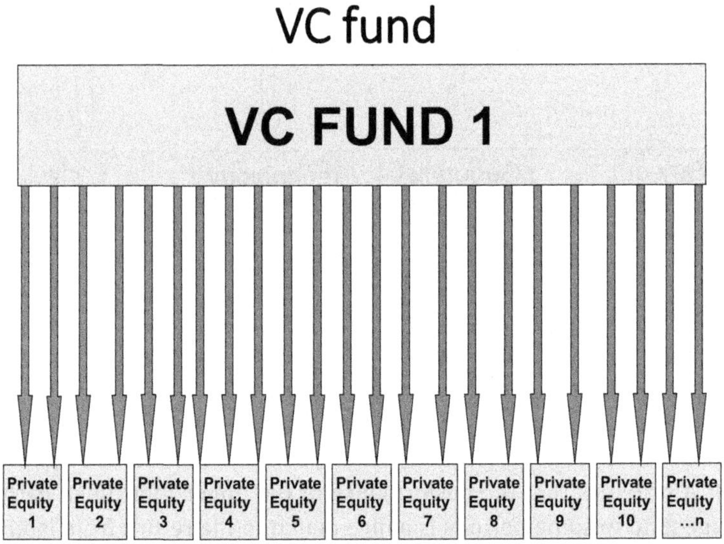

VC fund

Figure 1.7 Venture capital fund 1's investments in portfolio companies.

the management team knows from experience[30] that only a few will become the winner, but not which one!

It is reasonable to expect that the potential for capital gain is positively correlated to the risk. The risk exposure may be directly correlated to objective risk factors, or indirectly correlated with the price to pay for the shares in the portfolio company. So over the lifetime of a fund, some very bold investment decisions are to be made by the management team. These decisions are influenced by the potential for capital gain, but also heavily influenced by the underlying requirement of "not to underperform with respect to the hurdle rate". A precondition to raise a new fund is often based on a "proven past performance", which at least is equal to the hurdle rates. It put enormous pressure on short-term performance of the fund and avoidance of taking unnecessary risk. As previously mentioned, in this game a "balanced score card" does not exist. Over-performance

---

[30]Over both 10- and 30-year periods, the share of dollars invested, which go to losing deals, has been roughly 55%. Venture Capital Returns and Loss Rates, Bruce Booth, Pharma and Health Care, July 2012. Furthermore "lemons come before grapes", meaning the realised losses occur before successful exits are realised.

of a benchmark or hurdle rate is not rewarded in a balanced way compared to the "punishment" for underperformance.

1.7.2 Business Angels Risk Management

Let us then take a look at the business angels or the high net worth (HNW) individual, which is also a term often used.[31] Let us assume that these private investors are not investing for charity or offering grants. They invest in a professional way in order to make money and to have fun. However, they are willing to carry a certain risk, because they only put a small portion of their total assets into the private equity segment (Fig. 1.8).

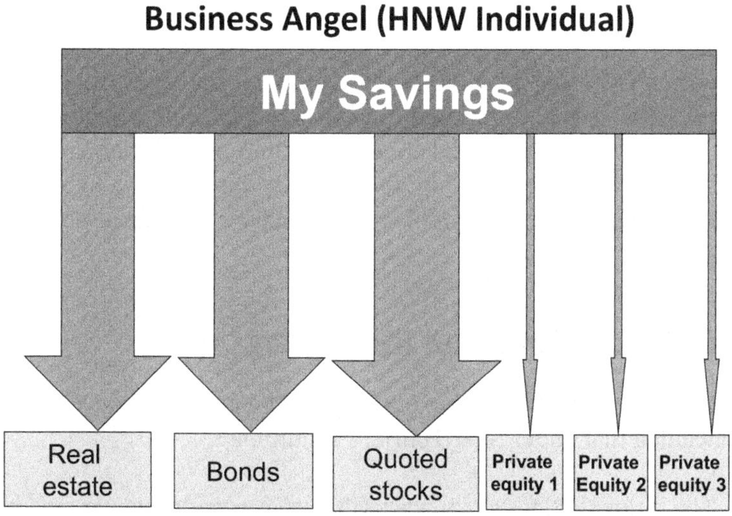

Business Angel (HNW Individual)

Figure 1.8 The investment strategy of business angels.

Although the term "business angel" is probably going to stay, it is such a nice term; many entrepreneurs receiving their money will realise that the money comes more from an "investor" than from

---

[31]Business angels and HNW individuals are not synonyms. Not all HNW individuals do business angel investments, and not all business angels are regarded as HNW by the special private banking section of the large financing houses.

an "angel" and that some "angels" are very demanding![32] Many entrepreneurs have been deceived by this "angel" term and are in for a big surprise when they experience a brutal but professional business behaviour from the "angel".

In our analysis, we have assumed that the rational behaving business angels will invest only a fraction of their total assets in the private equity segment. This fraction is determined by their private utility function in such a way that their utility will not be adversely impacted even if the investment is lost. Some business angels might have a greater appetite for risk, but that does not have any effect on the conclusion of our analysis.

As illustrated earlier, the business angels spread out their total investments in such a way that they achieve an acceptable and secure ROI from the majority of their assets. The rational business angels will only allocate a smaller part of their assets to high-risk investments. From a rational point of view, the total (relatively small) loss of the investment allocated to high-risk investments, such as private equity investments, will not severely impact the overall performance of their total assets. On the other hand, a substantial gain from this allocation will have a significant positive impact.

1.8 Conclusion about Risk Taking

In the analysis made in the monograph *Willingness to Take Risk*, we concluded that under *ceteris paribus* conditions:

- The rational VC fund manager will prefer to trade a lower upside against the protection of a downside, and hence aim at a risk-balanced portfolio strategy. Thus, increasing the chance of not getting fired or being unable to raise a new fund.
- The rational business angels, who have the major part of their capital invested in "low-risk" assets (quoted shares, bonds, gold, real estate), will allocate their limited risky private equity

---

[32]A successful Danish business angel even invests under the name "Black Wings" to illustrate that he or she does not invest for fun or charity, but for return on investment.

investment into projects with substantial upside potential and will be willing to take the associated risk.

Or formulated in a different way:

- Managers of closed-end VC funds which are capitalised through institutional investors will have a tendency to seek a risk-adverse investment strategy, and thereby protecting the "downside" of the hurdle rate.
- It is reasonable to assume that the same prudent investment strategy will be chosen by managers of evergreen funds capitalised on market conditions.
- "Classical/private" VC funds capitalised and managed by a few individual wealthy individuals/family funds will have a tendency to seek an aggressive "high potential" and "risk acceptance" investment strategy in order to over-perform market conditions.
- The rational business angels will allocate their limited risky private equity investment into projects with substantial upside potential and will be willing to take the associated high risk.

When looking at other differences between VC funds and business angels, when they make investments and investment decisions, it has to be recognised that the VC funds normally have the capacity to do a more structured and in-depth due diligence than the business angels. The VC funds will normally also have much more investment opportunities to choose from than the normal business angels. Statistics indicates that while many VC funds receive 300–700 investment proposals per year, and only invest in two to five projects per year (less than 2%), the typical business angels invest in a much higher percentage of the rather few projects which passes their doorsteps.

1.9 How Difficult Can It Be to Convince Investors to Invest?

Even if you adhere and adapt to the observations about investors, their preferences, rational behaviour and investment and risk strategy, it is evident that many good projects do not get funded. There are many reasons. Some are related to inadequate presentation of the investment opportunity to the investor community, and some are related to insufficient search for the right investor. Some are simply related to the fact that even the perceived "good" project turns out to be unrealistic or too risky.

Although it is a big challenge to make the right and convincing investor presentation and identify the right investor to approach, too many entrepreneurial teams favour the do it yourself (DIY) methods while searching for funding. This is another type of typical irrational behaviour which we can observe in daily life. Few people would sell their real estate without the help of a real estate agent or professional advisor, or cure a severe disease guided by Google search. However, when it comes to the hunt for funding, the attitude is "how difficult can it be?" Even if it is the first time in their life they are in search for funding and they have no prior experience or qualification, on top of the DIY method, many entrepreneurs often also address the financing issue too late. This lack of awareness of the problem can be called an "ostrich attitude": "If we do not recognise the problem, it may go away all by itself". It is often a result of the "super ego" of some entrepreneurs, or fears of meeting an experienced advisor and hearing his or her harsh verdict. Maybe the fear is similar to the fear of going to the dentist.

Other explanations may be found in a combined European cultural/social behaviour. Many Europeans do not like to ask for advice from other people, particularly not when it is related to money. When Europeans meet, they normally do not talk about money; talking about the weather is much less controversial. In the USA, you talk about money even in the lift! To ask for help on financial matters in Europe can be perceived as if you are not in command of the situation, and that the situation is controlling you. If we compare the European situation with that in the USA or Israel for that matter, the traditional US entrepreneur is much more inclined to seeking advice on financial matters than the European entrepreneur.

Whatever the reason, it is important to make it acceptable to speak openly about such issues and seek adequate advice. Experience shows that many more projects would get funding if a more professional investor search and negotiation process had been adopted.

1.10 Attracting Investors

Investors are attracted by exiting business opportunities which have the potential to grow and become valuable companies and which offer good opportunities for the investors to exit, meaning eventually sell their shares, after the company has either been listed on public stock exchanges (the IPO route) or is sold fully or partially to another company (trade sales).

The art of attracting investors—if the business case has these qualities—is to formulate the case in a short and convincing way and present it to the particular investors, where the case matches their preferences.

Investors look for all the same elements any competent management team of a company should look for. Therefore, it is not a waste of time to make a good analysis and presentation. It can also serve as a guideline for business development even if the funding is not found during the first attempt.

Investor search is often an absolutely new challenge for both start-ups and more mature SMEs, which are often managed by the founder or the founding team. Having external investors represented in the board might be an even greater challenge. If the development until now has primarily been based on "bootstrapping" or relied on the 3Fs funding support, there has been no need for external interference in the decision making. Among themselves and their team members, they know what they are doing, what their ambitions are and what they hope to achieve. Some even have been able to create a Board of Directors with good friends and relatives to support the venture.

Many successful family owned companies work in the same way. As long as business development can be funded by internal family sources or by a revenue stream from sales or licensing or drawing on a bank credit line, the business can live well in its own enclosed decision cubicle.

1.10.1 Explain What You Are Doing

However, if entrepreneurs want to attract external investors, they will meet new challenges. The first challenge is to explain and convince the investors what they do, why they do it and how this will be an even greater success with the new investor money. This is evident for themselves but not for external investors. Actually they might never have considered their business case in a structured way because the solution chosen has "just been obvious".

The three circles in Fig. 2.1, Chapter 2, are a good starting point for explaining "the obvious". It is not enough that there is a big market or a unique technology or obvious benefits for potential users. It all needs to be in place at the same time, the importance of which will be further discussed in Chapter 2.

The first thing the investors would want to understand is what value the services or products of the company are bringing to their existing or future customers. A convincing answer to this question will give an indication of the type of market the company is addressing and its size now and in the future.

The next obvious question is about what problem the solution solves, for whom and how and why. Not only the investors need to know why the company's solution is better/cheaper/easier than any alternative competing solution, but also the applied business model[33] needs to be convincing. It is also important for the investors to understand why the customers will buy "today" and not wait until a "tomorrow" which might be far away. Finally, the investors need to get a good impression about how the solution is delivered to the customers and how it is produced.

It is also important to provide a convincing impression of the experiences and quality of the management. Actually the more convincing and complete the explanation of the business case is, the more trust is created with respect to management competences.

However, the investor money is not a free grant. It is money looking for a potential return, which can also compensate for the risk encountered. Therefore, the investors will examine if the deal offered is more attractive than any other investment opportunities available. Only if the investors are convinced about the superior quality and opportunity offered, they would invite for a dialogue about the investment opportunity.

---

[33]See Section 2.12 for business models.

Chapter 2 further explains which types of more concrete information are required before an investor can make an informed opinion on whether the investment opportunity offered is of interest or not.

1.11 Investors and Funding

In order to attract investors' interest, it should be clear for the investors that an investment in the venture over time can satisfy their appetite for ROI. It is, therefore, advisable to make a few ROI calculation of the same type as the investors will be doing. If done before approaching investors, you will get a good impression on whether the deal you are offering could be of interest to investors.

For start-ups and early stage technology companies, the investor benchmark will often be between 30% IRR[34] and 60% IRR, to be realised in 5–7 years. One may wonder why the IRR benchmark is 30–60% when you can borrow money in the bank for 5–8%? Just try to borrow those money in a bank, particularly if you represent a young company with little bankable asset and no financial track record! However, this perceived high IRR benchmark can be easily explained via a risk analysis.

The example illustrated in Fig. 1.9 is the same VC funds and VC management company which were previously illustrated. Now we have just added numbers and made some fairly realistic assumptions.

- The institutional investors who are assumed to provide the money to the VC Fund I are assumed to expect a premium above Euribor[35] of between 10% and 12% as a condition to make funds

[34]The "internal rate of return" is the rate at which an investment project promises to generate a return during its useful life. The "minimum required rate of return" is set by the management. Under this method, if the internal rate of return promised by the investment project is greater than or equal to the minimum required rate of return, the project is considered acceptable; otherwise, the project is rejected. The internal rate of return method is also known as the time-adjusted rate of return method.

[35]The Euro Interbank Offered Rate (Euribor) is a daily reference rate published by the European Banking Federation, based on the averaged interest rates at which Eurozone banks offer to lend unsecured funds to other banks in the euro wholesale money market (or interbank market).

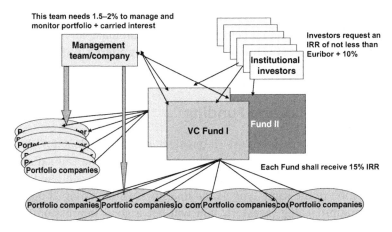

If risk is 50%, then each portfolio company shall have the potential to generate 30+ % IRR.

Figure 1.9 Risk and IRR requested, a VC example.

available for this asset class. The premium reflects the perceived risk and a premium for the illiquidity of the investment for the entire period of 10–12 years.

- The VC management team requires between 1.5% and 2% of funds allocated to cover the cost of operating the fund, making monitoring the investments in portfolio companies and exit from the investments. Often, if the total result of fund over its lifetime exceeds the "benchmark" (in the case Euribor +10–12%), the investors and the management team share the spoil in a ratio which might be 20/80.

- Combined, those two assumptions require that the result of the investment activity from Fund I needs to generate an IRR of not less than 15%.

Those are simple basic assumptions. The 15% IRR from Fund I shall be generated from investing and exiting from a number of portfolio companies. If we assume that the average success rate of these investments in portfolio companies is 50% and the money is lost on the non-successful investments, it is easy to see that the successful exits need to generate at least 30% IRR to compensate for the losses. If the risk is higher, the successful exits shall generate even higher IRR in order to create the 15% IRR, which is needed to cover management costs and return to the institutional investors.

In the case of seed and early stage investments, the success rate is often much lower than 50%. Hence, many early stage investors, in particular business angels, require an IRR potential much higher than the 30% IRR benchmark, before they even consider looking at a case.

Only solid high growth–oriented business ventures can match these expectations. And if the numbers do not match these expectations, it is better to revise the business plan and business concept or leave the dream of attracting investors as an unrealistic dream. However, intelligent tailoring of a business plan and business strategy can change the numbers. Likewise if the deal to be offered to investors can become more attractive, alone by offering the investors a large part of ownership of the company against their investment, then this option might be relevant to consider.

If the entrepreneur or the management team is not familiar with this type of calculations and analysis, they either need to learn it or team up with a good advisor who knows investors and how they think and act. The best advisor is a person with previous practical experience as an investor.

1.12 Funding via Debt, Equity or Public Grants

1.12.1 Introduction

In order to complete the innovation funding picture, it is relevant to quickly recapitulate the major type of funding sources. Not all are relevant to all, but before making a final choice, it is relevant to consider all possible alternatives. In principle, innovation can be funded in five very different ways, which many entrepreneurs tend to forget. When entrepreneurs are confronted with the following figure (Fig. 1.10), it always starts a lively discussion:

In addition to pure research grants, the public sector has, in recent years, made grants to companies available in various ways, as a means to stimulate innovation and company growth. Notably the US Small Business Innovation Research (SBIR),[36] which has been in place for decades, has had a substantial impact on the creation

---

[36]The Small Business Innovation Research (or SBIR) programme is a US Government programme, intended to help certain small businesses conduct research and development.

There are five ways of funding innovation projects:

The "hard" way
Bootstrapping: Secure that revenues from consultancy or sales can cover the cost of the innovation project.

The "Expensive" way—but also often the intelligent way
Convince investors to invest in the company and provide funding for the innovation project, and "give away" part of the ownership in the company.

The "strategic" way
Convince strategic business or industrial partners to provide funding, either as equity or in the form of convertible loans or similar financial instruments.

The "difficult" way
Borrow from a bank. Just try-you will find it is rather difficult. Banks love security-and hate risk. Remember, you will need to repay the loan!

The "smart" way
Apply for public or private "grants". You do not give away ownership. No need for repayment of the money, and evaluation criteria focus on opportunities-and if funded it might also attract investors!

Figure 1.10 Innovation funding.

and growth of new companies in the USA. In the European Union (EU), a new type of EU grants for innovative SMEs, the Horizon 2020 SME Instrument,[37] was introduced in 2014. This new innovative grant scheme has substantially improved funding possibilities for both business innovation and product and service innovation within the EU. The aim was to use the same success and selection criteria as those an investor would be using. Therefore, a good H2020 SME application shall, in principle, cover all the same elements as an investor presentation, except for a few special "investor criteria". Similar business innovation incentive schemes are also in place at the national level in Europe and around the world, or will undoubtedly pop up.

Later we will look at how such grants can coexist with and even support access to private or commercial innovation financing.

---

[37]The HORIZON 2020 SME "co-funding action" is a new "Champions League" grant programme aiming at (co)funding the first steps in the commercialisation process of excellent innovation by SMEs from the EU and associated countries. The application process is open for all SMEs, and through a professional and transparent evaluation process, only the selected best projects will receive funding.

1.12.2 Banks as Lenders and Investors as Providers of Private Equity

In order for a company to get access to the different types of funding, the suppliers (banks, investors, grant providers and others) will make their individual analysis while applying different types of criteria.

All banks are "very much alike" despite their attempts to differentiate themselves. Before providing loans, a bank will look at the accounts and budgets of the firm in order to establish whether it has the expected cash flow for the repayment of the loan, and in addition, the bank will look for ways of securing its loans against the assets in the case of default.

Like the bank manager, the investor will look at the assets and the debt service of the company but will also take into consideration the future value of the firm for the exit. He is primarily looking for an upside.

While debt providers will look for guarantee and cash flow coverage, equity investors will look to upside potential while benefiting from the leverage. They both rely and look at the same financials, and the material to be provided to them can, in many cases, be more or less the same. Good business performance for debt service will usually benefit shareholders as well. It will also increase debt capacity.

Debt financing is often the preferred way of financing if liquidity requirements are short term or limited. However, for larger liquidity requirements of more permanent nature, equity financing is often the preferred route. Debt financing is normally provided by banks and other traditional financial institutions but it can also be provided by equity investors as part of a combined equity/loan package.

It is not possible to give general advice as to which type of financing a company should choose besides grants, which most often are "free money with little strings attached". What has to be chosen depends on the individual situation of the company and the availability of the different types of financing. However, in many cases, the company might have no choice.

1.12.3 Loans

The advantage of debt financing is that no ownership to the company is given up if the needed liquidity is secured via loans. The other advantage is that it is the company which pays the interest and the repayment of the loan, not the shareholders. And finally, it is always a good idea to have close relations to a strong bank. Contrary to some people's belief, many companies have benefited from having long-lasting relations to a bank and its whole range of financial services. However, too heavy debt financing can have a negative impact on the balance sheets, and the suppliers and customers could become nervous. Furthermore, lenders might be difficult to find, especially if the company cannot present any guarantee, collateral or a steady income stream. It is also worth mentioning that the more risky the loan, the higher the interest to be paid. Furthermore, paying interest and repayment of the loan will have an impact on the liquidity of the company.

1.12.4 Mezzanine Debt

A "hybrid" financing vehicle called "Mezzanine loan" exists, which has some of the advantages of a normal loan. It ranks close to equity on the balance sheet. A Mezzanine loan is traditionally offered by a specialised financial institution or a venture fund. Normally, the loan is without guarantee or collateral; it has a low payable interest but a much higher roll-up interest to be paid at the maturity date. The loan is normally associated with a set of warrants to be exercised at maturity. The value of the warrants is by the lender expected to provide the extra return on the financial transaction which compensates for the risk involved. The repayment of the loan and interest payment is at the cost of the company, while the warrants become a "contribution" by the owners, who will suffer a dilution to their shareholding when exercised. Mezzanine loans are normally only offered to companies with a proven track record and steady sales. In the case of a default, Mezzanine loans normally include provisions that the lender can take control of the company in order to safeguard his loan.

1.12.5 Equity

Equity financing basically means selling shares of the company to outside investors. This means that part of the ownership of the company will be transferred to new owners. These new owners might also want to exercise control of the company relative to their ownership of the company. The advantage of equity financing is obvious. There is no money to be paid back, and the financing is "interest free". Dividends to shareholders do not have to be paid if the company does not make profit. An infusion of equity also strengthens the balance sheet of the company. The problem, seen from the angle of the entrepreneur or other owners, is that the ownership is spread to more shareholders, and consequently the current owners experience an ownership dilution. Equity financing is the "final form for investment", meaning that the money invested stays with the company. The analysis and considerations behind an equity investment are, therefore, of a completely different nature than the analysis to be conducted before offering a loan. The only way an investment can become liquid again is though selling the shares in the company. Dividends will seldom secure the full repayment of the investment.

In Chapter 3, we will examine the investment decision process more closely and also discuss an often overlooked risk associated with the early phases of financing: "the dilution problem".

1.12.6 Cost of Financing Should Not Be the Only Factor Influencing the Choice

When considering which type of financing to choose, it is equally important to consider the supplier reaction in the case of temporary or more permanent difficulties in servicing the requirements of the instrument.

If a company is defaulting with interest or principal payment on a loan, the conditions for the loan may be triggered or the entire loan might be called. If there is not enough liquidity to fully answer this call, the lender may try to cover his claim by calling the guarantors or take control of the assets underlying the collateral. In many cases, this can lead to a complete stop of activities of the company and eventual liquidation or bankruptcy. The interest of the lender is to secure the outstanding balance of the loan by securing all types of assets available as guarantee or collateral for the loan, in many cases also eventual deposits on other accounts in the same bank. Basically, the lender has no interest in trying to help the company out of its difficulties, in particular not if such supportive actions reduce the value of the guarantee or the collateral. Not all lenders will act like this, but the rational lender will take this path.

If a company does not live up to the expectations behind an equity investment, the investors can do nothing unless they are in control of enough voting rights to influence the decision of the Board of Directors. However, if it comes to calling for new money, they might be in a strong position to set their terms before new investors are invited to come in, or they themselves can provoke a substantial dilution of the founders of the company by setting their harsh conditions for an eventual rescue financing.

As explained, there is a substantial difference between the reactions of lenders and investors to mishaps. The lenders will try to grab guarantees or collateral to secure their claim, while the investors can only act by trying to make the company survive and infuse more money, or by starting a process of selling off assets. Therefore, the two different types of financing sources will also conduct their due diligence in a different way. The lenders will concentrate on guaranties or collateral, while the investors need to analyse the entire business model and can secure their investment only by getting direct or indirect access to influence the governance of the company.

In Chapter 3, we will discuss in greater details how combination of different types of financial instruments can play a part in the negotiation process with investors.

1.13 Grants as a Funding Source for Business Innovation

The common denominator for receiving a grant, either from a programme such as the SBIR (USA) or the H2020 SME Instrument (EU), is a good application, which covers in a convincing way all the elements in the commercialisation process of excellent innovation.

For the H2020 SME Instrument, the aim was to use the same criteria for getting funded as the criteria an investor would be using. Therefore, a good H2020 SME application should, in principle, cover all the elements in the so-called "business plan puzzle" except for the special "investor criteria". As you can see in Fig. 1.11, the two "puzzles" are almost identical; the only missing elements in the H2020 version are "investor return of investment", "agreements" and "investor exit" considerations.

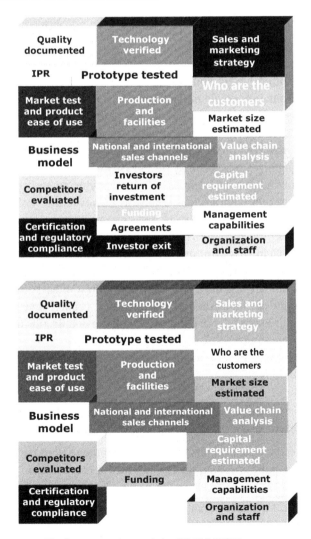

Figure 1.11 The business plan and the H2020 SME Instrument puzzle.

In Chapter 2, we will revert to the individual elements of the so-called "business plan puzzle". Therefore, even if an application for a H2020 SME grant is not successful, a substantial part of the job has been done for writing a good proposal to an investor. A further advantage is that investors will know that the selected projects which get funded via the H2020 SME Instrument have been evaluated by the same criteria as the investors would be using and have been selected for their excellence out of a pool of tens of thousands of applications. The same applies for public grant schemes in other countries/regions where the grant criteria are of similar nature as for the SBIR or H2020 SME grants.

However, a word of caution is needed. The public grant evaluation process is often based alone on a written application. This means that the evaluators solely make their decision based on the text in front of them. This also means that many applications are written by an expert consultant. This undoubtedly often increases the success potential. However, if the same consultant solution is chosen when approaching investors, this may be a grave mistake.

Investors might be impressed by a convincing written story presented to them in a professional way. However, the "evaluation" of an investment opportunity is not done only based on written material. It is done through a detailed due diligence process, covering all the underlying assumptions behind the business case, combined with in-depth discussions with the entrepreneur and his or her team. If it quickly becomes clear during the first of these meetings that the material forwarded is a "consultant report" and that the entrepreneur is not fully in command of all the details, this may well be the last meeting.

However, whichever way an H2020 SME grant is secured, there are two obvious advantages:

1. The first is the money, which in 2015[38] and the next few years is 70% of the project cost up to €2.5 million.

2. The second is the quality signal (also to potential investors) that this company is among the few innovative companies in Europe,

---

[38]H2020 SME Instrument Grants: Phase 1 up to €50,000, Phase 2 up to €2,500,000. The grant covers 70% total cost.

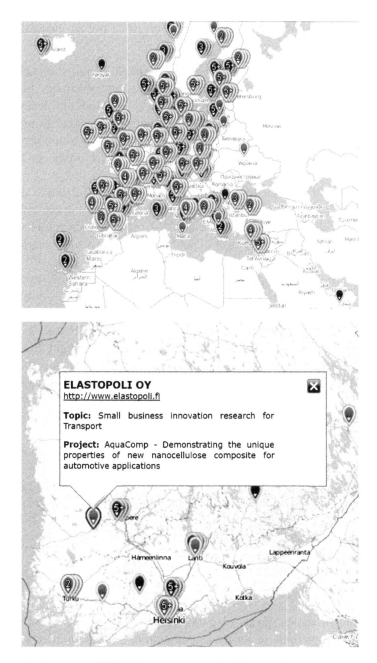

Figure 1.12 H2020 SME Instrument beneficiaries (June 2015).

which actually lived up to the very strict H2020 evaluation criteria.

An example of how a public entity like the EU Commission helps investors in finding these excellent companies which has been supported by grants is shown in Fig. 1.12. The Commission actually publish a list and a map of all the projects which get funded. A simple click on the Commission's interactive map will display to interested investors or industrial potential partners a short profile of the recipients.

The political objective behind a grant scheme like the H2020 SME Instrument is to reduce the risk connected to the funding gap called "valley of death" and create a "bridge" between research grants and private investments. The overall political objective is to strengthen European competiveness.

An H2020 SME grant can also be used to secure funding for a project which had been turned down by investors, because the investors had found that the combination of funding requirement and risk was too high. In many of these cases, however, the investors have indicated that they might invest if the funding from their side was reduced, and the gap filled by other sources. They did not propose to reduce the project budget. This interesting aspect has been formally illustrated in the official report in 2015 from the H2020 SME Innovation Advisory group, which I chaired.

The example illustrates a typical business case where it initially would have been impossible to secure investor funding; however, after an H2020 SME grant, the case became an attractive investment opportunity. This offers a win–win situation:

- For the investors who see the risk reduced and the "upside" increased
- For the entrepreneur who needs to give away less equity in order to attract investors' attention

One of the purposes of public innovation support is exactly to make it possible to secure exploitation of innovation, where no alternative funding possibilities exist, and make otherwise too risky projects attractive for private investors.

Box 1.1 Bridging the funding gap

In the example, the capital requirement for the new project is €2000K, which is sought from an investor against a 33% stake in the company. The budgeted value of the company in year 5 is assumed to be €23,000K. If the investor exits in year 5, his IRR will be 40%, which is a nice deal—on paper!

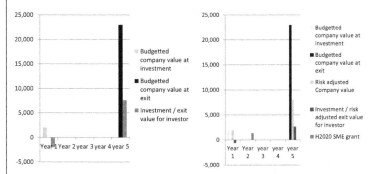

Investment case and company exit value 'as budgeted'

Investment case and company exit value 'risk adjusted'

However, budgets are often more dreams than reality. Hence, the investors in this example, based on previous experience, make a 'risk-adjusted' calculation of their expected return, using a risk ratio of 65%. This changes the expected IRR from 40% to 7%. Now it is no longer a nice deal.

If the company, in contrast, receives an H2020 SME grant to cover 70% of the total cost of the project, the entrepreneur can invite the investors to join the venture at the same 33% ownership conditions and only request an investment of €600 K. Now the investors will be smiling! Even if they maintain their original perception of risk of 65%, their IRR calculation now shows 45%.

	Expected Investor IRR
Private investment €2,000K; budgeted exit value realised	40%
Private investment €2,000K; risk-adjusted IRR if project risk is 65%	7%
H2020 grant €1,400K; private investment €600K; budgeted exit value realised	89%
H2020 grant €1,400K; private investment €600K; budgeted exit value realised; risk-adjusted IRR if project risk is 65%	45%

However, if life turns out as budgeted, the investors will get the jackpot—an IRR of 89%. This scenario creates a good bargaining position for the entrepreneur to secure a better deal than if the H2020 SME funding had not been available.

It has also become a heated political issue: Who is the real winner from, e.g. a public grant such as the H2020 SME Instrument, is it the entrepreneur or the investor? The typical argument from many politicians is "we will not use tax-payers money to support the 'rich' investors!" But is it, in reality, the investors who are supported by the grant or the entrepreneur? Can there be another angle to the public-funding issue, namely to preserve both the interest of the entrepreneur and the founding investors (e.g. the FFF or the small business angels)? Can public co-funding via grants during the most risky innovation phases support not only the entrepreneurs but also the early financial co-founders in situations where investors will request a high premium to cover the risk? If this is the case, public grants designed intelligently can actually promote the availability of more business angel investments.

1.13.1 Grant Optimising

An example can show how a public grant, such as an H2020 SME Instrument Phase 2 grant of, e.g. €1.5 million, when used in the proper way, can strongly support the interest of both the entrepreneur and the early investors (e.g. business angels) in a young enterprise.

In the example, we compare a funding scenario for a young company with and without public grants. In the case there are 2 type of investors, the founders (business angels) and VC funds. We assume in the beginning of year 1 that the founding business angels get 50% of the shares against an initial investment of €500,000 and the entrepreneur retains a 50% ownership.

The company needs a total of €3.5 million in funding during year 1 to 3; thereafter, it becomes cash positive. The shareholders are assumed to exit from their investments in year 6 based on an estimated exit value of €20 million.

Summary of the two cases:

- **Case 1:** Fully funded by business angels and 2 rounds VC fund investments.
- **Case 2:** The initial funding like Case 1 is complemented by a €1.5 million H2020 SME Instrument grant in the end of year 1. The remaining €1.5 million funding from a new investor in year 3.

The VC fund investors request a risk-adjusted IRR of 30%. The perceived risk in year 1 is considered high (50%), while the perceived risk in year 3, when the next funding round takes place, is reduced to 25%.

The required risk-adjusted IRR to compensate for the risk and to be used for calculations on the assumed budget looks like the numbers below:

	Year 1	Year 2	Year 3
Perceived risk	50%		25%
Investor risk-adjusted IRR requirement	30%		30%
Requested calculated IRR	**60%**		**40%**

If the business case should be funded only by external investors, they would require the above-mentioned benchmark return of investment. The cash outcome after exit for the entrepreneur, the founding business angels and the two VC funds (investors 1 and 2) would then look like "Year 6" column in the table Case 1:

Case 1

€1000	Year 1	Year 2	Year 3	Year 4	Year 5	Year 6
Funding requirement— exit value year 6	1000	1000	1500			20,000
Entrepreneur investment percentage part of exit value						600
Founders (business angel/seed fund) investment and part of exit value	500	0	0	0	0	600
Investor 1 investment and part of exit value	1500		0	0	0	15,000
Investor 2 investment and part of exit value	0	0	1500	0	0	3800

The reason is, in order to secure an attractive outcome from the investment while taking into consideration the perceived high risk, the VC fund investors need to acquire a big ownership in the company for their investments. This can only be achieved by using a very low "pre-money"[39] valuation at the time of investment. The table above clearly shows that the VC investors will take the bigger "slice of the exit cake" as a compensation for the risk they have taken.

This can be compared with Case 2, which provides a better "outcome" for the entrepreneur and the business angel /founders. In Case 2, Investor 1 funding is fully assumed to be replaced by an H2020 SME Instrument grant of €1.5 million. In this case, the entrepreneur and the founders benefit financially from not being diluted by "Investor 1 investment".

In Case 2, the initial business angel funding and ownership distribution is the same as in Case 1. However, it is now assumed that a €1.5 million H2020 grant replaces Investor 1 funding, while it is assumed Investor 2 invests at the same terms as in Case 1.

Case 2

€1000	Year 1	Year 2	Year 3	Year 4	Year 5	Year 6
Funding requirement— exit value Year 6	1000	1000	1500			20,000
Entrepreneur investment percentage part of exit value						8000
Founders (BA) investment and part of exit value	500	0	0	0	0	8000
EU H2020 grant	1500		0	0	0	
Investor 2 investment and part of exit value	0	0	1500	0	0	4000

We can also compare the outcomes of the two cases with respect to IRR and ownership at the time of exit:

---

[39]See Section 3.3 for definition and explanation of pre-money valuation. To illustrate the consequence of "high" and "low" pre-money valuation: high pre-money valuation = high price per share; low pre-money valuation = low price per share

Case 1

Fully diluted	IRR	Ownership
Entrepreneur	NA	3%
Founders (business angels)	3.1%	3%
Investor 1	46.7%	75%
Investor 2	26.1%	19%

Case 2

Fully diluted	IRR	Ownership
Entrepreneur	NA	40%
Founders (business angels)	58.7%	40%
Grant	0.0%	0%
Investor 2	27.8%	20%

The realised IRRs for founding investors and VC investors are shown in the tables above. When comparing Case 1 with Case 2, it is easy to see that because Investor 1's investment (where the risk is still high and, therefore, the "pre-money valuation" is very low) is replaced with a public grant, the entrepreneur and the founding investors (business angels) avoid being diluted. In this way, they also get a possibility to benefit from a high exit price. In Case 1, the business angel only gets a 3% IRR, while in Case 2, the business angel gets an IRR close to 59%, provided the expected exit value materialises.

It can, therefore, be easily concluded that public grant schemes such as the EU Commission's H2020 SME Instrument not only provide funding and protection against dilution for entrepreneurs but also support the interest of the early financial investors such as the business angels.

A number of similar cases can be made that will show similar results: Public co-funding of business innovation can, if used in the intended way, not only provide substantial funding possibilities during the risky phase of innovation exploitation, but also provide a possibility for the entrepreneur and the early financial founders to have a nice harvest from their risk taking and efforts.

A few word of warning. If a "grant-optimising" strategy is pursued to the extreme that company structure and localisation are also tailored to maximise the amount of grants, the blessings of "soft non-diluting" money can quickly turn into a burden. This will be further discussed and illustrated with a concrete example in Chapters 3 and 4.

Chapter 2

Business or Just a Dream: The Business Plan Puzzle

> This chapter deals with the elements which should be considered when compiling materials for presenting to investors. The "business plan puzzle" will guide you through all these elements. It summarises previous experiences from working with excellent business plans and findings from the many manuals and guidebooks found on international investors' websites. If you end up "ticking off" all these elements, you have a rather complete business plan, but this does not automatically imply that the business plan represents a good business case; it only means that the material is fairly complete!

2.1 Introduction to the "Three Circles"

When explaining an investment opportunity to investors, which is based on an innovative business idea, the three circles in Fig. 2.1 provide a good starting point. Using this structure makes it easy to explain to investors what is "obvious" for the entrepreneur but new to the investors. In order to have a good business case, it is not enough that there is a big market or a unique technology or obvious

How to Attract Investors: A Personal Guide to Understanding Their Mindset and Requirements
Uffe Bundgaard-Jørgensen
Copyright © 2017 Pan Stanford Publishing Pte. Ltd.
ISBN 978-981-4745-20-8 (Hardcover), 978-981-4745-21-5 (eBook)
www.panstanford.com

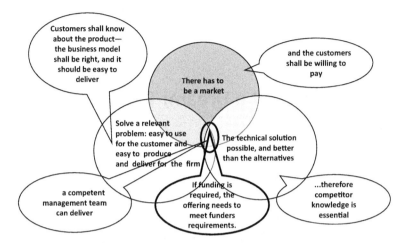

Figure 2.1 The "three circles" explained.

benefits for potential users. It all needs to be in place at the same time. This is illustrated where the three circles intersect.

When assessing a potential business opportunity, an analysis of competition and competing solutions is most often the key element. As long as the new solution is better, cheaper (much cheaper), more efficient and in other ways clearly stands out against any competing solutions, it is fairly easy to defend and explain the case. Data can probably be provided to assess the market size and potential. However, if the business case is a solution to unmet needs, the explanation becomes more challenging. It requires a special ability to feed the imagination of the investors, and the entire valuation discussion becomes very difficult. Last but not the least, even if the market and customers' willingness to buy is substantiated, it is also important to substantiate that the demand will materialize "today" and not sometimes in the future.

A number of interesting successful business cases are based on providing solutions to "unmet needs". Some of these have been analysed in details in the bestseller *Blue Ocean Strategy* by Kim and Mauborgne.[1]

---

[1]*Blue Ocean Strategy: How to Create Uncontested Market Space and Make the Competition Irrelevant*, W. Chan Kim and Renée Mauborgne, Harvard Business Review Press, 2005.

Following the success, this book has become the holy grail of many new business ventures. However, to copycat is not easy. Many ventures have failed simply because the business opportunity was not well examined, or competitors had already captured the market, or the solution was launched too early or too late. Another route to failure is when the management team does not have the stamina and qualification to do it right. It is also easy to forget that some of the very obvious "blue ocean strategy" successes, e.g. Skype, became a success because the timing was right, the supporting technology was suddenly available (bandwidth) and a few brave investors[2] believed in the team, actually some of them even believed more in the team than in the business case.

2.2 The Market

If you want to build a world-class business, it is not enough that there is a worldwide need for the services provided or the new product. There should also be customers who are willing to pay—today—and not in a distant future. Often it is not the user who pays but a completely different entity, who is the paying customer. But only if the solution also creates value to the customer, he or she will pay.

In the Skype business model, definitely the users do not pay. The value is created through the marketing value of having access to millions of users, their profiles and their accounts. The value of the direct access to millions of users made Skype a financial success and led to the acquisition of Skype by eBay in 2005.

With today's $2.6 billion purchase of Internet phone service Skype International S.A., eBay Inc. is making its boldest bid yet to remain the most potent force in e-commerce. The online marketplace, dogged by concerns about slowing growth in its core U.S. market, said Skype will help it not only recharge existing and new businesses within eBay, but help it ride an entirely new online communications business. "Together, we can pursue some very

---

[2]One of the early business angels in Skype, Morten Lund, said that he invested in the great team behind Skype. He had doubted the business case, but he was sure that if Skype did not become a success, the team would find another successful business venture.

significant growth opportunities," eBay Chief Executive Margaret C. Whitman said in an early-morning conference call. "We can create an unparalleled e-commerce engine."[3]

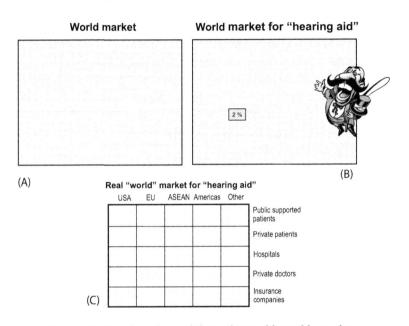

Figure 2.2 World market and the realistic addressable market.

Although Skype captured a large international market, most products or solutions do not have a "world market". As illustrated in Fig. 2.2, the world market is highly segmented, not only country wise, but also sector wise. This means that for each of the individual market segments, the company needs to establish sales channels, specific business models and competitor monitoring. In the end, the success of a new business venture often highly depends on choosing the right market to start, and from there build a strategy to expand into the other parts of the market.

To illustrate the challenge of market segmentation, we can look at a new "implantable hearing aid", from a new company created by an entrepreneur, whom we can call Mr. H. Ighhope. This new medical device is easy to put in place in the ear through light surgery and should make life more comfortable for the hearing impaired.

---

[3]Bloomberg, 12 September 2005.

Undoubtedly, the world market (A) for hearing aid is immense and an intended market share of about 2% (B) would create a very successful business. However, the "world market" does not exist. Any market is divided into segments which could be national states or regions (C). Within each of these vertical market segments, "users" and the usefulness of the new devise might be more or less the same, but the customers differ.

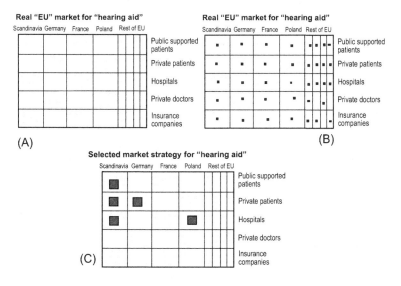

Figure 2.3 The addressable market.

If we now look, e.g. at Europe (Fig. 2.3), the target customers will also be different depending on the individual national health and social security systems and health insurance coverage. In some countries, the individual patient decides and covers all costs. In other markets, the national social health security system covers some but not all costs. To complicate matters further, in some countries and for some patients with severe hearing problems, all costs are covered. In other countries, the patients' costs are not covered unless a hearing problem is diagnosed by a doctor. Again in some countries, costs are reimbursed only via private health insurances. In those cases, the product, the need and the chosen solution are decided not by the patient and the doctor but by the insurance company and its internal approval processes. And there is no logic to why the situation differs so much other than political and cultural differences.

To illustrate the missing logic, in Denmark, where all costs connected to hearing aid were previously fully covered by the public, all types of glasses, irrespective of vision problems, are fully paid by the consumer, and so are dental bills, while all other medical services are for free!

Therefore, in cases such as with hearing aids and any other product or service, a detailed knowledge of the local market and institutional conditions is a fundamental requirement behind any international business venture.

For addressing all the potential market segments, special sales channels, partners and probably business models should be developed for each of the segments. The company should also know about the national regulatory frameworks for cost reimbursement in each market, and probably it will need individual approval for the reimbursement of product cost per country, but also for doctors/hospital fees if applicable. And to complicate matters more, if a lower price structure is applied to fit the opportunities in different markets, there is the risk that products sold cheaply in these markets are re-exported to the high-value markets.

One of my good friends is currently making a very profitable business from price differences. He buys standard drugs and medical devices from "low-price" markets in Europe and then re-exports them to "high-price" markets. The producers are not happy, but they can do nothing.

National rules and subsidies can also play an important role for a successful business development. An example is the hearing aid industry, where many wonder how a few Danish companies became dominant international players. Part of the explanation is to be found in a unique combination of technology excellence, excellent entrepreneurship and the very lavish Danish public health system. In Denmark, for many years, all major costs connected to the provision of hearing aid to hearing disabled patients have been fully reimbursed via the public health system. This created a very favourable home market for three of the world's current largest manufacturers of hearing aid technology.[4] This strong foothold in the domestic market provided an excellent reference platform to international expansion. The same lavish support system for clean technology for many years

---

[4]Videx A/S, Oticon A/S and GE Technologies A/S.

largely explains Denmark's strong position in the Wind turbine industry. E.g. the Danish company Vestas has become one of the world leaders in wind turbines.

The market for other products and services might be less complicated, but even more complicated for others. However, the general lesson learned is that the "the world market" is heavily fragmented, and estimation on sales potential cannot be based on estimates of "world demand". Sales potential needs to be aggregated from estimates of demand in each of the market segments the company has resources and talent to address.

2.3 Technical Solution and "Missing the Beat"

If we assume that solid market potential estimates are generated, is the situation then "home safe"? This is the only case if the solution is better, cheaper and easier to use or has other benefits compared to competing solutions, and this favourable situation shall exist in each of the market segments to be addressed. Even if the solution is better by all criteria, it might still not be possible to penetrate the target markets, if the competitors have implemented more favourable business models,[5] or service and support systems, or that the company or product meets unexpected certification or regulatory barriers.

All these issues should be addressed in the material to be presented to the investors. Not in great details to begin with, but later in the due diligence, all the details should be present. But the investors have to be convinced that in the future also, the solution, or new versions thereof, will have a competitive edge. Competitors do not stand still; they will constantly improve their products and services. If, e.g. the company of Mr. Ighhope is not likely to secure talent and resources for continued development of new excellent hearing aid products and services, the success might be short lived and the investor will not invest.

In most cases, if a product becomes obsolete in commercial terms, it is seldom connected to the product itself, but that competing products offer a better, cheaper and more flexible solution. In the

---

[5]See Section 2.12 for an elaborate discussion on business models.

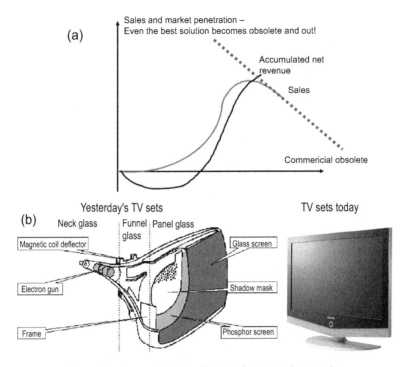

Figure 2.4 Commercial obsolete, in theory and examples.

ICT sector, technology advantages are driven by "Moore's law".[6] In principle, the moment when a product will become obsolete in commercial terms is determined (the dotted line in Fig. 2.4a) long before the product is introduced into the market.

It is not only small companies which "miss the beat". Household names such as Kodak misread the game changer from digital cameras and died! The giant Finnish mobile phone producer, Nokia, which dominated the market of mobile phones for many years, also missed a game changer. This "game changer" was created by smart phones. Motorola's mobile phone division was, for too long, convinced that the digital technology behind new mobile phones would not work. At that time, Nokia moved fast forward with the right technology and products, but still missed the next game

---

[6]"Moore's law" says that the number of transistors in a dense integrated circuit has doubled approximately every 2 years. This exponential improvement has dramatically enhanced the effect of digital electronics in nearly every segment of the world economy.

changer 20 years later. Why did this happen; the CEOs of these multi-billion companies were not dumb, but very experienced business leaders.

2.4 Connecting the "Dots" or Missing Them

There is no clear explanation for these mishaps, but in history, we have seen a number of similar situations where the people in control did not "connect the dots", a terminology used in the interesting book *What the Dog Saw*.[7] In this book, Malcolm Gladwell recalls examples from the attack on Israel in 1973 where all the intelligence was available to tell the Israeli officials that an attack from both Syria and Egypt was eminent. Even the Israelis knew that the Soviet families had been sent home during the week preceding the attack. But in the Middle East, at that time, all countries looked like ready to go to war—and it never happened—so why now? In fact, the Israeli intelligence did not see the pattern of Arab intentions, because on that afternoon of October 6, 1973, their intentions did not form a well-known pattern and the "dots were not connected".

The Al-Qaeda terrorist attack on the US Embassy in Nairobi in August 1998 was also pre-warned from many sources, but most warnings are dismissed as not credible because they were assessed individually and not put together in a "pattern of dots".

In hindsight, the information available showed a very precise picture of what would happen later, but the information was scattered among many services of the government.

History has a large number of similar "denials" of warnings, which in hindsight appears very clear and obvious and with "clear dots easy to connect". However, these "dots" were never connected.

Large corporations are, to some extent, like government. Management decisions rely on the filtered and selected information which reaches the "top of the pyramid". Management of, e.g. Kodak, Nokia, and Motorola knew very well that a new technology (the dotted line, Fig. 2.4a) was emerging but had no clear picture of how it would impact their products and market position. Because they

---

[7]*What the Dog Saw: And Other Adventures*, Malcolm Gladwell, Little, Brown and Company, 2009.

presided over so large companies with so large R&D departments, it seemed obvious to them that their companies own innovation strength, which had made them survive for so long and would again produce even better, cheaper and smarter solutions "using well-known technology". Therefore, facing the threat from the "dotted line", they reinforced their innovation activity by further refining their own "excellence". But in these cases, what killed the "old" technology and business case was not, per se, the technology, it was the way and speed with which customer habits changed, primarily because of other players' competing technology. Nokia, Kodak and Motorola managers did not "connect the dots" which combined technology and the real "game changer": *change in consumer behaviour as response to new technology.*

How could the "big elephants" have reacted? An example of how a "big elephant" decided to convert a part of its large corpus into the skin of a "gazelle" is the transition of Nestlé's office Espresso machine to become Nespresso.[8]

"Connecting the dots" and reacting to new patterns have become increasingly difficult during the last 10–20 years because of the rapid technological development and internationalisation. The ICT and Internet revolution and the impact of new solutions originating from nano- and photonic technologies entering the market with increasing speed create a rapidly changing and blurred picture of the future even if you have all the "dots" in front of you.

It is not unreasonable to say that if you today want to make a 10-year prediction of the "market and the technology future", it would be like predicting the market and technology situation of today from a position in 1985 or 30 years back. Would email, iPad, Facebook, carbon fibre fuselage for aircraft or low-cost carriers have appeared on your radar screen back in 1985? Therefore, "connecting the dots" and making decisions based on the emerging pattern are increasingly difficult for both large and small companies. If we go even 30–40 years back, a reasonable 10-year forecast could be built on the last 10 years' experiences. Today, the accelerated change pattern makes any new business venture riskier, as the future has become even more uncertain.

---

[8]See Section 2.10.

I have seen many times that agile small and medium enterprises (SMEs) with their "nose" deep into both the market and the most advanced new technology, and which were funded by large VC funds, had difficulties in changing strategy. They might correctly have "connected a series of dots" and observed that their original innovation strategy turned out to be inadequate, e.g. when facing unanticipated competition or new technical solutions. But if the relation between the entrepreneur or the management team and the investors is not build on mutual trust and flexibility, but primarily governed by adherence to contractual obligations about reaching specific milestones, there is the risk that the needed business strategy changes are not implemented in a timely manner.

In these situations, the entrepreneur might (wrongly) stick to the agreed plan in order to secure the liquidity from a milestone payment, which will flow into the company when a milestone is passed, instead of initiating strategy changes when it means that some contractual milestones need to be replaced with new ones.

Therefore, these small companies, particularly if milestones are considered as carved in rock, often have difficulties to get a new product strategy or market strategy accepted by their investors. In many of these cases, any proposed change will be met by severe punishment on company valuation. The reason is often that the investors, being far from the daily life of the company, cannot "connect the new dots" but see the request for change as a disappointment or management weakness. Sometimes these managers wrongly decide not to follow "their business instinct" and stick to the plan in fear of the investor reaction, even if the current plan now "stinks". In other cases, the entrepreneur decides to "jump ship", as we will see in Chapters 3 and 4.

Many investors have paid dearly from being too ridged with respect to enforcing a "stick to agreed plans" policy, often because they felt they were wiser and experienced than the entrepreneur.

Professional investors who make a living from investing in new technologies and innovative businesses are also not always good in "connecting the dots". In the mid-1990s, I was part of a small group of professional high-tech investors who formed part of the Board of Directors of the European Venture Capital Association (EVCA). At one point, we had a very intense (also funny in hindsight) discussion about email! What we seriously discussed at the board meeting was not "when" but "if" EVCA should get an email account and change communication with board members from fax to email. Many of us were in favour of sticking to fax primarily because we knew that it worked, but what was more important, without fax we would lose the paper trail for our archiving systems. In the end, the board reluctantly accepted the email account but emphasised that fax should be maintained to secure proper paper trails. That archives could rest in the Cloud a decade later was completely out of imagination.

The fax machine left the offices of EVCA many years ago, but the EU Commission still has fax number as one of the mandatory fields to be filled in when you register as an expert. More examples such as Nokia, Kodak and Motorola will come in the future and surprise us all, and we will ask why did they not see it—why did they not "connect the dots"?

However, you can also experience investors who are really good and who recognise the need for constant innovation and product development. When young companies looking for funding meet this type of investors, they can experience an unexpected feedback, when it comes to defining the amount of funding needed. These investors might, when a deal is being discussed and money is being asked for, present as a condition for investing that more money is to be invested than originally being asked for. This is because the investors know that only with enough resources available for constant innovation, the company can maintain its competitive edge.

However, more money always comes with a tag: "if more money is provided, more influence is requested".

2.5 Sales, Selling and Product Delivery

Even the best solution does not sell itself. It needs to be known to customers through marketing and actual sales effort. The optimal solution for the sales and marketing effort varies not only from product to product, but also from sector to sector. Even the same product is sold and marketed in different ways in different markets. The strategy is influenced by the competitor situation and also by country- and region-specific cultural differences and traditions.

What works well as a sales pitch in North Italy might not work in Sicily. Also the German businesspersons from Bayern differ in attitudes from the ones in Berlin or Hamburg. When it comes to actual sales, also language plays an enormous factor. If you really want to get close to French customers, speak French, and the same applies in Spain, Germany and Italy—not French, but Spanish, German and Italian.

In the book *Fish Can't See Water*,[9] the authors have made an attempt to illustrate certain characteristics of different national (and corporate) cultures. It is argued that predominantly US-based firms conduct business in accordance with what is called "masculine values" which evolve from the frontier spirit. These are in stark contrast with increasingly popular and viable "feminine values" which are deferred to in most European countries and many in Asia and Africa and to some extent in South America.

Typical type of masculine values	Typical type of feminine values
• Wealth, power assets • Material progress • Growth • Profits • Results • Boldness • Logic • Duties • Quick decisions • Individual career • Success • Leading others • Commanding	• Non-materials benefits • Social progress • Development • Reputation • Solutions • Subtlety • Intuition • Rights • Right decisions • Collective comfort • Quality of life • Nurturing others • Rendering services

Figure 2.5 Masculine and feminine values.

Hammerich and Lewis argue that if you have, e.g. a Swedish or Danish background, you have been influenced strongly from being brought up in some of the world's most equal and developed welfare states. Therefore, your understanding and reactions to business will

---

[9]*Fish Can't See Water: How National Culture Can Make or Break Your Corporate Strategy*, Kai Hammerich and Richard D. Lewis, Wiley, 2013.

differ not only from a person brought up in the USA but also from a person brought up in Italy or Spain.

About the French, Hammerich and Lewis find that it says a lot about the French mindset that their Minister of Culture André Malraux, when appointed by Charles de Gaulle in 1959, could declare in his first broadcast: "La mission de la France, c'est civiliser Europe".[10] Corporate leaders in France often emanate from elite business or management schools such as HEC, Ecole Normale Superieur or ENA (Ecole National d'Administration), and therefore bring with them the appropriate cultural baggage, a sense of history, deep respect for culture and languages and an in-built suspicion for and distaste for Anglo–American commercialism.

Still according to Hammerich and Lewis, among Italian leaders, you will find a large degree of flexibility, which is linked to other national traits such as humanitarianism, idealism and greater acceptance of delays than, e.g. in the German corporate culture. The German culture is influenced by a very scientific approach to problem solving, and they consider themselves as honest, straightforward and reliable. In general, Germans expect similar behaviour from their partners. The British have a great acceptance and admiration for individualism, inventiveness and engineering pride. The former strong class system is slowly being derailed, but the lingering insularity of the British is a more tenacious feature.

The unique Japanese business culture is derived from the exceptional historical and geographical circumstances as well as from their special thinking and reflection processes caused by a language very different from any others. Why are Japanese so different, not only from Europeans, but also from other Asians? A major factor was the 250 years of near-complete (self-imposed) isolation up to 1853. The culture is considered unrivalled by standards of honesty, loyalty, self-effacement, stoicism, unselfishness and unfailing courtesy. Westerners usually see themselves as individuals; many Japanese businesspersons see themselves representing a company, which is part of a group which in turn represents Japan.

Although this depiction of national characteristics by Hammerich and Lewis is an oversimplification, it is important to remember, when

---

[10]"The mission of France is a civilized Europe."

doing business outside your own cultural and historical comfort zone, that the partner you are meeting with may have a completely different background and also very different values. He may also not be able to understand your signals or implicit statements.

The materials presented to investors need to reflect deep understanding of the cultural challenges you will meet in foreign markets. These should also explain why the chosen business model will work in the particular markets of focus of your company and how you will take into consideration the local business traditions and cultures in these markets. And do not forget that the investors are also influenced by their background and upbringing. A Japanese looking investor who speaks fluent Danish might be born and raised in Denmark and carry Danish, not Japanese, values!

The material to be presented to investors should include a convincing description of how the product or service will be delivered to the chosen market(s). It should also reflect sufficient insight into how to overcome potential national and cultural barriers. If the "story" is not convincing, the investors might quickly back out. I have recently seen a marketing strategy of a company planning to sell high-tech photonic sensors to be installed in a specific medical equipment. They have selected industrial customers, and their marketing strategy is as follows:

> *"Online tools are being used to increase awareness at unparalleled pace and scale. Thus it is essential to use the leverage of these tools. We will use the mix of marketing approaches such as electronic referral tools, online awareness raising campaigns through blogs, Twitter, Facebook, and YouTube. We will participate in trade shows and technology fairs: these events are the best location for demonstrating new products and technologies to large and international crowds and to receive wide attention".*

This approach does not indicate deep insight into and knowledge on how efficient marketing is conducted in this business-to-business market segment. In this segment, access to key decision-makers is not created via Facebook or similar social media, but via direct personal contacts. Later established personal relations may be maintained via social media. Therefore, if a formulation like that is found in an otherwise well-formulated business plan, it could easily scare investors away, because it demonstrates fundamental ignorance about an important subject. The advice is, if you do not know enough about a subject, do not make unfounded assumptions as they may be wrong. It is better to explain that on this subject qualified assistance will be retained.

2.6 Textbook Management and the Team

There is a proverb in the investment community: "Rather invest in a good management team with a weak business case, than invest in a good business case with a weak management team". This saying holds some truth, because a very good management team will probably not involve themselves in a weak business idea. However, to judge whether a management team is strong or weak is not easy. The team experience and qualification which fit an ICT company may fail to manage a manufacturing company or a retail chain. Hence, management experience and qualification need not only be good but also relevant in the concrete situation.

There is a general agreement among investors that the following qualifications should be available within the management team. In the old management book by Adizes,[11] those roles "PAEI" were identified as follows:

P: the production and sales focus, experiences and will

A: the administrative skills

E: the entrepreneur or creator

I: the integrator, or human resource skills

---

[11]Adizes: Over the course of more than 40 years, Dr. Ichak Kalderon Adizes has developed and refined a proprietary methodology that bears his name. The Adizes Methodology enables corporations, governments and complex organisations to achieve exceptional results and manage accelerated change without destructive conflicts. *Leadership Excellence Journal* named him one of the top 30 thought leaders in the USA, and *Executive Excellence Journal* put him on their list of the top 30 consultants in the USA.

The team should include all these qualifications in various degrees, and the weight and required importance of different skills and qualifications vary throughout the lifetime of the company. The "P" can create results and produce products and services better than competitors. The "A" should be able to plan, coordinate, control and establish procedures for the organisation. The "E" is the person who develops the strategy for business development and the development of new products and services. He or she can adapt products and services to new market challenges and identify hither unseen opportunities. The "I" should be able to create harmony in the organisation and secure that the whole organisation develops with the right skills and qualifications and is moving in the same and right direction.

Those who have read the biography of Steve Jobs, the cofounder of Apple,[12] or the profiles of successful managers in the many books of Manfred de Vries[13] will notice that not all successful managers fit Adizes' profile of an ideal manager or leader of a successful management team. With respect to Steve Jobs, it has been said that *in the course of his rise, he betrayed his friends, alienated his allies and even mistreated his loved ones.* To some extent, his behaviour confirms the deep assumptions about the ultimate virtue of ruthlessness in the capitalist economy. It is also said that *as a person, he was heroic and despicable, and as a leader, he inspired loyalty and resentment, often from the same people.*

---

[12]*Steve Jobs*, Walter Isaacson, Simon & Schuster, 2011.
[13]Manfred F. R. Kets de Vries (born in The Netherlands) is a distinguished clinical professor of leadership development and organizational change at INSEAD. He is the founder of INSEAD's Global Leadership Centre, programme director of INSEAD's top management seminar "The Challenge of Leadership: Creating Reflective Leaders" and the scientific director of the programme "Consulting and Coaching for Change; Executive Master's Program". With European School of Management and Technology, Berlin, he is a distinguished visiting professor and director of their Center for Leadership Development Research. He is best known for bringing a different view to the much-studied subjects of leadership and the dynamics of individual and organizational change. Kets de Vries is also the founder of the Kets de Vries Institute, a partnership which counsels individual CEOs and top executive teams, using a clinical orientation to leadership coaching and organisational transformation.

A personality like him as the leader of a portfolio company of a VC fund would create both extreme happiness and severe nightmares. Hence, investors can make the most sophisticated test for entrepreneurial teams and hire the best head hunter to test the team, but in the end, it all comes down to trust and a good fit between the individual investor and the team.

Not all excellent management teams that look ideal on paper will fit well with all investors! In the end, excellent teams will seldom fit the profile in the textbooks. Many investors say: *A good management team shall make me feel good and confident. While I negotiate the investment deal with them, I get to know them and how they react under pressure and stress. All in all I get to know, if I can trust them. If not, I will not invest—irrespective of CVs and a skyrocketing interesting business plan.*

Therefore, if you are to attract investors, you and your fellow team members need to have the right experiences and qualifications. But you also need to have a personality and negotiation skill, which inspire confidence.

2.7 The Business Plan Puzzle

The "three circles" can function as a guideline for testing, if the business idea has a chance to survive or is best left as a sweet dream. When analysing a business concept, you need a structured approach. The purpose of the "business plan puzzle" is to get a structured overview of the entire business operation and to secure that all elements are ready for an eventual due diligence[14] by interested investors. This does not mean that there is a need to compile all the information in a comprehensive and nice-looking business plan. But whether you want to attract investors or just "bootstrap" and manage a successful company, it is a good idea that all the pieces in the "business plan puzzle" (Fig. 2.6) have been addressed. It is also important that the knowledge and conclusion related to each piece of the puzzle can be retrieved, when asked.

---

[14]See Section 3.3, Chapter 3, for more information on the due-diligence process.

Figure 2.6 The business plan puzzle.

Investors will question and explore all the nitty-gritty of the business and its underlying assumptions, and this might happen even during the first meeting. This could be a meeting at the office of the investors, or it could be one of the frequently organised "elevator pitch" sessions at conferences, where invited entrepreneurs are given the opportunity to present for a panel of investors. Many entrepreneurs expect an unchallenged presentation at these first encounters with investors. In the end, they therefore often fail to make a convincing appearance "because they did not expect to be examined in all the details so early in the process".

If a large part of the presentation and the business plan has been compiled and written by a consultant and the financials are put together by an accountant, many entrepreneurs look bewildered and appear naked when asked about details. If the entrepreneur's strategy focuses on a brilliant presentation and complicated questions are expected to be referred to the consultant, the confrontation may be unpleasant and the meeting might be very short and with no invitation to meet again.

Many entrepreneurs believe that a thoroughly developed business plan is a waste of effort and time if it does not attract investor interest. This is true only if you think about the design efforts and time to make the document "look good". However, even if the effort does not result in the expected investor contact and funding, the exercise of "solving the business plan puzzle" alone often provides insight into the business opportunity in a new and more structured way. An examination of the individual pieces of the "puzzle" will show that many of the individual pieces are closely interlinked and often overlap each other. The exercise has often led to unexpected and new ways forward for the business strategy, with different and sometimes even less financial requirements.

However, the analysis may also lead to a quick abandonment of the venture if it turns out not to be fundable or impossible to "bootstrap". Although it might be a disappointing result, it is still better to avoid spending time and effort on a losing case.

As with most puzzles, the order in which you put the puzzle together is not so important, although grouping the subjects together makes life easier. What is important is that all pieces eventually come into place. In my opinion, it is the business plan that eventually describes the business "strategy" by converting all the elements in the puzzle into a winning business case. The "puzzle" puts all the elements together. The "plan" converts the elements into a convincing strategy.

Normally, the many pages of a business plan will not be read by investors during the initial screening process. Therefore, to stir the appetite and interest of the investors, all the highlights (of interest to investors) in the business plan should be extracted and converted into a short "investment summary" of a few pages. This is the document that should be the first material to present to investors, eventually combined with a short attractive PowerPoint presentation.

It is easy to disintegrate the puzzle into four major elements: (i) product and production; (ii) sales and marketing; (iii) funding, liquidity and investors and (iv) management and related issues, plus a separate important element related to competitors.

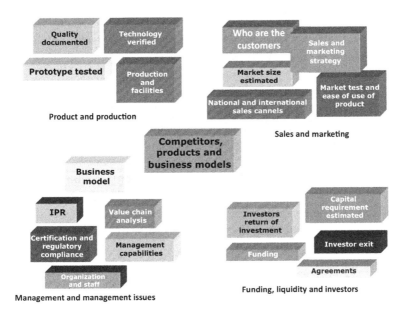

Figure 2.7 Structuring the puzzle.

There is not only a need to analyse the competitor's products and services, the competitor's financial strength, their business models and sales and marketing strategies should also be analysed.

2.8 Competition and Competitors

Even for "Blue Ocean" business strategies, competition needs to be analysed. Although it is difficult to remember for many people, in particular young people, that life went on before emails, smartphones and the iPad changed our lives. Even without these new electronic gadgets, we managed to communicate with each other. But we did it in a different way. We sent letters with brief marks on or telexed or faxed. Hence, competition is often not a direct competing product/ service but a different way of solving a problem. This also applies to high tech such as nanotechnology and photonics. It is possible to fry a steak on a non-Teflon-coated frying pan; actually good cooks prefer cast iron or copper! This broad definition of competition is often forgotten by entrepreneurs who argue that "there is no competition" because there is no direct competing product/solution. The competitor to the excel spreadsheets and the electronic calculator is doing calculations by hand and using pen and paper.

Kim and Mauborgne demonstrated in the original book *Blue Ocean Strategy* a new way of analysing competition. They did not see it from the product feature side, but from the customer side, and they used the customers' assumed needs and preferences as the yardstick.

When a product using a new technology or providing a new service is developed and its functionality is well understood, it is essential to understand who the end users are and why will they buy—today or sometimes in the future. In other words, what value is created and for whom and when?

In the "B2C" (business to consumer) market segment new products and services are often more "nice to have" than "need to have", hence sales and marketing efforts becomes closely interrelated. In the "B2B" (business to business) market segment, we often see that even if the solution is "need to have", purchase decisions might still be postponed. In order to secure the short term sales, it can be relevant to identify customers with a "burning platform", which means a purchase decision cannot be postponed. The "burning platform" market can sometimes be very different from the large "long term" market—but it can make the company survive until the "long term" market "takes off".

Actually, it is pretty smart to make this analysis before the product is developed, although this is not always the case in real life. Hence, some results of an innovation process end with the question "could you please help me finding a problem which matches the solution". Sometimes this "strategy" actually works out. One of the most well-known examples is 3M s "post it" product. This product was originally the result of a development process for a new type of glue which failed, but what a successful failure.

For a proper competitor analysis, you need to understand what value is created for the end users to make them chose your solution. If the user is not paying the bill, then there is a need to understand why and how someone else will pay the bill. Actually the one paying the bill is the real customer. It is, therefore, always important to

remember that the end users who benefit from the product or solution might not always be the one who make the purchase decision.
The following analysis should be carried out:

- Which market segment is addressed and who are the users and customers?
- If the "customer" is different from the end user, you need to understand both the value which is created for the end user and the value which is created for the customer.
  - » **End user example:** a solution creating welfare improvement for elderly persons
  - » **Customer example:** savings or value creation for the municipality which provides and pays for these welfare services

In the Danish hearing aid example, the users were the hearing impaired persons, and the "customer" paying the bill for many years was the public health authorities. Actually if the hearing aid was to be pre-paid by the patient, it was automatically reimbursed. So in this case, the user made the direct purchase decision although the purchase price was fully refunded. It is therefore likely to believe that functionality was the determing selection citeria, not price. In many cases, this first user/customer analysis will show how to get the sales and marketing strategy and pricing policy right the first time. The analysis can sometimes lead to a revision of product functionality, price assumptions, business model and overall business strategy.

The next step is to compare product features and customer/end user preferences and compare with competitor product features and business models.

- Which end user problems are solved and what value does it bring to the end user or the customer (if different)?
- Which end user segment(s) is (are) best served by the new product?
- Who are the competitors and how does our product compare to their products?

In the next example, the "blue ocean strategy" is used to analyse if customer preferences are aligned with product features. The example is from real life and illustrates a bad alignment of the first version of product features with customer preferences. The product is a machine which targets fruit, wine, almond or olive oil farmers. The machine can collect and process pruning[15] left on the soil. The first part of the analysis is about alignment with customer preferences.

Customer preferences

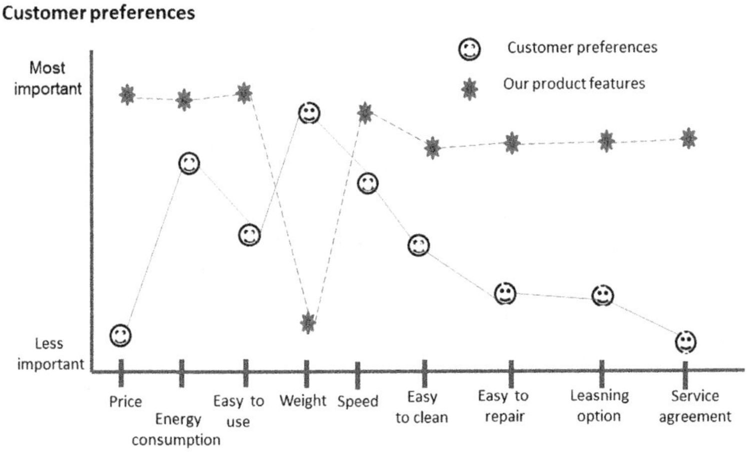

Figure 2.8 Farmer preferences and pruning collector features.

Figure 2.8[16] should be read in the following way:

- For the customer, the purchase price is not so important, while operating costs such as energy consumption are important. Also weight is an important factor; because of soil conditions, weight needs to be minimised. Also relevant are features such as ease of use, speed, ease of cleaning, while repair possibilities, leasing options or service agreements are of less importance.

---

[15]For example, fruit tree pruning is the cutting and removing of parts of a fruit tree.

[16]The analytical model is similar to the ones presented in the book *Blue Ocean Strategy: How to Create Uncontested Market Space and Make the Competition Irrelevant*, W. Chan Kim and Renée Mauborgne, Harvard Business Review Press, 2005.

- With respect to the product in the example, emphasis has been put on purchase price, while ignoring the weight. In addition, functionalities are offered, which are not considered relevant/ highly valued by the customers.

The value of a customer alignment analysis is that it describes customer preferences and concerns in a structured way, and it also helps to structure the sales process or marketing process.

With respect to competitor analysis, the same analytical tool can be used to identify where and how our own product compares/ differs from competing solutions.

Figure 2.9 illustrates how a customer views two products aiming to solve the pruning collection problem. It should be read in the following way:

- The purchase price and conditions of our product are higher than those for the competing product. Our products' energy consumption is also higher than that of competitors, but it is easier to use. The two products weigh the same. Our product seems to work faster than theirs and is more easy to clean and repair, and is offered with better leasing and service facilities.

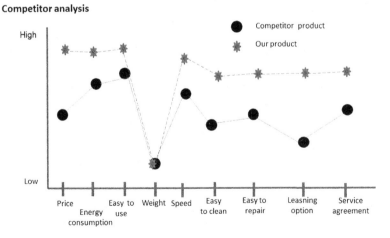

Figure 2.9 Comparison of competing solutions.

The value of a competitor analysis is that it not only gives insight into what competitors are doing, but it also helps in the sales process or marketing process. Competitor analysis identifies the very special features which distinguish our product and service from other products or solutions. It also provides a structure for the potential investors to make their own assessment of the potential and competitive strength of the new venture.

Actually, if a good competitor analysis is not included in the first presentation to investors, they will begin to make their own comparison, which might be wrong, because they might not have full insight into the product features and customer preferences.

The advantages of included customer preference alignment analysis and competitor analysis in the investor presentation is that it leaves few items open for the investors to make their own assumptions. You never know what they would do, and they might chose the wrong assumption and, therefore, arrive at the wrong conclusion.

Competing business models are also important to consider; therefore, a whole section[17] in the book is focused on business models.

2.9 Innovation, Products and Production

Many investors are interested in investing in products, services or solutions which are results of an innovation process if it can be demonstrated that there is a market and the team behind the innovation has the capacity and experience to get it into the market and make a profit. In many business plans, the section about products and solutions is the best described part, as the innovation effort and the management focus concentrate on those issues. In order to create investor confidence, it is important that the presentation of the "maturity" level of the product or the solution is also described in an open and honest way.

There is a big difference between testing a prototype of a product under laboratory conditions and testing it in real life in the fields. The same applies for new types of services. There is also a big

---

[17]See Sections 2.12–2.14 on business models.

Fishbone

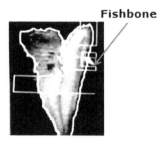

Portioning

Figure 2.10 Fish bone in fillets and automatic portioning.

difference between a test carried out by the team which made the innovation and a test carried out by a potential customer under real-life conditions. This also goes for quality testing, product longevity and requirements for services, repair and maintenance.

A few years ago I experienced how difficult it is to conclude that an innovative solution is actually also the solution the customers wanted. In the concrete case described as follows, the problem was identified by the potential customers, and the innovative solution was developed (actually tailor made) aiming at solving the identified problem for these potential concrete customers. However, it was not until the solution was installed and demonstrated in real life that the customers realised that the robot developed was not the solution to their problem.

The case is from the fish-processing industry. In this industry, it is a quality mark (higher price/less potential liability) that no fish bones remain in the processed fish fillets. The filleting process is largely manual, and quality control is a serious and costly issue. The innovation company in which we had invested had developed a robot, to be placed at the end of the filleting process conveyer belt. It could automatically identify and remove fish fillets, which still had bones in them.

The industry wanted to get these "off spec" fish fillets separated from the good ones and have the "off spec" reprocessed. It was expected that the introduction of the robot would reduce cost and improve quality control. Hence, its functionality met the identified and expressed needs. However, when the robot was finally tested in a fish-processing plant, the managers realised, by looking at the pile of rejected fillets, that only one of their problems was solved: the removal of "off spec" fillets. However, in order not to lose the value of these fillets, a new manual process to remove the fish bones from the "off spec" fillets had to be started. Making a quick calculation, the plant manager found out that the time used to reprocess the "off spec" fillets did not vary much from the cost of the manual quality control they had previously been using. And the robot was dismissed, as a product not solving the problem!

With hindsight (which is often very easy), it was easy to see that this result could have been predicted. But this was difficult to see in advance "how the dots" should have been combined, and one "dot" did probably not appear before the robot was installed: The advanced vision and software technology of the robot identified many more fillets as "off spec" than the manual control had, and the "reject pile" became bigger than anticipated. Good for quality, but bad for business.

That this first fruitless attempt to build a robot for the fishing industry later led to the development of a bigger and more advanced robot is another story. This new robot could not only remove the remaining bones but also cut the fish fillets automatically in predefined portions. But the development also cost tenfold more than the development cost of the small one and took a few years to make it right. Unfortunately, when all the technical problems were solved, the business model which was finally applied turned out to be wrongly chosen. We will return to the rest of the sad story in the section of business models.

Experienced investors have learned similar lessons many times while involving in innovation processes. It is seldom that what customers actually need or want is also what we think they need and want. But it is also not always what a customer actually says that he wants, that turns out to be what he needs or will pay for, when the product presented to him, and he tries it out in real life. Therefore, investors are so interested in knowing the result of actual user testing from close and real contact with end users. If a "real-life test" has not been conducted, investors will mentally add additional risk factors to the business venture.

Even Steve Jobs from Apple did not get it right the first time. Actually he got it wrong many times, not necessarily because he misread customer preferences, but because the technology to meet the needs/expectations was not yet available.

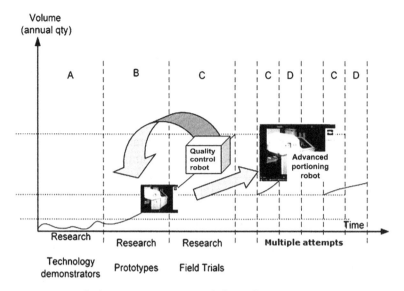

Figure 2.11 The bumpy innovation road: from idea to commercial product.

Investors, in general, consider themselves wise and with a good eye for the next technology wave. However, many investors declined to invest in Skype when they were presented with this business opportunity. And as previously stated, even the Board of Directors of the EVCA reluctantly accepted to use email in the mid-1990s; this was a new technology which we did not really trust or saw a bright future for. Therefore, the fax machine was kept in the offices of EVCA for many years.

Investors know that a successful result of an innovation process is uncertain, and results are complicated to achieve and most often also very costly. The first outcome of the innovation process is often believed to be a hit by the team behind the innovation, at least sometimes in the future. But this first innovation result might still be far away from the final product the customers will buy.

Because investors have this experience, they want assurance that the result of an innovation process leading to a commercial product has been tested and demonstrated in real life. If this "real life demonstration" has not been conducted with "real life customers," the risk of a commercial failure is higher. Therefore, in the absence of a solid and happy customer feedback, the investors will put a lower value on the investment opportunity.

The remaining part of the puzzle on production and production facilities also needs to be in place. It is important to consider and describe the needed production facilities, both in the short run and with a longer time perspective. If it is relevant, considerations should also be made about service and maintenance solutions, product liability and guaranties. If the product is costly or of special importance to the customer and the company is new, it might be difficult to sell unless backed up by a solid capital structure or to have a costly insurance to back up eventual guaranties. These eventual costs or conditions should be reflected in the budgets. These and many other requirements are valid for both physical products such as the food robot and for software.

In speaking about "production capacity", not only machines and physical installations are important, but also the availability of staff with right qualifications, professional credibility and at the right cost. Location might play an important role in getting access to qualified staff. Often it involves a delicate trade-off between a location where qualified staff is in abundance (competition for qualified staff is high as it is easy to jump from one job to another) and a more remote location where it might be more difficult to attract staff with all the required qualifications (however, when employed, they stay and have a great company loyalty). Deciding the location from a convenience point of view of the entrepreneur cannot be considered a qualified argument. However the headquarters and also often production facilities of many successful companies are located in "funny" places, because the founder was born there, and it was there it all started.[18]

2.10 Marketing, Sales and Internationalisation

If the team behind the business concept cannot demonstrate substantial knowledge and experience about sales and marketing and internationalization or, in other ways, have access to these resources, it will be difficult to convince potential investors that the budget and sales assumptions are realistic. We have previously, on an aggregated level, dealt with market, market tests, market analysis and the

---

[18]The headquarters of household company names like Ferrari, LEGO and DANFOSS are still located in small provincial cities where it all started.

difference between users and customers. The investors know that market test often provides for surprises, but might also lead to interesting business opportunities, not only for young companies but also for large and mature companies.

The first investor contact will therefore often focus on how the team can substantiate the sales assumptions and customer reactions, including the reason for the choice of business model(s). In other words, you will be asked: "why the chosen sales and marketing strategy will work". This section provides a number of relevant examples which can illustrate typical challenges and how to exploit opportunities.

The book *Business Model Generation*[19] describes the interesting example of the now successful company Nespresso. Originally, the Nespresso system was designed to bridge the gap between the instant coffee market, where Nestlé is the dominating player, and the roast and ground coffee segment. Nestlé wanted to provide a dedicated espresso machine which could conveniently produce restaurant-quality coffee. Having failed to enter the restaurant market, Nestlé created the organisation Nespresso, which started marketing the system to offices. However, this attempt quickly sagged far below expectations. Osterwalder describes in his book that the company was only kept alive because of its large remaining inventory of high-value Espresso coffee machines. Then Nestlé appointed a new CEO (Jean-Paul Gaillard) at the helm of Nespresso. He completely overhauled the previous business model with a few major changes. First he shifted the focus from offices to high-income households, and then he started selling coffee capsules directly by mail. He combined it with introducing high-end retail channels located at premium locations such as Champ-Èlysées in Paris. This business model proved successful and resulted in a high profitable growth rate.

From this and other examples we can learn that the sales and marketing solution and the chosen strategy are closely connected to the choice of a successful business model. In the end, the basic Nespresso technology more or less remained the same throughout

[19]*Business Model Generation: A Handbook for Visionaries*, Alexander Osterwalder and Yves Pigneur, Wiley, 2010.

this roller coaster of business development, while it was the business model that underwent dramatic changes.

The preconditions for business objective and international growth may often depend on factors not directly related to the product, the customer interest and market potential.

For example, the value of solid investors in the shareholder group of a company can be a precondition for a young company when it tries to enter a new international market; it can make the difference between success and failure.

Back in the 1990s, one of the portfolio companies (PPU Maconomy) of the venture fund I managed got the opportunity to sell an integrated CRM/accounting system to the marketing division of American Express. This unit was situated in the World Trade Centre, New York. The customer had found that the solution offered by PPU Maconomy was a perfect match with their needs. However, their IT department was, for good reasons, lukewarm to purchasing and introducing new administrative and time-recording processes for a large department of American Express based on a solution from a small and young Danish software company, which furthermore had no long track record and still a fragile balance sheet.

At that time the saying was that IT managers never got fired by choosing an IBM solution, but they might risk their neck if they selected a different supplier and something went wrong. At that time, we were the major shareholder in PPU Maconomy. Hence, we decided to go to a meeting in New York and speak directly with the American Express team. At the meeting, I explained that a large Danish financial VC fund stood solidly behind the "small" PPU Maconomy. That made the trick; we removed a serious perceived risk factor, and the company got the contract, not because of us but because the product had superior quality and functionality, combined with the right price. There is no doubt that PPU Maconomy did not manage to rein this contract in without the direct intervention from its major shareholder. No product insurance guarantee could replace the needed confidence in the financial survival of the company. As investors, we recognised that not only a US order, but an American Express order for our "little" company would be the "blue stamp", which could lead to even more serious orders from major US clients. We were proven right!

2.10.1 Marketing and Sales

The business potential for introducing new products, services and solutions has been high since the turn of the century. SMEs can play a significant role in bringing new products and solutions to the market. Also Microsoft, NovoNordisk, LEGO, Apple, Ryanair, IKEA and TetraPack were once SMEs, and right now investors are looking for the future global winners. All these now well known household names were not only good to do product development, develop sales and marketing and secure rapid internationalisation. But their management teams also knew how to get funded along the route to success.

The opportunities are, in principle, big in almost all sectors. If we, as an example, take the water sector, the market potential for new solutions is vast and growing. Water is developing into a scarce and valuable resource globally: The world market for water technologies represented €190 billion in 2005 and is expected to reach €290 billion by 2020. The EU global market share is currently around 60%, and the sector includes more than 1 million workers plus 300,000 indirect workers. There are similar opportunities for solutions addressing climate change, conditional maintenance of infrastructure or for providing services and solutions for the rapidly growing elder population in many countries in Europe and Asia.

However, the risk of such "world market estimates" is that the business case for the company may be presented in an unrealistically positive way. Less experienced entrepreneurs often meet with the statement: "If we can get just 2% of the world market, it is going to be a fantastic business case". The problem is that the total realistic addressable market for all SMEs is much smaller than the world market, often just a very small fraction. As illustrated in Section 2.2, an in-depth market analysis and market segmentation strategy will help the company achieve more realistic benchmarks.

Marketing is, in principle, simple. It is about communicating the value of a product, service or brand to customers or consumers for the purpose of promoting or selling that product, service or brand. The oldest and perhaps the simplest and most natural form of marketing is word of mouth (WOM) marketing, in which consumers convey their experiences of a product, service or brand in their day-to-day communications with others. These communications can, of course, be both positive and negative.

Nowadays, the Internet has provided a platform for mass, electronic WOM marketing (e-WOM), with consumers actively engaged in rating and commenting on goods and services. However, marketing can take many other forms, from product reference lectures by doctors and scientists at international medical congresses, to affiliate marketing[20] often used by international online gaming and betting companies.

If a management team does not have previous experience from practical sales and marketing, it is wise to consult one or more of the numerous books written about the subject or, even better, to team up with a knowledgeable and experienced colleague. As any marketing strategy is so closely related to the execution of each individual business case, it is not possible to provide any general advice or recommendation.

On the other hand, it is also important that the subject is dealt with in the material to be presented to investors in a very concrete manner. When investors probe into the reasoning behind a particular sales and marketing strategy and find that it is more based on vision and "wishful thinking", the credibility of the entire business plan evaporates in thin air.

For the customers purchase decision there is a big difference between "nice to have" and "need to have", in particular in the B2B market segment it is relevant also to look for customers with a "burning platform". For the company it is important that the first sales estimates are based on "need to have" customers rather than "nice to have" customers.

Recently I have been advising a number of SME, all of them with advanced technology solutions and substantiated large market

---

[20]Affiliate marketing is a type of performance-based marketing in which a business rewards one or more affiliates for each visitor or customer brought by the affiliate's own marketing efforts. The industry has four core players: the merchant (also known as "retailer" or "brand"), the network (which contains offers for the affiliate to choose from and also takes care of the payments), the publisher (also known as "the affiliate"), and the customer.

potential. However, the challenge for all the companies was that although the solution could create substantial savings (= value) for the customers, it was a clear "need to have", but it was not a "burning platform", meaning that although the value created was big, its solution could always wait until "next year". Therefore, the companies all had to shift the short term sales strategy to other customer groups where immediate "burning platforms" could be identified. This also lead to minor changes in product features but to substantial changes in business models.

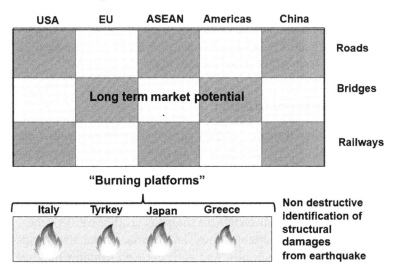

Figure 2.12 Tool for preventive infrastructure maintenance.

An example: A company has developed a novel tool for non-destructive analysis for preventive maintenance processes for different type of infrastructure installations. If the process was implemented it could extend the lifetime from 30 years to 50 years. The market potential was large, and the savings from moving to preventive maintenance enormous. Hence a big world market and high value creation for the customers, who owned the infrastructure. However, a decision to implement changes in maintenance procedures "can always wait until next year" and the savings are "long term savings". Hence also the decision to buy can wait "until next year". But a thorough discussion with the management showed that the tool could also be used for non-destructive analysis of potential structural damages from earthquakes. Here the company had hit a "burning platform" but for a different type of customers: the national and local authorities and fire and rescue brigades in earthquake prone regions in countries like Japan, Italy, Turkey and Greece. As the need was urgent, a quick sale and initial revenue stream could be realized, while the large "preventive maintenance" market matured.

For an innovative company with high ambitions, exploring how to release the potential for international success is a vital step, which needs to be founded on analysis, understanding of customer needs, insight in competitors and a solid executable plan. This applies whether the goal is building a company for long-term growth or to provide for short-term exit for the investors.

2.10.2 Internationalisation

In general, the strongest motives behind internationalisation are improving the firm's presence across markets, increasing competitive advantages or achieving larger-scale and, therefore, improved cost efficiency. Done properly and with adequate initial research and preparation, efficient sales and marketing efforts combined with internationalisation will enable the company to achieve exactly these goals and become profitable. However, the process contains a wide range of executive decisions. And each decision contains multiple pitfalls with strategic and financial implications. These implications may impact the company's position not only in the new markets but also in the home market.

In particular, with respect to internationalisation, it is important to understand that internationalisation adds complexity to the company's core processes, products and services, business model, strategy, budgets, etc. Even more important is the considerable amount of time the management needs to allocate to the internationalisation plan and its execution. If substantial management time and resources are not available for this particular purpose, I have often seen that the internationalisation process has led even to killing promising companies.

Therefore, in the material to be presented to investors, the company's general vision and business strategy must also demonstrate the financial resources and management's realistic commitment for the internationalisation strategy. It must be possible for the investors to assess whether the potential benefits of internationalisation exceed the risks and the costs related. The complexity of the internationalisation process leaves no uniform and "right" decision. When deciding which markets to enter, when to enter and at what scale to enter, the decision is unique every time. However, there are a number of standard factors to take into account. An analysis and planned action related to all those factors should be possible to present to the investors at request.

Designing the right strategy for capturing international markets requires a comprehensive plan which considers objectives, goals, resources and policies for a time horizon which makes it possible to achieve solid business results in the market place, often within 2–4 years. The entry strategy should consider the following decisions:

- Defining the most promising market
- Defining the product: standardisation or adaptation
- Choice of entry mode
- Marketing plan

2.10.3 Promising Markets

Defining the company's most promising markets requires in-depth understanding and analysis of the individual potential markets. A range of tools and checklists are available, just to name a few:

- The first step is to gain an overview of the macro-environmental factors which the company should take into consideration, i.e. political, economic, social, and technological (PEST) factors in a given market and helps the company prioritise which markets to enter (also known as the PEST analysis). The growing importance of environmental factors and regulatory/legal factors should also be considered.

- Subsequent to the macro-level analysis, the next step is to look into the competitive landscape within the relevant industry. A widely used framework for industry analysis and strategy development is the "Porter's five forces analysis".[21] The analysis is used to define the competitive attractiveness of a market by analysing the intensity of five forces: (i) competitive rivalry within an industry, (ii) threat of new entrants, (iii) threat of substitute products, (iv) bargaining power of customers and (v) bargaining power of suppliers.

- With the overview of the macro-level and the competitive landscape in mind, it is possible to make a solid analysis of the company's strengths and weaknesses along with the external opportunities and threats (also known as SWOT analysis).

Markets are attractive when the product in question satisfies an unmet need, but even though the company's products may be a huge success in the domestic market, it is not guaranteed to become a success internationally. Exploring how competing products are positioned in the new market is essential. Also, pricing issues should be considered: transportation costs, product packaging, legal concerns, trade barriers, etc.

One of the key barriers to international trade is language. Many SME internationalisation strategies are based on the limited language skills of senior management and sales managers. This decision pattern means that a wide range of market opportunities are not utilised in countries with "difficult languages". It is an irrational decision criterion to choose market primarily based on management language skills. If the right market opportunities are present, the company should acquire the relevant language skills through recruiting.

In the initial market selection and in order to get an overview of the potential success of the markets, it will be beneficial to set up measures to benchmark and rank the different markets, so they can be easily compared to each other. The measures will be of how well the market supports and is ready for your firm and products. A

---

[21] Michael E. Porter. "The Five Competitive Forces that Shape Strategy", Harvard Business Review, January 2008.

simple and widely used tool for market prioritisation and selection is the "selection with multiple criteria" analysis.

This approach follows three steps:

1. Define three to five most important criteria for market selection (e.g. competition intensity, legislative issues, language barriers, distances, customer density, "nice to have" versus "need to have" current network of company) and list these criteria in columns. Choosing the criteria is rarely straightforward, and the PEST, SWOT and Five Forces analyses may guide in this process. If necessary, the criteria may be weighted differently.

2. List the potential markets in rows.

3. Brainstorm how each market matches each criteria and score on a scale of, e.g. 1–5. Some scores will be obvious, whereas other scores will require additional analysis. In order to facilitate these discussions, individual scoring can be used prior to the team brainstorm.

In the end, a comprehensive analysis will have been developed for further discussion, a discussion which often provides surprising results and insight. While the results gained from this analysis will be highly valuable and take many important factors into account, the results should not stand alone. The exact scores and results are not as important as the management discussions that accompany the scores. The scores can never substitute sound management decisions.

However, it has to be admitted that despite ranking, benchmarking and selection criteria and the comprehensive analysis, at the end of the day, the method mostly applied by SMEs, and often very successful, is pure opportunism—meeting the right contact person at the right time. However, leaving success to the "lucky punch" of meeting the right contact person at the right time is not a convincing story to tell investors. Therefore, a comprehensive analysis is required. It should include findings from actual visits to the relevant markets. This also increases the chance to meet the right contact person, and perhaps even the investor network can help.

2.10.4 Standardisation or Adaptation

When the relevant new markets have been identified, the next step is to define whether the product can be marketed in its current form (standardisation) or whether changes are required (adaptation). Whether and how to adapt the product should be decided after addressing a range of issues about the buyers, users, sales processes, after-sales requirements, tariffs, taxes, legal or technical requirements, positioning compared to competitors, etc. Most often, technology manufacturers will need to adapt their products to some extent to gain a satisfactory level of buyer acceptance in the foreign market.

Adaptation may be related to the physical product, packaging, marketing or sales processes or the support and service functions. However, adaptation is costly, and for an SME with limited resources, this strategy may not be a viable option. Instead, the company may want to keep products the same across national markets and seek to adapt buyers and users to the company's product. Such a product standardisation strategy keeps down the costs of adaptation but incurs higher costs of marketing and promotion.

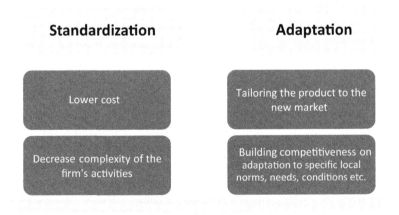

Figure 2.13 Standardisation or adaptation.

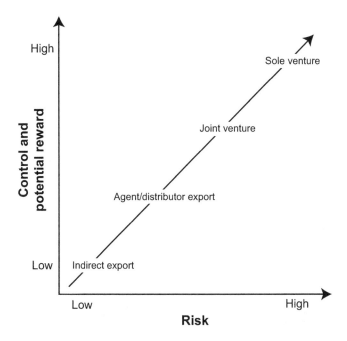

Figure 2.14 Risk and control choices.

2.10.5 Choice of Entry Mode

A company can arrange entry into a foreign country via:

- **Indirect export entry mode or export via agents and distributors**: The final product is manufactured outside the target country and then transferred to it via middlemen or directly from producer to buyer. This includes long-term non-equity agreements between a company and an entity in a foreign country which enables transfer of technology or competencies.
- **Investment entry mode**: This involves ownership and management control in the foreign country and may be either sole ventures with full ownership and control by the parent company or joint ventures.

SMEs most often face a higher level of resource constraints than multinational corporations in terms of financial and management resources. These constraints make it difficult for SMEs to pursue the investment entry mode and instead most often force SMEs to seek alliances in the international market place in order to succeed with market entry. These alliances range from simple purchaser/ supplier relationships to joint ventures and all types of agreements in between.

Strategic alliances facilitate entry into a foreign market, allow firms to share the fixed costs (and associated risks) of developing new products or processes, bring together complementary skills and assets which neither partner could easily develop on its own and can help a firm establish technological standards for the industry, which will benefit the firm.

Exports via agents and distributors are also commonly used. It is important to distinguish between these two channels.

- An agent is an independent middleman who represents the exporting company in the target market. The agent does not take title to the manufacturer's goods and he or she seldom holds any inventory beyond samples used for sales and marketing purposes. The agent is basically a salesperson, who is most often rewarded through a sales commission.
- A distributor is an independent merchant who takes title to the manufacturer's goods for resale. The distributor may also assume ownership risks and stock inventories, promote and extend customer credits, process orders and deliveries as well as carry out product maintenance and repair. The distributor is rewarded by his or her profit margin.

Choosing between the two channels requires careful analysis of the agent's/distributor's business terms, competencies, reputation in the market, financial strengths, etc.

In the previously mentioned food-processing robot company, it was decided to use a "distributor model" for sales in the US market of a more advanced portioning food-processing robot. The chosen distributor got exclusivity for the entire US market and was, therefore, eager to push the sales forward. The business model selected was direct sales, combined with an option to return the robot if it did not perform as promised. This business model was aligned with the distributor's normal sales strategy. By choosing the distributor model, it reduced our influence on which business model should be applied in practice. We had serious discussions about adequate business models, but the distributor was used only to use a straightforward sales model and definitely not a "try it first and buy if you are satisfied" model. He argued that if this model is implemented, he fears his other products would be exposed to the same request from his large customers. And as he was backed up by the Danish company's return policy, he faced no risk if a customer becomes dissatisfied. At that time, the robot had only been tested in real-life conditions in the fish-processing industry, but we felt confident that it would also work in the poultry and meat industry as well. As we shall see in Chapter 4, Section 4.4, the chosen business model did not work.

One of the other challenges of dealing with agents and distributors is that these middlemen represent other suppliers who provide proven and recurring revenue streams. In order to achieve true commitment from the middlemen, it is important to design an incentive structure which works for both parties in the start-up period, which often inflicts more costs than benefits, as well as in the long run when the cost of sales decreases and benefits outweigh costs.

Though strategic alliances come in many forms and are mainly beneficial through shared learning and technological improvements, the main motivation lies in seeking alliances which reduce market entry and overhead costs, which would have been costly for the individual firm. The shape of the alliance is not as important as the gains which come through the fact that technology and knowledge change organisations.

A major determinant of how much a company gains from an international alliance is its ability to learn from its alliance partners. Once a partner has been selected, the alliance should be structured in a manner which allows for skills and technology swaps with equitable gains, but also in a way which prevents the transfer technology not meant to be transferred, with contractual safeguards against the risk of opportunism.

The success of an alliance is basically a function of the partner selection, alliance structure and manner in which the alliance is managed. The right local or international partner will work with the firm to achieve its strategic goals and has the capabilities the firm lacks and that it values. It should also share the firm's vision for the purpose of the alliance, and it should be unlikely that it would try to opportunistically exploit the alliance for its own ends: i.e. to expropriate the firm's technological know-how while giving away little in return. The right partner can really help guide the firm to avoid a range of pitfalls in areas such as legislation, intellectual property, tax, cross-cultural management, governance, foreign business etiquette, etc. With the wrong partner or alliance, achieving success will be equally difficult.

If the choice of investor is right, the company may also "piggy back" on the personal international network of the investor, or use the investors' financial strength to gain a foothold in foreign market, like in the PPU Maconomy and American Express case previously described. However, an internationalisation strategy need not be implemented before investors are approached, but it needs to have been analysed and thought through. It may then be changed when the investors get on board and their contact network is added to the network of the company. But your own analysis can be a good starting point.

2.10.6 Internationalisation and Marketing Plan

Having decided which markets to enter, which products to promote, and which entry strategy to apply, the next step is to define how to sell the product. Traditionally, this is analysed in the marketing plan, which describes product, pricing, channels, promotion and logistics. These factors are highly interdependent, i.e. a change in product packaging and pricing may easily have an impact on promotion, and the choice of distribution channels and incentive structure for middlemen go hand in hand with decisions on logistics and pricing towards end customers.

One of the key decisions is pricing and entry pricing strategies. Several factors should be considered before determining the price structure. How sensitive will the sales volume be to the product's pricing in the market? What are the competitors' pricing policies? Does the potential product advantage allow the company to charge a premium price? Are initial discounts necessary to facilitate market entry? Which pricing strategy best fits your thoughts and choices on promotion, logistics and marketing? How do we price towards agents and distributors, and which pricing flexibility do we allow for middlemen? Do we need full control of the promoted end user price? Will our pricing policy be legal or will it attract government investigation and possibly regulation?

Promotion is about how the company communicates its core messages to end users, agents, distributors, partners and other stakeholders in the market place. What do we say, how do we say it and to whom? A key communication issue to consider when expanding abroad is about the "made in . . ." images which the foreign users and partners have of the company's home country. Studies show that people are inclined to ascribe favourable characteristics to their own nationality and less favourable characteristics to other nationalities. A "made in France" signal may be interpreted differently in Scandinavia and North Africa. And a software company indicating "made in Denmark" does not get much added value from this statement. If it was a wind turbine, the impact could be different. "Made in Germany" might have got a new flavour after the Volkswagen scandal in September 2015 with the cheating software build into diesel cars in the US market and elsewhere. Awareness of "made in" creates different perception in different countries and where cultural settings differ. Therefore, a knowledge about local "origin" perception is valuable when designing promotion strategies.

2.10.7 Monitoring of the Process

For the internationalisation process, each decision step should be closely monitored and reviewed regularly by implementing a management control system. The purpose of this control is to monitor operations and identify any differences between actual and planned performance, diagnosing the causes of variances (especially when the discrepancies have a negative impact), and defining action plans to eliminate problems.

The key control measure is the budget and comparing the budgets to actual results, not on a yearly but monthly or quarterly basis. Planning and budgeting an internationalisation process is extremely difficult, and most often due to optimistic forecasts, there will be significant (negative!) discrepancies between budgets and actual results. Product changes, channel agreements, customer uptake, etc. will often take considerably longer time than budgeted, which should not be kept as a secret for the investor.

Another important and often underestimated control measure is competence mapping. Have new issues arisen during the internationalisation process which require a different management skill set than originally anticipated?

If the management team responsible for international sales was initially hired based on their track record in aggressively opening new doors and building partner relations and the focus is now on incremental process improvements and fine-tuning of pricing and promotion strategies, it might be a good idea to reconsider the management team's competencies.

2.10.8 Fish Cannot See Water: The Challenge of Cultural Differences

A huge number of business deals are lost every day around the globe due to cross-cultural blunders. Most international sales managers will be able to supply war stories of basic mistakes made by themselves and their colleagues in foreign cultures. Having the right business etiquette in the foreign setting is crucial for success, i.e. knowing how to give and receive a business card the proper way in Asia, knowing how to handle the culture of giving gifts in the Middle East, understanding when to use first names and surnames in the USA and France ought to be basic knowledge for an international sales representative, yet it is often the source of lost opportunities and deals.

A couple of basic guidelines when approaching foreign cultures: Prepare yourself before your visit, communicate with respect and genuine interest in the host culture and its people and show empathy for the attitudes, values and ways of thinking. Listen before you talk and be careful applying humour, e.g. irony which may work so well at home might easily offend your customer or local partner. Patience and persistence are required. To succeed, it is most often necessary that the country manager in the foreign country knows the foreign language in order to successfully interact with employees, customers and other stakeholders. Deep knowledge of the foreign culture and language increases the chance of getting it right and avoiding local pitfalls. The way to glory and business success of the previously mentioned international household names were also filled with pitfalls and blunders, but they learned from it all.

2.10.9 Currency Risk

International sales activities often involve fluctuating foreign exchange rates, in particular if the company wants to trade outside its own currency zone (e.g. euro). The fluctuating value of foreign currency can affect the success of the sales effort in the foreign market, the actual revenues and costs generated by the business transactions and, therefore, the entire profitability of the internationalisation effort. The decision about whether the importer or the exporter will bear the currency exchange risk is important. Both the buyer and the seller would typically prefer the sale to be denominated for payment in their local currency. Therefore, choice of currency is an important parameter in the sales and negotiation processes.

In both developing countries and emerging markets, the risk of currency fluctuations should be of particular concern to the exporting company. In these countries, it may be very difficult to analyse the risk and severity of changes in the value of the local currency, and it may be difficult to offset foreign exchange risk. Abrupt political changes, trade deficits, foreign exchange shortfalls, freezes on payment of imports and other activities may lead to a sudden devaluation of the currency. The willingness and ability of a country's central government to support its currency are factors in assessing foreign exchange risk.

Banks and other financial institutions offer to offset the exchange risks contracts which "hedge" against fluctuations. However, the process adds additional costs to the exporter and is also time consuming.

2.10.10 Law, IPR, Regulation and Jurisdiction

When deciding on which markets to expand to, it is important for the investors to know that you are aware of the foreign markets' legal and regulatory systems. Antitrust regulations, corporate governance codes, transparency and financial disclosure laws all determine how attractive/risky a country is to operate in. Lack of legal protection from local governments and the ability to enforce a suitable remedy are other important factors. The most intrusive form of legal risk in foreign investments is expropriation, where the local government seizes or erodes ownership of assets.

Entering a new country unaware and uninformed of potential legal traps is a certain road to failure and has cost many companies their investments. It is, therefore, highly recommended to ally with legal resources with local knowledge. Usually embassies and chambers of commerce can be a good and inexpensive source of information and can help avoid the most common pitfalls.

Typical legal matters to address are international contracts, distribution agreements, joint venture agreements, setting up foreign companies, import compliance programmes, seizures and forfeitures, corruption issues and employment laws.

Often one of the first legal challenges a company meets, when going abroad or establishing a partnership with a foreign partner, is related to the first exchange of confidential information. This often needs to be preceded by a signed non-disclosure agreement (NDA). In principle, it is a small and simple agreement, but before signing it, there should also be an agreement between the two parties about the choice of legal framework to govern the NDA. For many companies, it is also an invitation to better understand the importance of getting access to solid legal advice. With respect to the NDA, the question arises (or should arise): "Which legal system should govern the NDA?" Should it be the legal framework of your own country or that of your potential partners' country? Both parties have an interest in solving potential conflicts using their own well-known legal framework. However, this is, in principle, also an invitation to give one of the parties an advantage to carry out the "fight" on their home turf. In order to secure a level playing field and avoid too obvious invitation for one of the parties to start a fight, it can be a good idea to agree upon letting a third-country legal system govern the agreement. If this should be a long-term solution, it should be part of the following business agreement to be established.

For a technology-based company with international ambitions, special attention must also be directed towards the issue of intellectual property rights (IPR). Entering new markets may represent significant risks. There are international frameworks in place to help harmonise national IPR laws and regulations, which is increasingly happening. But despite international attempts for harmonisation, the exporting company may be exposed to surprises.

Even if a product has been sold for years in the domestic market and a few neighbouring markets without any IPR violation claims being raised, you still risk facing IPR violation problems when moving into new markets. When the company enters a new foreign market, the same product might now be met by claims of IPR infringement, because a competitor only had registered for IPR protection in a few key markets, and now you enter its protected market, where it has legal means to defend its IPR position. You may also be in the opposite situation that your IPR protection is limited to a few countries where you have been able to operate peacefully, and by entering the next market, you move outside your own protective IPR shield.

An exporting company whose products benefit from IPR protection will also experience that not all countries have the same interpretation of the IPR rules and regulations or follow them at all. The attitude and approach to IPR in the Western economies are very different from those in Asian and Southern African Development Community (SADC) economies. Most IPs are registered in the Western economies, especially in the USA, but also in Japan. Many of the developing countries have a more liberal view on IPR, and a culture where copying and plagiarism are considered the norm. It is, therefore, essential for the international company to be aware of how to protect its IPR.

To conclude, internationalisation may be the right route to glory and growth. Unfortunately, the route is not always paved with smooth tarmac, but with sharp and unstable rocks and stones.

2.11 Operations and Management

This section, in general, deals with investors' expectations related to management and organisation. In particular, the difficulties of assessing management experience and quality is discussed, as this represents one of the greatest challenges for investors to cope with.

2.11.1 Management Team

The examination of all other elements in the business plan puzzle by the investors leaves these elements unaffected;[22] however, the check of the management team represents a special challenge. The management has a direct interest in the outcome of the examination. Hence, its role is double: it is the "sales team" for the investment opportunity and, at the same time, it is the most important element in the entire puzzle, which should be objectively analysed. What is even worse is that it has a personal interest in the outcome of the examination.

The investors know that the team wants to present itself in the best possible light and hide any weaknesses (including internal disagreements) which could make the investors walk away. The investors, on the other hand, are interested in knowing about the real strength and weakness. It is not always that an apparent weakness makes the investors walk away. However, if the weakness is deliberately hidden, the alarm bell rings when the investors find the weakness. The confidence is lost if this happens after the investment is made, and then life with investors can become very difficult.

As a starting point, the investors will be looking at the CVs of the entrepreneur or the management team and consider if the qualifications and experiences of the team and the entire organisation are balanced and relevant. They will also examine if the entire organisation has the same belief in the potential success of the

---

[22]When you look at a sales forecast, it does not react when you are examining it, but when you want to explore management capabilities through interviews or indirect negotiation, the management reacts and might change its behaviour while being observed.

venture, as is expressed by the lead entrepreneurs with whom they get the first contact.

The investors will be looking for relevant experiences, training and education. They will check if the individual team members with whom they get in contact have a realistic perception of their own strength and competences. Most investors strongly believe that they can quickly see through if a team member presents himself or herself as a "Champions League" player instead of the "Series F" player he or she actually is. However, a Series F player who aspires and has the ambition and talent to become a Champions League player is fine. It is all about realism and perception.

In real life, judging if the entrepreneur is the right leader or the entire management team is the winning team is the most difficult part of the whole evaluation process. Not only because evaluating personalities and human behaviour in itself is very difficult, but also because of the dual role of the entrepreneur or the management team as "seller" and "object of purchasing".

In essence, the investors are looking for the "entrepreneurial and leadership gene" of a Bob Noyce, Bill Gates, Steve Jobs, Mark Zuckerberg, Ruben Rausing, Larry Ellison, Ingvar Kamprad or Richard Branson, and who can convert a business case into a new Intel, Apple, Microsoft, Facebook, Oracle, TetraPak, IKEA or Virgin Airlines.

Leadership is, in essence, an exercise of power, which again requires professional competence, conceptual skills, vision and imagination and the capacity for creating interpersonal relations. Good leadership is also often combined with personal characteristics such as charm, humour combined with strong determination.

Therefore, an important by-product of a lengthy and complicated investment negotiation is that it gives the investors a possibility to check if the right personal characteristics and profiles are present in the management team.

Although "heroes" such as Jack Welch, Richard Branson and Steve Jobs are all men with "fire in their belly" and are what the investors are looking for, they may, at the same time, be afraid to team up with such strong personalities. And in the end, they may revert to prefer "the man in the grey flannel suit" because he communicates at the same wavelength as the investors.

2.11.2 Leaders and Imposters

One of the challenges for the investors is that these "heroes" in reality possess some of the same qualities found in the imposter. According to Manfred de Vries,[23] the term "imposter" has two connotations, which are often concurrent. An imposter is a person who deceives, swindles or cheats, but can also be someone who assumes a false character and passes himself or herself off as something other than he or she really is. There are situations where the two roles are combined, but there have been many cases with individuals who pass themselves off as someone else without obtaining any visible benefits. They seem to reject and devalue their own identity, despite their awareness of their own genuine gifts and talents. In fact, they frequently make use of these talents to develop their imposturous behaviour. In many cases, when the illusion is broken and the money (other people's money) is lost, it turns out that psychological gratification often seems to be much more important than the material advantages which can be won by imposture.

After all, entrepreneurs act in many aspects in the same way as imposters. They are both trying to turn their fantasies into reality. "In their intense need to pursue a vision and convince others of their ideas, they may slightly resort to distortion of facts. Nevertheless the enthusiasm they generate in selling their dreams—unrealistic or ill-defined as they may be—is important because through it they can be catalyst for change and if successful, also agents for economic improvement."[24] Successful entrepreneurs, like good imposters, have talent to describe visions or fabricate illusions and to make them convincing. Often there is a thin line between a vision and an illusion.

Therefore, many investors have a fear of being fooled by the magic of imposters. Imposters such as Anthoney de Angelis, Refaat El-Sayed, Stein Bagger or Kenneth Lee Layby and Jeffrey Skilling have all (for a limited time) been considered business "wunderkind". These special personalities were, among many others, considered "business stars" by bankers, accountants and the financial press for

---

[23]*Leaders, Fools, and Imposters: Essays on the Psychology of Leadership*, Manfred F. R. Kets de Vries, Jossey-Bass Publishers, 1993.
[24]Ibid.

a long period. Their falls were, in all cases, a "big surprise" which no one had seen coming. But they managed to do a lot of harm to many people's finances before their true personality and the illusionary magic surfaced.

De Angelis' manipulation of millions of gallons of non-existing salad oil sent two Wall Street brokerage houses into bankruptcy and led to plummeting futures prices on commodity markets in New York and Chicago. Nobody understood how he could make money by selling salad oil at so low prices, but he managed to convince the world's shrewdest bankers, brokers and businesspersons to lend him money to conduct transactions they did not understand. The whole scam exploded in 1963.

El-Sayed became chairman of the Swedish Biotechnology company Fermenta. He dazzled the Swedish financial and industrial establishment, the media and the public at large. He was voted "Swede of the year" in 1985. However, soon thereafter, a small article in an obscure newspaper questioned whether El-Sayed had obtained the doctorate he previously flashed to the public. For many, this small deception was hard to take, and after a short disbelief, those involved in his various financial transactions took a closer look at the deals and the man. Quickly, a number of announced deals fell through. Eventually, it became clear that El-Sayed had sold merely dreams and promises and that the stock price of Fermenta, which fell like lead at the Stockholm Stock Exchange, was built, to a large extent, on thin air rather than on substance.

Bagger became CEO of the Danish IT Company, IT Factory, which became the subject of considerable media attention in November 2008 after it was revealed that the company was involved in a spectacular fraud linked to the CEO. The fraud caused the company to declare bankrupt on 1 December 2008. Until the fraud surfaced, the company enjoyed much positive attention in the IT industry due to its impressive growth performance. In 2008, IT Factory was voted Denmark's best IT company by Computerworld because of impressive economic performance. In the same year, it was also voted the Entrepreneur of the Year by the accounting firm Ernst & Young.

Lay and Skilling played a leading role in the corruption scandal which led to the downfall of the US energy company Enron

Corporation. Lay, Skilling and Enron became synonymous with wilful corporate abuse, accounting fraud and corruption when the scandal broke in 2001. Lay was the CEO and chairman of Enron from 1985 until his resignation on January 23, 2002, except for a few months in 2000 when he was chairman and Skilling was CEO. At the end of 2001, it was revealed that its reported financial condition was sustained substantially by an institutionalised, systematic and creatively planned accounting fraud, known since as the Enron scandal. The severe prison sentences following the abuse did not compensate for the losses endured.

These imposters, and any imposter for that matter, have in common great showmanship, verbal virtuosity, personal charm and an ability to be a good listener. Through listening, they knew what the audience wanted to hear. They were good to get their audience to suspend disbelief, and they mastered the creation of excitement about the proposed success of their vision. They also mastered the skill to make people believe that they understood complicated explanations, which in reality was a cover up for the illusion. They did not act alone. They managed to get the whole organisation to believe in the illusion and act as it was real. Another interesting aspect is that actually many of these imposters got so captured by their own illusions that the illusion became a reality for them.

In all these cases, the applauding "audience" included experienced investment bankers, accountants and leading financial editors.

I have not met the imposters mentioned above in person, but they are all well known in the financial world. However, I have, in real life, dealt with imposters, but of smaller scale. The venture fund I managed invested in a few business illusions which looked like promising business visions. From the outset, they were all credible, had a big growth potential and were managed by "great leaders"! However, it turned out later that the vision was founded in thin air. Actually in one of the cases, we were later told by people from the CEO's local community that he was known for embarking on projects which were pure illusions! However, no one had told us. Had we done more background checks, the alarm might have rung, but we relied on our standard due diligence procedure and had listened too much to "the song of the sirens".

It can be very difficult to spot an illusion and may require a very specialised background, as the following example shall illustrate.

More than 10 years ago, as part of an EU project, I worked as advisor to a "talented" and charming apparent imposter, Mrs. Olderst (name disguised). The solution she had developed, and which looked like an exceptional business opportunity, used a proprietary software code to produce geological mapping on the basis of electromagnetic data retrieved from satellite imaging combined with gravity data retrieved from the Ørsted satellite. The software code enabled her to extract hitherto unknown correlations in these satellite data to map deep geological structures with a high confidence level. The solution was the result of a masters' study conducted at a well-known French technical university and had apparently high confidence level. It was also based on concrete comparative studies covering areas where relevant geological data were available.

The solution would reduce the cost connected with the search for deeply located natural resources, particularly valuable minerals and hydrocarbons, in remote and inaccessible areas. Another advantage was that the search would not require a survey or exploration permit from local or national authorities. To add realism to the solution, she pointed out that although the method was revolutionary, it could not quantify the exploration potential of the finds. To do so by using only satellite data would have been completely incredible! However, having an easy tool for the pre-identification of potential hydrocarbon reserves would be worth millions of euros for the exploration companies and billions of euros for national governments, when selling exploration licences. Hence, this solution represented a unique international business case—almost too good to be true. Even that we were not 100% sure of how the technology actually worked, the upside was enormous. Therefore, we considered it worth supporting Mrs. Olderst as advisors.

She had asked me, because of my background in the energy sector, to coach her in the process of finding investors and identify interested exploration companies who could help with test cases. Besides her masters' degree from this well-known French technical university, her "credentials" were good as she had won an important French business plan competition the year before. It added to her credibility that the first focus of Mrs. Olderst's effort was not investor money but to secure a few full-scale comparative "blind test" analysis, where potential customers could compare her method with actual geological data. Hence, the strategy was to find one or two international exploration company partners (e.g. Maersk, BP, StatOil or GDF) who would give us access to their confidential data. In the search for these test cases, we visited the R&D departments of quite a few of the world's leading companies with exploration departments.

It was easy to arrange for meetings with the R&D departments, particularly after having described the new method and its convincing results. The reaction was that if it worked as promised, it could be the method companies had been dreaming about for years. The presentation went well in all cases, and the findings presented impressed our hosts. However, when the exploration experts present at the meetings began asking direct questions about the software, the theory behind the software models and the quality of the data used, and when they wanted to peep into the software "black box", Mrs. Olderst always closed down like an "oyster". She explained that if she provided this information, these experts would, with their large organisations behind, easily replicate her solution and her business case would evaporate. She argued that the material she had presented was proof of the technology and the concept and that it was an offence to require a look into her "secrets". All meetings ended like this, and no collaboration was established. As potential customer endorsement of the technology could not be obtained, the investor search was put on hold.

In the meantime, I independently contacted a few relevant leading university scientists about the concept. Their feedback indicated that the method could simply not work in practice because the data captured apparently conflicted with basic physical laws. Unless they got access to the "black box" and were allowed to examine all the data and calculations in detail, they could only consider the solution as an illusion. Their request for access to the "black box" data and software models was denied.

So our ways departed. I had to conclude that the business case was dead and that I had once more been fooled by an imposter.

All investors have met both real and apparent imposters and fear to react to "the song of the sirens promising wealth and reputation".

Manfred de Vries makes another interesting observation that the traits in the personality of imposters like El-Sayed are, to some extent, the lifeblood of society. They see new possibilities where others fail to do so and help to re-evaluate existing practices and patterns. The problem for investors looking for exceptional investment-ready business cases is to distinguish between vision and illusion and to control their internal greed, when being presented with the visionary opportunity of their dreams.

The investor preferences are often highly ambivalent when it comes to whom they prefer to work with. In reality, they would like to invest with an honest, trustworthy and experienced entrepreneur or manager, who has good technical and administrative skills and is easy to work with (the grey flannel man). But at the same time, he or she should also have a great vision and strong and ruthless leadership skills to quickly build a world-class company, which will change the world and the rules of the game for doing business. This does not correspond to the profile of the "grey flannel man".

For investors and us all, when "the sirens promise wealth and reputation", it is a challenge to maintain our capacity for reality testing and prevent us from being swept away by emotional forces and greed. Even if the story is about deals based on promises and assurances which do not really make sense, it still often tempts us to suspend our disbelief. Investors are also normal human beings behind their shield of financial jargon and cool professionalism. Also investors are potentially easy prey for imposters if they do not watch out.

The fear of being captured by illusions is one of the reasons why it is so difficult for the exceptional business case to get investors' undivided attention and to make them believe in a vision, which still needs to come true. This is, in particular, difficult if not all assumptions behind the vision are explained in a comprehensive and trustworthy way.

The investors also know, even if they could spot the entrepreneurial and leadership "gene" they are looking for, that conversion of a business vision into a financial success requires the presence of special market circumstances and technology preconditions.

Therefore, in the final negotiation process, the focus is on the three "if s":

- **If** these special market and technology circumstances are present
- **If** the entrepreneur or the entire management team has "what it takes" to guide the company on the journey to success
- **If** they can be trusted

Investors know that even in recognition of these difficulties connected to assessing the entrepreneur and his team, it is important also to safeguard the downside of the investment. They will, therefore, often check if the standard "textbook"[25] or similar required competences (PAEI)[26] and experiences are present or can be made present in the organisation and with the right assigned roles.

Depending on the company's level of development and size, these skills will have a more or less dominant role to play. This means that some of these qualifications play a more important role in some stages of company development than others. What is important for the investors is not only the presence of these competences but also a clear recognition by the team that the importance of these roles will shift over time.

Size of organization

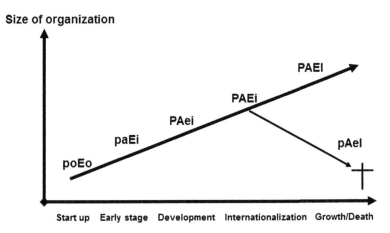

Figure 2.15 Shifting of management role relevance.[27]

---

[25]See Section 2.6 about Adizes.

[26]P: production focus, experiences and strong will; A: administrative skills; E: entrepreneur or creator; I: integrator or human resource skills.

[27]How to read the figure: **capital letters**: strong need, **small letters**: need to be there, **0**: no need right now.

It is clear that entrepreneurial skills dominate the first phases of the life of a newly started company, and you also need to know how to turn the innovation into a product or service. When the company begins or has real customers, administrative and accounting skills are also needed. When the company enters the development stage, focus needs to be on getting the production and sales and marketing effort right, while new innovations and products have less importance (right now). This is also the time where human resource qualifications are needed to secure continued organisational growth, which should match the growth of the business. Later in the life of the company, hopefully before it hits the "dotted line" (mentioned in Fig. 2.4) unprepared and its products become obsolete, innovative skills become essential to secure a constant and relevant innovative development in the products or services of the company. If the company misses the beat, it might end like Kodak and disappear.

When a company grows above 10–15 employees, the previous informal structure is difficult to maintain. The company also moves from a situation where "all know each other and have a common language and experience" to a new situation where only a part of the organisation has a common memory of "how it all started" and personal relation with the entrepreneur, while another part of the organisation has no similar memory. This is a challenging situation, when for the first time, a part of the organisation is old and the other part is new. It requires good personal skills to manage this transition. Later, as the company grows, there will be many of these flex points.

The material to be presented to the investors does not need to have solutions to all these situations, but the investors will need to be convinced, and by understanding the mindset of the entrepreneur or the team, that these challenges are recognised and that there is willingness to cope with these even if it means that a role can shift from CEO to, e.g. CTO, or original key members need to leave the management of the company. Steve Jobs experienced this faith but returned later in glory.

If the investors experience that this type of flexibility and problem recognition are not found in the management team, they might refrain from investing. As we shall see in Chapter 4, a stubborn investor attitude about "how it normally should be" can lead to grave mistakes. Remember that not all investors have a degree in psychology.

In general, investors are good in making human assessment. However, this is not only done via desk research of the business plan and the forwarded CVs, or by Googling or checking LinkedIn or other portals. Nor are results of eventual conducted personal tests decisive.[28] The assessment of the intangible "human factor" is primarily done during the due diligence phase and during the investment and the shareholder agreement negotiations. From the side of the investor, this part of the process is not only about securing the deal at acceptable terms, but also a test of how it is to work and negotiate with the entrepreneur and his or her team. The process is also used to fight the imposter fear and to probe into how much "illusion" is included in the proposed business vision. If this process becomes unpleasant and difficult, investors might at the very late moment decide not to invest, even if the entrepreneur in the end gives in on all the original investor requests.

The investors know that in the end, it is impossible to predict how an entrepreneur or a management team will behave and operate when faced with all the different challenges of business leadership. Manfred de Vries concludes "the more leaders I encounter, the more difficult I find it to describe a typically effective leadership style". Not only is each specific situation in which the uniqueness of a leader shows unique, but the peculiarities of a specific national culture can also lead to great variations.

Therefore, limiting the definition of good leadership to a list of a few common dimensions (as is done too often in research on leadership) is, in reality, an insult to the intelligence of the readers of this books.

The Adizes dimensions mentioned above are, therefore, only to be seen as illustrative examples. The lack of a definitive list does not imply, however, that there are no common requirements for good leadership behaviour, but they are all case dependent.

If the investors, in the end, feel that the entrepreneur and the team are not transparent, flexible and honest in their dealing, if they

---

[28]If you are ever asked by investors to participate in this type of test, say yes, by all means.

see signs of imposturous behaviour or if they experience that there is no common ground for ideas and ambitions about the business venture, even the best deal gets a sour taste.

2.12 Business Models and Value Chains

This section deals with two of the most used—and misused—business terms, which actually only few non-professionals really understand, namely, "business models" and "value chains". However, investors know all about value chains and business models which worked and those which did not perform as expected. Therefore, any investor discussion will sooner or later focus not only on the business model but also on why a particular business model was chosen. So let us start getting the terminology in place.

A "business model" is a buzzword that everybody used (or rather misused) during the dotcom boom. In fact, poorly thought out business models were the downfall of many dotcoms. The term business model dates back to the earliest days of business; it merely describes the way in which a company makes money. A business model can be simple or very complex. A restaurant's business model is to make money by cooking and serving food to hungry customers. A website's business model might not be so clear, as there are many ways in which these types of companies can generate revenue. For example, some make money (or try to) by providing a free service and then selling advertising to other companies, while others might sell a product or service directly to online customers.

A "value chain" is a set of activities that a firm operating in a specific industry performs in order to deliver a valuable product or service for the market. The concept comes from business management and was first described and popularised by Michael Porter in 1985. The idea of value chain is based on the process view of organisations, the idea of seeing a manufacturing (or service) organisation as a system made up of subsystems each with inputs, transformation processes and outputs. Value chain analysis can also be made for entire sectors, as done in this book. How value chain activities are carried out determines costs and affects profits.

The commercial realisation of new ideas and technologies or exploitation of an untapped market potential does not happen through "wishful thinking". It requires careful examination of the opportunity identified. As previously explained, at least three elements (the "three circles") need to be considered.

1. There has to be a market (= demand + willingness to pay) for the product/technology or service. This market may already exist or it may be a whole new market opportunity not yet exploited.

2. The product/technology or service needs through "the eye of the user/consumer" to be better or cheaper than any competing solutions.

3. The product/technology or service needs to be easy to use and also easy (cheap) to produce/deliver.

The best business opportunities are where there is an overlap of the three requirements. In order to make an assessment of the business potential, you need to examine:

- Is there a space in the entire value chain for this new business idea, which can also generate enough value to cover the cost and effort to start commercial exploitation?

  » Value chain analysis

- What is the best way to bring the product/technology or service to the market, and what does it require with respect to product specification, organisation and funding.

  » Choice of business model

- Which competing solutions exist and why is your solution "better" and in which way?

  » Competitor analysis

When these analytical steps have been covered, it is possible to make a first assessment of the realism behind the identified business opportunity.

2.12.1 Value Chain Analysis

Suppose someone asks you: "Can we make a business by developing tools or services which can convert pruning residues from olive trees, fruit trees or vineyards to a combustible biomass and sell it to energy consumers?" How would you approach this challenge?

Besides establishing a good understanding of the market opportunity in the relevant potential markets, the next step is making a "value chain" analysis. The following example is easy to understand: Farmers regularly prune their olive trees, almond trees, fruit trees or wine yards. This pruning material is normally left on the ground, and the question is can it be turned into a valuable biomass. This requires knowledge of whether the soil is deprived of valuable "vitamins" by the removal of pruning materials and whether the farmer has machines which can collect and process the pruning material. The farmer also needs to have access to final customers who will use the biomass, e.g. for energy purposes or for production of biomass-based products.

The value chain can look like Fig. 2.16. In the example, Fig. 2.17, it is assumed that the final customers will use the biomass for energy purposes.

In order to create a more operational background for financial and logistic analysis, this generic "value chain" can be easily converted into a more operational structure which eventually can be converted into an economic analytical model.

In the example, it is assumed that we have six different types of parties involved. Four are directly involved in the value chain: farmer, storage, transport and energy users. The other part is (to the left) the supplier of technology, equipment and services to the other parties, and the last part (right) is the sales and marketing activities. These functions can be undertaken by an independent party or by one or more of the previously listed parties.

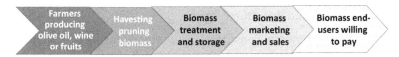

Figure 2.16 General value chain for pruning waste.

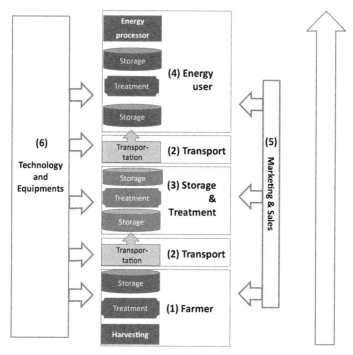

Figure 2.17 Detailed value chain analysis for exploitation of pruning biomass.

Explanations of the different parties and their roles are as follows:

1. A farmer who harvests/collects the pruning residue and provides its initial treatment and stores it for further transportation at the farm gate.

2. The transporter who provides transportation from the farm to a central storage/treatment site and further to the "energy user gate".

3. A central storage/treatment site where the pruning residue is first stored, then processed (dried/converted to pellets or other treatment) and then stored again.

4. End user (energy consumer) who stores the material and makes further treatment before the biomass is used for energy processes. The end user might have additional cost related to

adaptation of conveyer bands, burners and other adaptation cost.

5. Marketing and sales and associated services are also involved, either as separate entities or as a service embedded in one or more of the other entities.

6. Supplier of technology, equipment and services to the other parties without which nothing would happen.

Fundamental to the value chain analysis is the estimate of the maximum price the end user is willing to pay for the energy biomass. In this example, the "substitution cost"[29] is the maximum price the "energy end user" is willing to pay for the treated biomass at his or her plant gate.

The next step in the value chain analysis is to make assumptions regarding the cost of services for each of the parties involved. In some cases, a market price can be used if such price exists for the service. In other cases, the industry sector data might be used.

Based on this "value chain" structure, it is in principle easy to make a simple excel model for a "first level" economic feasibility analysis. In practice, there is "only" a need to make assumptions regarding total amount of ton pruning residue produced at the farm level, and

*   The energy content/ton raw pruning material
*   Harvesting/collection cost/ton
*   Treatment cost/ton, including assumptions regarding potential change in BTU/ton
*   Storage cost/ton/days
*   Transportation cost/ton/km
*   Sales and marketing cost associated to each "transaction point"

The model could look like the excel spread sheet in Fig. 2.18.

In principle, if all the general parameters have been established, it is possible for an enterprise, which is considering to develop a new "pruning collection and processing" machinery, to analyse in a very

---

[29]Substitution cost = cost of using alternative fuels (e.g. coal, fuel oil, natural gas or other types of biomass).

Olive (50%)

Processing unit	Process	Price l/kWh	Total kWh	kWh/ton pruning	Moisture content	Weight reduction via treament	Ton pruning	Treatment cost / ton pruning	Total treatment cost	No of storage days	l day/ton	Total storage cost	l ton/km	Distance in Km	Total transportation cost	Total value chain revenue & cost
	Cost of collecting pruning in fields						100	7.40	740.08							740.08
	Extra cost of harvesting "energy" pruning				-		100	0.00	0.00							-
	Cost to take bales out of field						100	2.88	288.36							288.36
	Costs to store in distribution hubs (R=3 km)						100	6.00	600.00							600.00
Farming cooperatives	"Raw" pruning at farm		229.000	2.290	50%	10%	100									
	Ton pruning after reduction/loss						90									
	Avoided costs (such as mulching)				-			0								
	Value removed from farm (such as mulch)						90	0								
	Storage before farm gate (fields)						90			10.00	0.000	0				
Total farming crop costs																1628.44
	Load and transport to storage						90						0.333	0	0.00	-
Logistic operator	Storage (open air)						90			120.00	0.017	180				180.00
	Treatment		340.200	3.780	25.0%	17.3%	90	6.567	591.00							591.00
	Ton pruning after treatment						74.40									
	Load and transport to delivery						74.40						0.078	0	73.32	-
Total logistic operator costs																771.00
Energy company/ Consumer	Storage cost pruning delivered at storage area						74.40			365.00	0.00	73.32				73.32
	Energy consumer treatment cost		281232.00	3.780	25.0%	1.0%	74.40	0	0							
	Ton pruning after treatment						73.66									
	Pruning to be consumed		278419.68	3.780			73.66									
Total energy company costs																73.32
Financials / Viability	Max price consumer is willing to pay	0.0159	278419.68													4419.36
	Sustitution price (natural gas)															
Value remaining to the farmer after harvesting and pre-teatment cost before farm gate																1946.60

Figure 2.18 Value chain analysis: example for calculating the potential of commercial exploitation of pruning.

detailed way if there is a potential market, and also where and which customers (farmers) it is worthwhile to approach first, because their fields are within the "economic" distance of the end consumers, the customers who will use the biomass as a source of energy.

For almost all sectors and business cases, similar structured analysis can be made by starting a conception value chain analysis (Fig. 2.16). In the next step, break it down into its individual components (Fig. 2.17). From this analysis, it is practical to convert it to a simple economic model (Fig. 2.18). The next step is then to assess if the results can be exploited commercially and through which business model.

In principle, investors will assume that this type of analytical exercise has been conducted in more or less details and that it is a result of this type of strategic thinking, which is the fundament behind the chosen business model and business case presented to investors.

2.13 Business Model Concept

This leads directly to a discussion of what would be the optimal business models for a new technology or service provider. Very often investors like to challenge the choice of business model in order to fully understand why this business model has been chosen and not another. Hence, it is important to be able to explain the entire process which has been conducted before a conclusion has been made, and also you need to explain if and how the model has been tested in "real life" or are "ideas still on the drawing board".

In our pruning example, even if the global value chain analysis shows that a great potential net value could be harvested from using the pruning residue as energy biomass, nothing will happen unless each of the five parties in the value chain is individually able to "see a good business opportunity". For some of the parties, it might make sense to consolidate more activities into one (e.g. combine transportation with storage, treatment, marketing and sales services); for others it is best to run an individual operation.

The business case for each of the parties in the value chain depends not only of this party's chosen business model, but also on the business model chosen by the other parties. In our example, we are looking at the supplier of new technology for the harvest and treatment of pruning, and we assume that this supplier is a company with strong financial resources, so funding is not a limiting factor when choosing the right business models. In principle, at least five completely different business models could be examined. This is illustrated in Fig. 2.19.

- *Harvesting and treatment unit that converts pruning residue to energy quality biomass—the same technical solution but 5 different business models:*

Model 1
- Provide all the crucial components for the harvesting and treatment unit at a central warehouse. The farmer buys the equipment and use the technology at own risk. The farmer buys consumables (e.g. standard "knives") for the treatment unit from supplier or from third party
- **Ikea model**

Model 2
- Deliver and install the harvesting and treatment unit at the farm and leave operation to the farmer. Provide ongoing service and supply of consumables (special "knives") for the harvesting and treatment unit.
- **Turn key supplier**

Model 3
- Provide harvesting and treatment services to the farmer at a fixed "operators fee". Same business model as used for harvesting cereals and other crops, where the harvesting machinery is expensive and only used for a short period of time.
- **Service provider**

Model 4
- Install, operate and finance the harvesting & treatment unit at the farm. Provide the harvesting and treatment services. Assist the farmer in selling the treated biomass and receive x % of sales revenue as payment for services provided to the farmer.
- **ESCO type model**

Model 5
- Install, operate and finance the harvesting unit at the farm and operate the unit for both the harvesting and treatment process. Provide all transportation and sell directly quality biomass at commercial terms to energy users. The biomass company pays the farmer for the right to harvest and further handle and sale the pruning waste.
- **Biomass company**

Figure 2.19 Same technology but five different potential business models; no financial constraints.

Each of these business models requires different financial resources, different design of the product and services, and very different management capabilities. In particular, the Energy Service Company (ESCO)[30] business model and the biomass company business models require different financial resources, different design of the product and services, and very different management capabilities.

---

[30]The ESCO model was originally developed within the energy-saving sector. The initial Energy Service Company (ESCO) started in Europe more than 100 years ago. Over the last 10 years, there has been an increased interest within Europe for the provision of energy services using the ESCO business model. See more in Section 2.17.

However, if the company which developed the machinery was small and with limited financial resources the options would have been fewer and of different nature. In particular, the feasibility of some business models, e.g. licensing, depends entirely on the level and strength of obtained IPR protection.

The choice of business model is not a "free choice". In many cases, the best business model is out of reach because of financial constraints, IPR issues, regulatory barriers or lack of adequate internal resources. In practice, the choice or selecting or developing the right business model is a "work of art" and not formal science!

2.13.1 Business Models and Product Adaptation

It is not possible to outline one unique process for identifying and developing the right business model or strategy for commercialisation. Real-life situations represent such a variety of challenges that a one-size-fits-all approach will never work. Even if the common definition of a business model is fairly straightforward:

A "business model" defines the manner by which the business enterprise delivers value to customers, entices customers to pay for the value, and converts those payments to profit.

It is not a straightforward process to determine and reflect what customers want, how they want it, and how an enterprise can organise to best meet those needs, get paid for doing so, and make a profit. The challenge in assessing relevant business models and their potential success is connected to finding a common ground between:

- What customers want and how they want it delivered
- How an enterprise can organise to best meet those needs and get paid
- Make a profit at the same time

Choosing the right business model for a new business, the launch of a new product or the introduction of a new technology, is more important in most cases than any technology-related choices. Unfortunately, in most cases, when transferring R&D results to business, more emphasis is put on technology than is put on the choice of the right business model.

For many technology-focused entrepreneurs, the term "business model" remains a mystery. Although there has been so much hype about the term, particularly in the vague of the previously mentioned successful books *Blue Ocean Strategy* and *Business Model Generation*, business models are not often a key subject at technical high schools and universities. Even among trained economists, the implications of different business models are not always well understood. It requires understanding of not only economic and market mechanisms, but also of social, psychological and organisational behaviour.

Good examples of successful business models are found in very different businesses. Not all of these companies found their "successful" business model in the first attempt; nor did the eventual successful business model last forever. It had to be adapted to new market conditions. Business modelling is an ever-ongoing process. Key to continued business success is constant adaptation to changing market conditions. A few examples might be best to illustrate the complexity and variation in successful business models.

Many years[31] before the term "business model" became fashionable, the successful entrepreneur Isaac Merritt Singer introduced an entirely new business model for his sewing machine. Isaac Singer is famously associated with the invention of "the eye pointed needle".[32] However, it was the business model for his Singer sewing machine which made him rich. His sewing machine achieved more fame than his competitors, not because it was better and had sharper or longer needles, but because it was offered on hire–purchase basis. This was a business model which had not been seen before. For a small down payment of just $5.00, a purchaser could take the machine home and on the same day start making money as a private seamstress. The Singer sewing machine became the first home appliance, and the Singer Company became one of the first

---

[31]We are back in the 1850s in the USA, at the very beginning of the industrial revolution.

[32]Few remember that Isaac Singer did not make the invention. He licenced the right to use the "eye pointed needle" from Elias Hower. But it was Singer, not Hower, who made a big business by commercialising the invention.

American multinationals, not thanks to the technology, but thanks to the chosen business model.

When Xerox invented the Xerox 914 in 1958, one of the first plain paper copier, it was priced too high for the market. So Xerox developed a new business model. It leased the machines at $95/month, including 2000 free copies, plus 5 cent per additional copy. Clients acquired the new machines and started making thousands of copies each month. Years later the machine price went down, and then the "bait and hook" model was developed. Today the printer/copying market is dominated by cheap printing/copying machines but costly toner cartridges.

Starbucks was originally founded in 1971 using the entrepreneur's own financing and "bootstrapping". Back then, the company was a single store in Seattle's historic Pike Place Market. From just a narrow storefront and the name inspired by Moby Dick, it evoked the romance of the high seas and the seafaring tradition of the early coffee traders. In 1981, Howard Schultz (later Starbucks chairman, president and chief executive officer) first walked into a Starbucks store. From his first cup of Sumatra, Howard was drawn into Starbucks and joined a year later. A year later, in 1983, Howard travelled to Italy and became captivated with Italian coffee bars and the romance of the coffee experience. He had a vision to bring the Italian coffeehouse tradition back to the USA. He left Starbucks for a short period to start his own Il Giornale coffeehouses and returned in August 1987 to purchase Starbucks with the help of local investors, and then the Starbucks adventure as a franchise concept took off. While brand, design and quality coffee are still the profile of a Starbucks café, the product and services you get are constantly adapted to local cultures and new trends. This franchise business model concept is also far from the original 1971 Starbuck business model.

We have previously described Nestle's struggle to convert its research labs patent for the Nespresso system into a booming business.

The previously mentioned young software company PPU Maconomy, which succeeded in selling to American Express, was created in Copenhagen in 1990 by three young entrepreneurs. Their aim was to create new standards for financial and administrative

Mac-based software to the professional creative business segment. The development took place in close cooperation with Apple Computers and financially supported by the VC fund I was managing. We invested in the Mac solution because our market analysis had shown a big empty space for accounting solutions for professional Mac users. One of the founders wanted, for fun, to demonstrate that the special software-building tool on which the company was founded could also be used for the Windows platform. Fortunately, the management team and the board accepted that also a small Windows version of the accounting solution was tested by selected customers. Ten years later, the company went public with a Windows-based enterprise resource planning (ERP) product as flagship and as the key revenue driver. However, it was the Mac version sold to American Express which helped to open the international market for the company. But in the end, it was the Windows-based product which eventually moved the company from an entrepreneur-driven and VC-backed company to its initial public offering (IPO). In 2010, the company was delisted and fully acquired by Deltek Inc. An interesting observation can be made from this case:

- Had the team originally presented a Windows ERP solution to us as investors, we would have turned the venture down because

  » at that time, a Windows-based solution developed by Navision[33] was quickly gaining market dominance and

  ◊ the son of one of my VC fund board members was one of Navision's founders.

- The transition from an Apple focus to a Windows solution was not planned but happened only because one of the Maconomy founders, in his spare time, "played with the idea also to build a Windows prototype of the Mac solution also".

In 2001, Apple launched its iconic iPad brand of portable media players. The device works in conjunction with iTunes software enabling the transfer of music and other content from the iPad to a computer. It also provides seamless connection to Apple's online

---

[33]The Danish software company was later fully acquired by Microsoft.

store, so users can purchase and download content. This solution gave Apple a dominant market position. Yet Apple was not the first company to bring portable media players to the market. Competitors such as Diamond Multimedia with its Rio Brand of portable media players were successful until they were outpaced by Apple. How did this happen? Apple competed with a better business model. On one hand, it offered users a seamless music experience by combining its distinctively designed iPad devices with iTunes software and the iTunes online store. On the other hand, to make this value proposition possible, Apple had to negotiate deals with all the major record companies to create the world's largest online music library. The twist? Apple earns most of its music-related revenues from selling iPads, while using integration with its online music store to protect itself from competitors.[34]

The so-called ESCO[35] model was developed as a special way of delivering new technology or services to customers. The ESCO was originally a private company or consortium which offered solutions for energy renovation of public or private buildings and guaranteed a certain amount of energy saving. The purpose of ESCO projects was typically to reduce energy consumption in buildings/industrial processes and save customers from making heavy investments themselves. ESCO got paid via the documented saving obtained. Later, the ESCO concept broadened to other sectors while maintaining its name and nature, and the original meaning of the term ESCO is long forgotten.

Although these examples are very different, they are similar in one aspect: In each case, the business model was developed based on:

- Deep insight into market conditions, competitors and competing solutions
- Knowledge of how different products were used
- Flexibility in adapting to market reaction
- Understanding of the type of risk involved
- Insight into how and why customers were buying and using them

---

[34]See more examples in the book *Business Model Generation: A Handbook for Visionaries*, Alexander Osterwalder and Yves Pigneur, Wiley, 2010.
[35]See Section 2.17.

- Insight into eventual regulatory barriers and requirements
- A good insight into customer concerns, desires, objectives and behaviour

The many business models which have been successful should serve as inspiration for developing new concepts. Unfortunately, it is impossible to identify all the conditions which have made some of the most well-known business model successful.

The major lesson to be learned with respect to business model is

Don't copy, study and get inspired!

2.14 Business-Modelling Process

The objective of the business-modelling process is to turn a new technology into a commercial product and develop a successful business concept. The objective from the business-modelling process is to develop a range of relevant business models. Investors want to understand not only the advantages of the chosen business model but also why it was chosen. In other words, they want of know about the process which led to the final choice.

The excellent book by Osterwalder and Pigneur, *Business Model Generation*, has a number of useful tools and tips about business model canvassing and generation, which can serve as inspiration for the business model discussion. However, in the end, the results have to be converted to numbers, which can be inserted in budgeting models in order to see if the "ends meet", also from a financial point of view or if a revision or adaptation to the cruel financial reality is required.

The process of analysing relevant business model is, in principle, straightforward. Start by identifying the different elements in the business case.[36] In principle, there are two different types or analysis to be conducted: whether the product/service is a "standalone" product/service or if the product/service is "embedded" in someone

---

[36]Identification of relevant business models can also be made by using the Osterwalder business model canvassing tool. *Business Model Generation: A Handbook for Visionaries*, Alexander Osterwalder and Yves Pigneur, Wiley, 2010.

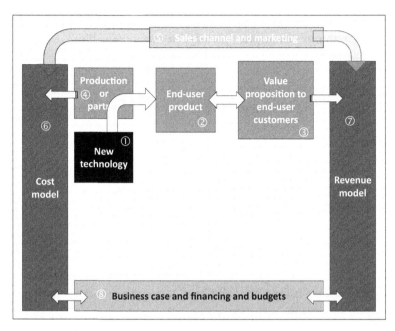

Figure 2.20 Steps in defining the relevant business model (new technology = new product).

else's product. In order to get familiar with the businesses-modelling process, we start with the "standalone" product/service.

Steps 1 and 2

When a commercial product using new technology has been developed and its functionality is well understood, it is essential to identify the end users and "why would they buy". In other words, what value is created for the end users to make them or the customers buy the new product. It is important to understand that the end users might not always be the one who makes the purchase decision (= customer).

The following analysis shall be carried out:

- Which market segment is addressed and who are the customers?
- If the "customer" is different from the end user, what value is created for the end user and what value is created for the customer?

» **End user example**: welfare improvement for elderly persons
» **Customer example**: savings in providing these welfare services

In many cases, this first analysis will lead to revision of product functionality, price assumptions and overall business strategy.

Step 3

This step involves a comparison between product features and customer/end user preferences, and comparison with competitor product features and business models.

• Which customer problems are solved, and what value does it bring to the customer?
• Which customer segments are best served by the new product?
• Who are the competitors and how does our product compare to their products?

To make this analysis, it is relevant to adapt the analytical process from the *Blue Ocean Strategy* book.[37] With respect to competitor analysis, the same analytical tool can be used to identify where and how our products compare/differ from those of the competitors.

Step 4

This step includes an analysis of the requirements for production and the cost associated. Also consideration regarding potential partners in the production process is relevant.

Step 5

This step is a review of how the product is brought to the market and which sales and marketing channels are relevant:

• How to make the customers aware of the new product/service?
• How will customer relationship be established and maintained?

---

[37]See Section 2.8.

- How will eventual local regulatory barrier or requirements be overcome?
- How are the products/services delivered to the end user (e.g. direct sales, agents, distributors, via licence or directly via Internet)?
- What are the typical priorities and concerns of the decision-maker, which can be both the customer and the end users?

This analysis will also often result in a revision of the business strategy or the business model.

Steps 6 and 7

In Steps 6 and 7, you build a cost and revenue model which provides input to the financial part of the equation:

- How the value created for the customer converted to a revenue stream?
- Which local support/subsidy schemes can be exploited?
- Which resources are needed to secure the sales and when?
- What are the total costs of the planned operation?
- Which key activities are needed in order to achieve the business objectives?
- Which partners and partnerships are required to achieve the business objectives?

It is relevant also to analyse if the organisation is tailored to implement the plans and if adequate and qualified staff is available.

Step 8

1. When all the previous steps are completed, it is now possible to make the first financial analysis. At this step also, a first estimate of the required funding can be made, which should lead to the following question: Can a credible investment case for this funding requirement be generated?

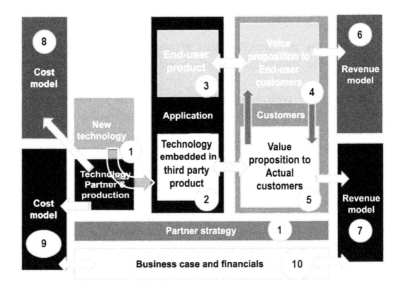

Figure 2.21 Steps in defining the relevant business model (new technology = embedded product).

The next step is to analyse the investment case[38] and analyse if it can appeal to investors or commercial lenders. As previously discussed, lenders will provide loans only if sufficient security for the loans is available, and investors are interested only if they can be convinced of a good chance to make more money by investing in this project/business than by investing in other projects available for investment.

All these business-modelling processes involved a number of iterations before a credible result can be included in the business plan to be presented directly to investors. Investors will be equally interested in hearing about the chosen business model, be even more interested in hearing how you reached this particular conclusion, and which alternatives you have been considering and why they were abandoned. Some good ones might have been abandoned because of lack of money, but this constraint can be removed by an investor!

---

[38]We deal with this subject in Chapter 3.

The more complicated, but equally relevant, exercise is connected to the so-called "embedded product/service" case. This is characterised by a situation where a product or a solution is part of someone else's product/service. In this case, you do not have direct contact with end customers, but your revenues might be entirely dependent on how this third-party product in which your product is imbedded is sold. In order to optimise your business model, you actually need to make an assessment about how much extra value your solution is bringing to the final product, how much of this extra value is captured in the selling process, and how large slice of this extra value can you lay your hands on.

Steps 1 and 2

When a new supporting technology, e.g. a heat sink[39] or a new micro-battery for hearing devices, has been developed and its functionality and efficiency are well understood, it is essential to identify how this new product can bring value to the end product (e.g. laptops/hearing aids) producers. The business idea is to secure replacement of "old technology" (mechanical ventilation/power supply) with the new heat sink/micro-battery. The challenges are to assess the value of eventual production saving, or additional value created for end users (you or me), because new laptops with the new device built in will now become more stable and silent, or a new hearing aid will last longer without recharging. If we deal with complicated products, such as laptops or advanced hearing aid technology, the production process is normally highly automated and the technical design is not something which is easily changed. If the end product is, e.g. ISO certified, then even the smallest redesign might require an entirely new re-certification process.

In practice, you need to convince an internal "local champion" in the laptop or hearing aid company about all the benefits your solution can provide. And you need to do it in a way that he or she can see his or her opportunities and make the internal "sell in". You also need to make the offering to the laptop or hearing aid producer,

---

[39]A nanoparticle-based small unit, which can be built into, e.g. a laptop, which can disperse heat generated. In principle, it can replace the traditional ventilation unit.

right at the moment where a redesign process is taking place. Many pieces of luck need be combined, but it can be done!

Most investors will expect that the following analysis has been carried out and with a positive result:

- Identification of the product(s) which will benefit most from the new technology.
- Which market segment is addressed and who are the customers?
- Which value/saving is created for the customer, and is it significant or only marginal?
- Sales strategy defined, e.g. market to all laptop producers, or strike an exclusive deal?

In many cases, this first analysis will lead to revision of product functionality, price assumptions and overall business strategy.

Step 3

This step involves a comparison between current technology solution and your new solution, and identification of design and production staff preferences, including the normal sequences for product redesign.

- Which customer problems are solved, and which value does it bring to the customer?
- Which customer segments are best served by the new product?
- Who are the competitors and how does our product compare to their products?

To make this analysis, it may be relevant to adapt the analytical tools and processes from the *Blue Ocean Strategy* book.

Steps 4 and 5

These steps summarises the value created for your customer, and how your pricing capture part of this extra value created.

- How to make customers aware of the new product/service?
- How will customer relationship be established and maintained?

- How are the products/services delivered to the end user?
- Which are the typical priorities and concerns of your customers and decision-maker?

This analysis will also often result in a revision of the business strategy or the business model.

Steps 6 and 8

You will probably never know how your customers' cost model is impacted in the end, or how it has influenced their final revenue model, but you can make qualified guesses. The final business model which will be attractive to your customers also depends on how you sell. For example, you can "sell" via a licence agreement (they can make it all by themselves and get full control of the value chain), or you sell "by the piece". In the latter case, you determine the price and your cost. Your customers have less control over you and their value chain, but you can sell to other customers also, depending on the agreement with the first and hopefully major customer.

Steps 7 and 9

Steps 7 and 9 combined is used to build your own cost and a revenue model which provides input to the financial part of the equation:

- How the value created for the customers can be converted to a revenue stream?
- Which local support/subsidy schemes can be exploited?
- Which resources are needed to secure the sales and when?
- What are the total costs of the planned operation?
- Which key activities are needed in order to achieve the business objectives?
- Which partners and partnerships are required to achieve the business objectives?

It is relevant also to analyse if the organisation of your customer is tailored to implement the plans and if adequate and qualified staff is available.

Step 10

When all the previous steps have been completed, it is now possible to make yourfirst financial analysis. At this step also, a first estimate of the required funding can be made, which should lead to the following question: Can a credible investment case for this funding requirement be generated?

2.14.1 Processes Described in Textbooks Do Not Replace Need for Imagination

I was recently asked by a group of investors to structure their business model analysis for a French innovative company. They wanted to enhance its chances to become a market leader within its field of technology. When embarking on this task, the analytical structure outlined in the section above secured that all relevant elements were encapsulated in the process. But as always, when "theory" becomes confronted with "real-life challenges", it can only help in structuring the process, not function as a "manual" which, if followed, will guide you to the right solution. Real-life choices require substantial additional imagination.

The company in question had developed a superior micro laser-based engraving technology, which could carve exceptionally refined surface structures on metal surfaces, which are used for production of high-end consumer and industrial goods and products. This technology can fully replace the traditional etching process.

The company wanted to find a business model for rapid growth, not only targeting the high-end market for metal products requiring advance engravings but also for the larger mass product market where sophisticated surface treatment is required.

The company had the following range of business models under consideration:

1. Maintain the current French engraving service centre to be servicing customers worldwide.

2. Creation of a number of fully owned "satellite" engraving service centres in key countries/regions.

3. Creation of a number of partner owned "satellite" engraving service centres in key countries/regions.

4. Creation of a "laser-engraving" franchise service centre concept with local managers.

5. Produce and sell laser-engraving machines and associated software to individual engraving service centres around the world.

Each of these alternative business models and perhaps many more business models would create different management and staff challenges, different funding requirements including different requirements for technical design of software, machines and tools.

First of all, a close analysis of the competing etching technology (and competitors) needed to be conducted, identifying the type of products where micro laser-based engraving has significant advantages compared to etching, either from a cost point of view or from a production point of view. With respect to the latter, speed, flexibility and accuracy could each be elements where laser technology has clear advantages compared to etching. The analysis could be refined, indicating:

- Advantages, including cost savings compared to today's etching and traditional laser technology
- Competitive advantages using "next year" improved laser technology and lower cost

This analysis could then be combined with geographical identification of design departments of the companies which need engraving in their production process and their geographical location. We should estimate the expected "lifetime" of current production facilities, which could provide an indication of ongoing market for new and replacement sales.

These analyses together could give good indication of potential "customers" and an input to evaluate market size and potential growth. This identification could also provide a clear indication of where eventually micro laser engraving could take place, compared to the current costly solution where the engraving took place in

France. The analysis would also provide an indication about where the "low-hanging" fruits in the engraving market are first to be harvested.

It was clear that the current "France-only" solution puts a severe constraint on growth possibilities. The analysis provided a first outline of where eventual local laser-engraving service centres could be localised and also estimates of the size of local business. Combined with this analysis, it was possible to make estimates of cost and investment requirement and develop a business case for each entity. Based on this information, it became possible to first understand whether profitable local service business cases could be created and where to start benchmarked against the competing etching technology.

The business cases for 4 competing business models were identified, including strategies for getting the information needed for further assessment of pros and cons:

Business model 1

French engraving service centre servicing all customers worldwide

- Identification of market size and growth limitation following this solution

Business model 2

Creation of a number of fully or partially owned "local" engraving service centres in key countries/regions, Identification of localisation

- Cost and investment and general business potential analysis
- Management requirement

Business model 3

Creation of a "laser-engraving" franchise concept with local managers but all software and machines/tools delivered from HQ in France

- Identification of localisation and franchise takers
- Cost and investment and general business potential analysis

- Training and quality assurance
- Management requirement

Business model 4

Produce and sell laser-engraving machines and associated software to individual engraving service centres around the world

- Design and production of standalone laser-engraving machines/ tools and associated software
- Price setting in order to compete with etching technology
- Sales, marketing and service structure and associated costs
- International service and maintenance solution

For each of these possible business models, the current management strength and weaknesses were evaluated, also capital requirement was estimated combined with an assessment of realistic possibilities of obtaining the required funding.

In the end the investors decided for the last option primarily because the strength of the management was in developing and producing advanced laser technology, not in operating and managing service companies around the globe. The process also secured a better alignment of the ambitions and intentions of the investors with that of the management.

2.15 Timing

The "dotted line" previously discussed in Fig. 2.4 illustrates the need for continued product and service innovation, as all existing products or services will hit "the dotted line" sooner or later and become obsolete from a technical or functionality point of view. However, when analysing the potential of a successful business model, you also need to include the "timing" issue. This relates to the problem of implementing the chosen business model at the right moment, namely, not too early or too late.

Arrival at the market "too late" may be caused by your business idea being launched too late because you got the idea very late. However, we often see entrepreneurs who get the right idea at the right moment and still do not make the "jackpot". They are typically those who want to minimise the funding requirement or want to "avoid losing control to investors". They, therefore, "bootstrap" during the development phase, and by doing so have less resource to get the product ready in time for market launch. As the "dotted line" always exists, they often come into the market too late and, therefore, only get less-than-expected sales before their version of the product becomes obsolete.

However, it is equally dangerous to come to the market too early; your costs are running and sales do not materialise as expected because the market conditions are not yet ready. In the 1990s, I participated in an investment in a promising Danish software company Autograph. The credentials of the management team were "on the spot". They were experienced managers, also in sales. Some of the team members were even active in the international standardisation group which formulated compression and other standards for colour and image handling and colour printing standards. The colour printer manufactures would in their specifications adhere to these standards. The product and business concept was to licence printer drivers with a combination of unique compression technology and colour optimising for the new generation of home colour printers. The compression technology made it possible to use it on normal home computers, which had limited CPU capacity at that time. The solution would make it possible to print quality colour screen image using the new small home colour printers, which the big printer manufactures such as HP, Canon and Fujichi were expected to release on the market 2 years after our investment. At that time, colour prints from small printers never looked like what was on the screen. If you wanted "what you see is what you get" type of quality, the only solution was the large professional colour printers.

Hence, everything looked good, and we visited the big printer manufactures in the USA and got clear confirmation about the planned launch date for home colour printers. The development of the new printer driver had started, and all the sales preparation was lined up for the "big bang", and then the launch of these home printers was postponed, first for 1 year and then again for another year. In order to keep the small company's key staff members and sales team

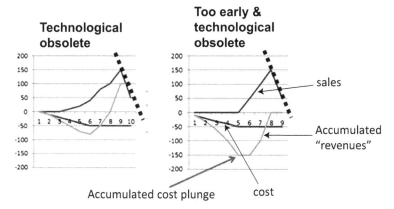

Figure 2.22 Technology obsolete and coming too early in the market.

operational, the burn rate was still high. When we had experienced the launch delay for the second time, the bank account was at nil, and a decision to put more money into the venture was required. A close examination of the situation showed that one of the key unique selling propositions, the compression technology, was not needed so much anymore. All new computers now had much more CPU power. Hence, there was not any longer the urgent need for the unique data compression technology (we were hitting "the dotted line"). The investors decided not to increase the investment exposure. The company was drastically downscaled, and the investors had to write off their investment. Nothing was wrong with the business model or product, but the company hit the market with a product 2 years too early and wasted via the high burn rate its reserve liquidity, which could otherwise had been used to re-adjust product strategy.

Although this particular product was not a real "embedded" product, the example illustrates another risk for products where sale is entirely dependent on the decision made by other companies on which you have no control. In this case, it was the printer companies that delayed the launch of the product (colour printers), which should have secured the demand for and sale of "our solution".

Investors have, in many costly lessons, learned this type of lesson. Hence, they will always make very detailed examinations not only of the sales forecasts in a budget, but of each of the underlying assumptions behind the sales estimates.

2.15.1 Competitors and Funding Pitfalls

The budgets associated to a business model, which eventually can lead to a business plan, should outline both the short and the long funding requirements. It is prudent always to make budgets for the first years on a monthly basis. The peak in liquidity requirement during the months of the year can easily exceed by a factor of 2 the "liquidity requirement" which is estimated based on a 1-year budget. This also has implications for the business model chosen.

A company could decide, in order to sustain its market introduction efforts and beat aggressive competitors, to choose a customer-friendly credit policy. The reason could be to overcome customer reluctance, when buying a new product. The chosen customer-friendly credit could give the customers during the first year a 2-month credit. This "hidden rebate" will not show on the profit and loss account: "it is only a bit deferred payment". Such a policy, however, compared to a 1-month or 15-day credit policy can severely put the liquidity of the company in danger, particularly if new customers pay late. Hence, detailed budget and liquidity simulations always need to go hand in hand before, e.g. the sales and marketing guys begin to offer creative solutions to new customers, if sale does not perform as expected.

In Section 2.21, we will go deeper into the budget and liquidity challenges.

Liquidity and cash flow considerations are, therefore, important elements to include during the discussion on the "right" business model. Sometimes, liquidity concerns may prevent the choice of the best business model.

2.16 Competitor Analysis with Respect to Products and Business Models

The "no competition" situation never occurs! Although young people might not believe it, life went on before SMS, Facebook, Google, mobile phones and iPads came into existence. For all new products and services brought to the market, you always face competition from solutions which the customers used before or lived well without. Even the supplier of clean water from a new water hose in a Maasai village will face competition from the free water collected at the old well or in the river. And similar and competing products may appeal in very different ways to the customer depending on the business model chosen.

With the risk of oversimplifying the competition analysis, two major types of analyses are required.

In the first one, you need to analyse if your product or service creates differentiation from your identified competitors by product differentiation (functionality, design, price, efficiency, brand, quality) or by tweaking established business models.

In the second, you need to analyse and fully understand if you create new, uncontested market space through the creation of new benefits and services to the customers, while simultaneously reducing cost by eliminating less valuable features or services.

In the bestseller *Blue Ocean Strategy*, the authors called the first option "red ocean strategy" and the second "blue ocean strategy". To achieve this "value innovation", you need to challenge both the industry conventional wisdom and the established business models. You need to analyse:

- Which of the factors the industry takes for granted can be eliminated?
- Which factors should be reduced well below the industry standard?
- Which factors should be raised well above the industry standard?
- Which factors should be created that the industry has never offered?

You should try to explore non-customer groups and tap untouched markets.

Around 2012, a new "online language-teaching" product was brought to the market. In principle, the product represented a good example of a potential "blue ocean strategy" with a great potential for "innovative online language teaching". However, it turned out that these services were brought to the wrong market and too early.

- Classroom teaching forms the basis for most foreign language teaching. The classroom and the location limitation could be eliminated via online video-backed tools, a good broadband and a simple Skype connection. In principle, the argument to the language schools around Europe and elsewhere was formulated like: your students are everywhere; you need not limit yourself to make money from your classroom teaching constrained by classroom capacity and availability.

- In principle, only Skype and a laptop with a camera were required to conduct online live tuition. No real estate/school buildings were needed, and teachers could work from home on flexible hours.
- The solution brought full flexibility on teaching schedule and removed physical classroom availability restrictions.
- It provided worldwide reach for the language-teaching classes and no restrictions on students to travel to meet the teacher. Hence, the potential market was apparently big.

The other competitive tweak in the "live online language teaching" offering was that the big language schools, e.g. Berlitz Corporation, could afford to develop this online solution by themselves. But small independent language schools, e.g. in Malta, Cyprus, Australia or elsewhere, would not have this possibility. Hence, the offering would, from a technology point of view, bring the small language schools "on par" with the big multinational schools and at a very low cost.

The first test and target market was the large Malta-based English language industry because the entrepreneur happened to live in Malta. Here there were more than 50 small language schools which could add this new functionality to a well-established language-teaching business. Malta is an attractive language education place, which attracts 80,000 plus students to this sunny island every year. By implementing this solution, this local language industry could reach out to the entire world and service all students, who either would not or could not fund the cost to travel to Malta. A laptop, a video camera and a few hours of training of local teachers could service the thousands of students in Europe, Asia, Africa and South America who could not afford to go to Malta.

The product was simple and the business model well described, but when the product and the service were launched, it turned out that it did not fit with the business models of the local language industry in Malta. This industry makes a substantial part of their business not through teaching but by providing travel services, hotel rooms and local entertainment services to the language students. In reality, for a large part of the students, the language course in Malta was also an excuse for having a "great time in Malta" for a couple of weeks, maybe more than a serious attempt to learn English. Hence, the solutions did not support the current business models of the language schools, and they would not buy!

This example illustrates how difficult it is for an outsider to a business sector to rationalise the local decision-maker's motives, business models and incentive drivers. In this segment of the language industry, the business model was a combination of language teaching, travel arrangement, accommodation and fun creation. Hence, addressing one part of the language schools' business model with "online teaching" would destroy other part of the business.

What we learned was that there are more important factors to take into account when making a competition analysis than the one which is related to the technology. One misconception which is often experienced is that competition will come from a competing technology with the same functionality. The online tuition example illustrates very well that other similar (but not so good) online products were not the competitors, but the real competitors were the conventional language school classroom teaching and in particular the associated business connected.

Fully understanding this industry like many other industries requires "insider knowledge". No one doubts that supermarkets sell goods to consumers, but the real business is shelf-edge management! A technology which can replace the cost of publishing and distributing "weekly offer" magazines from a supermarket chain disregards that it is often the suppliers of the goods advertised in the magazine that pays for these cost and that the supermarket also makes a profit here, so no savings here!. Too many tech entrepreneurs forget that industry knowledge is as important as technology excellence, when it comes to building a successful business case.

The key to any analysis of relevant business models is the identification of the relevant customer segment and to fully understand how the current needs of customers or end users are served by existing solutions, suppliers and business models. You also fully need to understand all the elements of the business models of your competitors. In this process, you will find out how (and if) your solution and business model are better and how it might serve additional, even unrecognised, needs. You need to fully understand the future "battlefield", including your opponents. Each situation requires special tools, resources and strategies.

The relevant competitors to watch may easily change over time. While the low-cost airlines such as EasyJet and Ryanair in the beginning were competing directly with the traditional airlines with a "blue ocean strategy", now they are facing traditional fierce price competition from other low-cost airlines and even from the big "flag carriers", who have lowered their prices.

The strategy behind a competition analysis should also take into account where your new solution/product is placed in Fig. 2.23.

Each of the existing competing solutions should be identified and described with respect to price, functionality, quality, design, business model and other relevant product features. When this list is completed, your own product/solution should be compared to each of these elements. The previous funding/liquidity example has illustrated that sometimes features as simple as payment terms might be an essential business differentiator, and a differentiator where the capital requirement to implement a flexible payment term might kill a small company.

If a structured competitor/competition analysis has been conducted, it should be possible to identify the major differentiators between your solution (all factors taken into account) and any competing solution. This comprehensive survey should then form the basis for a reassessment of the chosen business model and business strategy.

Even if the solution which you want to promote is "far better" on all factors, it might still not be attractive to pursue this business opportunity, if the potential profit from operation is not sufficient to justify the risk of the endeavour. It might then be necessary to go through the entire process once again in order to make product adaptation or develop an alternative business model, which can be funded.

Under all circumstances, it is irrelevant to pursue a business plan which cannot be funded. *Hence the bottom line of all analysis is financial analysis.* If the business case needs money and you cannot borrow from the bank or do not have a rich benefactor, you need to make the "investor readiness test". If this does not give a positive result, revise the business case and the underlying assumptions or find something else to do!

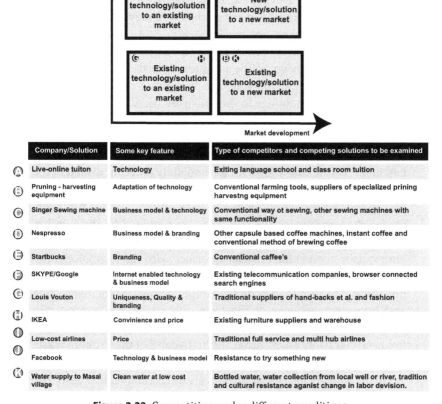

Figure 2.23 Competition under different conditions.

2.16.1 Customer Preferences and Business Models

The complete analysis of relevant business models should include an analysis of the best way to deliver the product and service to the customers and to understand which type of value the product or service is generating. Customers not only look at the product "per se", but also look at the way they buy it. Louis Vuitton would not have existed if product functionality was the only decisive factor when buying a new handbag.

The very different business models illustrated in the pruning example[40] were based on the same technology and solving the same problem: "harvesting and treating pruning waste". But the different business models delivered the product to the customers in very different ways, and leaving the customers with different financial and risk exposure. The business models also may differ in the way they address technology and market risk.

If we look at the so-called "IKEA" model, this business model requires special design of the products in order to make it easy for the individual end user to use it without external support/ service. While the supplier in the "Turnkey" model both takes care of instalment and instructs the user on how to use/operate the product. Only when it works, he or she has finished the sale and product delivery and can leave the day-to-day operation to the customer. This model allows for a completely different design of the product, as it is not the customer who needs to understand how to assemble the product and make it work. In the "Service provider" model, the services for the customer are provided by the supplier and the customer is not directly involved in the process. Hence, less emphasis is needed for the user interface with the technology. The supplier is in full control and the customer pays a fixed fee and has no risk. In the "ESCO" model, the supplier provides the harvesting and treatment services at the farm and shares the market risk with the farmer, but the farmer makes no investment and has no financial risk. Only an eventual alternative use of the pruning waste represents a small risk to the farmer. The last model, the "biomass company" model, is actually an entirely different business case. The biomass company simply buys the raw material from the farm and develops this raw material into a product which is sold directly to energy users. The farmer is not a "customer" in the traditional sense, but a supplier of raw material.

---

[40]See Section 2.12.

Each of the five business models requires different organisational structure and financial strength from the supplier of the new technology. And each model might have very different appeal to different customers.

The final choice of business models and sales strategy also needs to take into consideration the motivation and concerns of the decision-maker at the end user level. How will his or her comfort, responsibility, liquidity, risk or career be affected by buying the new product?

2.17 ESCO Model as Remover of Customer Risk Concerns

Customers buying new technology or new solutions always run the risk that the solution does not fit to their requirement or does not function as expected. Both the perceived and the real risk will often prevent the customer from buying if the risk is not removed one way or the other. Prudent investors will ask if the chosen business model addresses also this obvious market risk. If the product costs €10, the risk is low, but if the product or solution is costly or requires process adaptation at the customer's site, the risk element can play a decisive role in the purchase decision process, irrespective of how good it is and how many relevant problems it solves.

An example might help to understand this issue: Let us consider a local farmer who owns and operates a large olive oil farm. He is considering alternative ways of treating the organic waste from pruning. An obvious and easy solution is "to do nothing". An alternative solution might be to buy a pruning waste harvesting and treatment technology for his estate. He will consider both the performance and the savings or revenues the new technology provides and the financial risk he is exposed to by using his limited financial means to buy/rent the new technology: It might not work as expected on his particular fields, or the value of the pruning waste is less than expected.

As previously mentioned, the ESCO business models were originally developed for the introduction of new solutions and technologies within the energy savings sector, particularly energy-saving technology for buildings. The ESCO business model has since become popular also outside the building sector for which it was originally designed.

In its original form, an ESCO[41] provides its products and/or services with the following four fundamental operational features.

1. First, ESCO guarantees the energy savings and/or the provision of the same level of energy service at a lower cost by implementing an energy-efficiency project. A performance guarantee can take several forms. It can revolve around the actual flow of energy savings from a project, can stipulate that the energy savings will be sufficient to repay monthly debt service costs for an efficiency project, or that the same level of energy service will be provided for less money.

2. Second, the remuneration of ESCOs is directly tied to the energy savings achieved.

3. Third, typically ESCO either finances or assists in arranging financing for the cost of installation of the energy project it implements under the ESCO contract.

4. Last, but not least, ESCOs retain an ongoing operational role in measuring and verifying the savings over the financing term.

Under an Energy Performance Contract (EPC), an ESCO develops, implements and finances (or arranges financing for) an energy-efficiency project or a renewable energy project, and uses the stream of income from the cost savings, or the renewable energy produced, to repay the costs of the project, including the costs of the investment. The overriding principle of the ESCO business model is "that remuneration is based on demonstrated performance". This appeals to many other innovative solutions which have not yet got a firm place on the market; therefore, it has spread rapidly to other sectors.

An ESCO business model might, in some cases, have greater chance to succeed than an "IKEA" business model, in particular with

---

[41]An ESCO is a company providing its products or services via the ESCO business model.

new technology or innovative solutions on which customers have no prior experience and which is to be introduced in a conservative industry sector. In the "IKEA" case, farmers have to buy the new technology and do everything themselves, including taking the risk that the machine does not work well on their particular soil, or that their personal business model of selling the collected pruning material does not work. The ESCO solution removes the financial and technological risk from their shoulders, and they still share the potential "upside". In the IKEA solution, they have to trust the guaranties provided by the supplier and hope for the best market price for their pruning waste.

On the supplier side, the ESCO business model creates very different financial/liquidity and risk challenges than associated with traditional sales. However, a big technology supplier might have a better insight into the entire value chain and the risks associated than the individual farmer. And a big company might also have the financial muscles to secure its funding. Hence, in some cases, unconventional business models might be the only solution to get new technology accepted in a conservative sector.

To conclude, the ESCO model removes the risk from the customer, who is faced with a risky purchase decision related to new technology, and passes the risk to the supplier.

The ESCO model should, in principle, be a "win-win" solution. The customer has no risk, so why not say yes? In real life, however, we have observed that customer reactions are based on a very complex set of reasoning and arguments. These may include many other considerations than those which are "cool cash" or "perceived risk" related. In a number of cases, the customer reaction to the ESCO model was negative. The argument was "if a product cannot be sold on normal terms, then the product is probably not good"!

It is, therefore, reasonable to conclude that one business model might be applicable during the introduction phase of a new technology or while moving into an entirely new market. Later, it might be relevant to shift to other business models when the new technology becomes accepted and is considered an efficient "standard" technology. In other words, the choice of "business model" broadly speaking is a complex choice to make and requires substantial information, not only of the market, the decision process

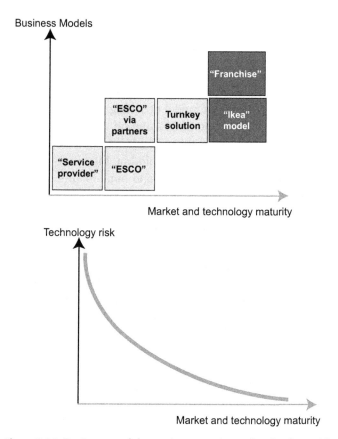

Figure 2.24 Business models, market maturity and technology risk.

at the purchaser level, but also about the business models applied by competitors. The relevance of different business models also changes over time, as illustrated in Fig. 2.24.

With respect to "early stage" projects originating from R&D activities, it is seldom that all elements in a business model analysis can be thoroughly analysed right from the start. But those elements which are not covered should be put on a "to do" list for later consideration. Before any strategic business decisions regarding business model and financial requirements are made and before investor contacts are made, all relevant elements which have been listed in the previous sections should be examined in more or less detail. This is much more cost efficient than the traditional "muddling through"[42] method, which often leads to financial disasters.

Fortunes have been made by companies who got the business model right. Among the most well-known "prototype" business models, we find:

- Gillette model—razor and blades
- Bait and hook model—cheap printers, expensive toner cartridges
- Coca-Cola model—franchise and no registered formal IPR (patent) on recipe
- Nespresso model—sell cheap equipment, but "high-end branding" and make money on consumables
- IKEA model—warehouse with easy-to-assemble furniture, do it yourself (DIY)!
- Turnkey model—complex solutions made ready to function before handover
- Skype/Google/Facebook model—Free service, make money on data and advertising
- iPad model—unit sales combined with content control
- Component/embedded business model—quality/performance; "Intel inside"
- Franchise model—McDonald's, 7Eleven, Starbucks, etc.
- Low cost model—Ryanair, Easy Jet, Cabin Hotels
- ESCO models (Energy Service Company)
- Affiliate marketing models (particularly used in online gaming marketing)

We also need to mention all the traditional business models which you find in most management textbooks and which have always been around:

- Leasing
- Direct sales
- OEM solutions
- Sales via agents

---

[42]Muddling through: first we try one model; if it does not work, we try another and so on.

- Service contracts
- Licensing (only if strong IPR)
  » Strategic choice between small upfront/large royalty versus large upfront/small royalty and so on

2.17.1 Summing Up

Too many business failures and negative investor response have been caused by the wrong choice of a business model. Too often the choice of a business model is based on "I have heard that this business model is very successful" or "this is the standard in our industry" or "this solution is the only possible solution with the financial resources available". None of these arguments represents "good reasons" to choose a particular business model.

The right choice of business model should reflect a thorough understanding of the customers' preferences and decision process or decision situation and a relevant mapping of competitors and competing business models. The best way to start the serious "business model" discussion is to bring forward a few concrete and relevant examples and discuss "pros and cons" in relation to the "value chain" and force a process of "thinking outside the box".

Companies such as IKEA, Apple, Skype, Nespresso or Ryanair would not have been in business today without a lot of "out of the box" thinking. Business history tells us that it is (almost) never the new technology which makes the difference between a success or failure. It is the business model (in combination with technology, e.g. Singer, Apple and iPad) which makes the difference.

It is not possible to identify a few "key types" of business models which have greater chances of being successful than others simply because business situations differ too much, also over time. What can be proposed is, in a structured way, to compare the "pros and cons" of any chosen business model against the other potential business models relevant for the individual case. If it is done in an intelligent way, it is possible to derive a semi-rational justification of the "pros and cons" of different realistic models, including the financial/funding consequences/requirements of each model.

The penetration or uptake of a new technology, service concept or process also depends on whether it is "nice to have" or "need to have" or if you can find the customers "burning platform". If you are not a business sector "insider" and try to rationalise customer behaviour or preferences within that business sector or industry, the risk of making a big mistake is high. Inventors of new solutions or technologies often live with the misconception that everybody will immediately be "in love" with the new solution. They often forget that life has been pretty comfortable and also easy before the new solution became available. Creating a "market pull" for a new technology or solution often takes time. Even the success of the iPad did not come "overnight" although it may looks like today.[43]

2.18 IPR and Freedom to Operate

2.18.1 Introduction

Too many entrepreneurs and researchers believe that having a patent or any other IP protection is like having your own private goldmine. Nothing is more wrong. The only thing which is 100% sure, if a person wants to go all the way to patent an invention or protect a trademark, is that it costs a lot of money, but in some cases those cost are insignificant compared to the value it protects—but you do not know beforehand! Basically, patents may be compared to insurances. If a company has a patent protection, it is in principle "protected" against someone stealing or copying their invention **but** (contrary to the insurance analogy) only if the company can afford to enforce the protection provided by the IPR. You need to go to court to enforce your rights and eventual get compensation for losses endured. It is also important to remember that a patent is not a value creator by itself, but a protector of a (potential) value. You never know upfront what will be the value of a discovery or invention, especially not in the high-tech sectors. It can take a decade or more before the discovery can be developed into a successful and valuable product. It also has to be taken into consideration that by taking out a patent, the description in the patent application will disclose detailed information about the invention to the outside world.

---

[43]To get an impression of the many "trial", read *Steve Jobs*, Walter Isaacson, Simon & Schuster, 2011.

Only few patents are very valuable and generate a substantial revenue stream. The distribution of income from patents and licences is extremely skewed. Not all patents lead to licences which give at least some income, and fewer lead to an income covering the costs many universities and companies currently are paying for the IP protection. Sometimes it might be more relevant to publish to prevent other parties to take out a patent on a similar discovery. For companies, the benefits of patenting activity might be valuable even if the direct income stream from the protected invention might be less obvious. With respect to universities, the example from Stanford University provides facts for thoughts: The licence history of Stanford has been followed for many years. Even in the long run, only one out of 20 licences bears its own cost and one patent out of thousand brings in the "big income" covering the total economy of these operations. It should also be noted that even the often-cited Stanford success story took really many years until the accumulated income could meet the accumulated cost.

A recent study[44] of the patenting activity of Danish SMEs has indicated that only companies with strong growth and revenues are able to convert patented innovations into commercial products with a positive impact on profit. The least profitable companies could not justify the cost of patenting through an impact on profit. According to the author, the conclusions from the study seem to have European-wide relevance. However, patent protection is sometimes the basis for a strong revenue stream for the very successful companies. Hence, there is no general answer to the question: Patent your invention or not?

2.18.2 Patent Strategy Consideration

IPR strategic considerations are essential for entrepreneurs and academics interested in the commercialisation of new technologies. Besides offering protection for intellectual property, patents and other type of IPR may be the key to opening the door for strategic business discussions with large corporations and investors. This is

---

[44]A study of 320 patenting and 6997 non-patenting companies in 2006 by Prof Ulrik Kaiser, Institute for Business and Economics at South Danish University.

particularly pertinent for large corporations, as many will not engage in a discussion about technological sales (e.g. licence strategy) or enter into a partnering discussion unless the solution is protected, or an IPR application has been filed. Investors will normally only consider a patent to have significant value if it protects a strong potential revenue stream, or has a major strategic position.

2.18.3 Intellectual Property Rights[45]

There are many types of IP protection:

- Patents
- Utility models
- Copyright
- Trademarks
- Design, "registered" and "unregistered"
- Trade secrets

As European patents are examined and published by the European Patent Office rather than simply registered, patent rights are more certain than many other forms of legal protection available for inventions. For example, if a patent is infringed, the patent holder can sue for infringement or file for a court order for customs to intercept imports of the patented products. On the other hand, it should be noted that the cost associated with the legal battle for patent enforcement can be substantial.

A short description of each of these different types of IPR can be found in Annexure 2.

2.18.4 Intellectual Property Protection

The individual types of intellectual property are connected to different aspects of intangible assets and can potentially help an inventor to protect an innovation. For example, an inventor might use a patent to ensure that his or her company is the only company

---

[45]See more about types of intellectual property and intellectual property infringement in Annexures 2 and 3.

that can offer certain features or products; trademarks and design patents are able to communicate to consumers the unique feature(s) of a product or service; trade secret law protection may benefit inventors who wish to keep aspects of the production process secret (often requires significant effort to ensure secrecy is maintained).

In today's economy, intellectual property and its protection through IPR are crucial for the successful growth of new ideas, products and solutions. Start-up companies use IPR to protect themselves from industrial competition and to make themselves more attractive to larger corporations. Large companies also use IPR in order to secure and protect the benefits of their investments and to establish a strategic position forwards competitors. Use of IPR can be seen across all industries, including, e.g. traditional industries such as steel manufacturing, which might use IPR to protect their intangible assets, such as process formulations.

In order to use an IPR to attract funding, the invention and associated IPR must have the potential to generate income or have a special strategic value. Ideally, the intellectual property protection should be robust and relatively easy to defend. With no intellectual property protection, competitors are likely to be able to replicate the product(s) or service(s) at a lower cost, as they are unlikely to have made the significant investment in research and development, which is required to generate new innovations.

Intellectual property laws allow the owner to transfer the right to use the intellectual property to another party, i.e. to grant a licence. Licensing is very common, yet the conditions under which the licence is granted are open for negotiation and depend on both parties' mutual interests as well as strengths. Intellectual property protection can also be used to enforce public ownership of intellectual property. For example, open source software developers rely on intellectual property protection (copyright) to ensure that others who choose to build upon their work adhere to certain terms.

2.18.5 Value and Use of IPR Protection

It is evident that a patent or a registered trademark can be a powerful tool to protect a product and business if the patenting is part of a business strategy. However, patenting "just because the technology can be patented" might not justify the cost. But alone, the process through which you obtain an IPR will provide an insight into the world of technology and business in which the company is operating, and you will receive an overview of the IPR protection others might have achieved. Hence, a patent can be a valuable *protection* of value created by the technology and the products covered by the patent. The patent process also provides an overview of areas where other companies' IPR might prevent a company from entering. A strategic patent might also become a strong bargaining tool if there is a need to get access to third-party technology which IP is protected, e.g. via a cross-licence agreement.

Patents can be used to prevent competitors from launching a competing product or technology in the market. This also goes for trademarks, as we shall see later. It is important to bear in mind that while you might use the information from a patent analysis to identify competitors, it can also be used to identify potential partners with complementary technology. A new business concept was developed by a young technology company from Grenoble[46] a few years back. The service it offered was using artificial intelligence software to combine citation indices from scientific articles with patent information. In that way, it could find both potential partners and competitors and identify clusters with special high patenting activity within certain sectors. The methodology was also used to identify new staff members to portfolio companies of venture funds.

In order to attract the right investors and obtain the right valuation of a company prior to a VC investment, a well-structured patent protection might be a powerful tool if, at the same time, it is proven that there is a large market for the products of the company, and that a reasonable profit can be made by selling products/services in that market.

A word of caution: only a few entrepreneurs with an idea or a new technology which merit patent protection can complete the required strategic analysis in a professional way. They will need advice from experts with business insight and experience. Universities embarking on the "patent route" for a number of their

---

[46]TechKnowMetrix SA.

researchers should also bear in mind these considerations and have a realistic view on the potential revenue stream from licences. In many cases, it may take longer than expected. Hence, substantial funding and "staying power" from these universities are also required; not all universities can quickly develop a track record similar to that of Stanford or MIT!

In some countries in Europe, we have recently seen that universities are trying to cover their substantial IPR protection cost by only offering licence to protected technology and solutions via heavy down payments. The heavy down payment is then nicely combined with a light royalty percentage. However, for SMEs, this policy in practice creates an unbalanced competition for the access to research-driven IPR between big industries (with deep pockets) and SMEs eager to exploit the IPR but for liquidity reasons cannot afford the heavy down payment. It is easy to understand the business rationale of the universities; however, it is not supportive for the creation of new IP-based growth companies. Actually the same policy prevails for spin-offs from universities, whose funding possibilities become even more difficult as a large portion of eventual funding is to be set aside for the IPR down payment. It is interesting to see how often national policies for research funding and business development conflict in Europe.

2.18.6 "Freedom to Operate" Analysis

The "freedom to operate" analysis is another way to approach the whole IPR issue. It serves the function of assessing the external (legal) risk of someone using IPR's to stop you from exploiting your technology or business model. It is also an evaluation of the open space available for you to establish your own IP regime. Your own IP regime serves the function of making your business model exclusive, thereby increasing its value. Even if the company does not expect to have any technology or methods which merit patent protection, it is important to analyse whether the activity of the company is violating the IPR of other people or companies. Today many investors will ask if a "freedom to operate" analysis has been carried out, and the answer is too often: "What is a 'freedom to operate' analysis, and is this really needed as we have nothing to patent ourselves"? Nothing is more wrong than this attitude. The "freedom to operate" analysis provides an overview of all patents and other IPRs which have any relation to the business activity of your company. It examines if any of your products or methods risks violating such IPR protection, and it identifies the owners of such eventual IPRs. The analysis provides a background for strategic decisions which may be either to ignore the IPR conflict and cross fingers that nothing will happen, or to seek licence to the IPR or to use different logos, technologies or methods.

A "freedom to operate" analysis is also an efficient way of avoiding unnecessary costs. It may be an expensive endeavour if a company is forced to alter production processes, products or simply just logo and design because of IPR violation. Therefore, it is better early on to secure a free highway to operate on. This can reduce the risk of being prohibited to conduct business as planned solely because the activity suddenly appears on the IPR "radar screen" of a competitor which holds a strong IPR, which your business concept or technology is violating.

Both a patent search and a "freedom to operate" analysis must be conducted in order to establish whether or not an individual or a company is free to use their patented invention or just launching a new product/service into the market. As illustrated below, even when having a technology patent protected, it does not necessarily mean that you can launch a new product to the market without infringing other patents.

A simple example can illustrate the situation:

Assume you have invented "the wheel" and got it patented. Another guy now invents an inflated rubber tube to put on the wheel in order to make a softer riding. His patent will prevent you from selling a wheel with an inflated rubber tube; however, the other guy will not have much use of his patent without the wheel to put it on. But if you are both wise guys, you enter an agreement with cross licensing and together you have the entire wheel with rubber tube market covered and protected.

Figure 2.25 Cross licencing (© CartoonStock Ltd. 2016).

It is, therefore, advisable to conduct a "freedom to operate" analysis before commencing the often costly development of a new product. This ensures that time and efforts are not wasted by duplicating what others have already done or have protected. If in doubt, it is best to consult a patent professional or patent attorney for advice.

Given the enormous number of patents which exist today, it is quite difficult for many companies to ensure that their products do not unknowingly infringe upon an existing patent. Therefore, companies have no option but to carefully search for and analyse existing patents.

2.18.7 Rights Conferred by the Patent

The patent owner has the right to prevent others from making, using, offering for sale, selling or importing a product that infringes the patent for a limited amount of time. But he has to go to court to ensure the enforcement of his rights. The patent owner also bears all costs associated with securing effective policing and protection of their patent. Even after having won litigation, the patent owner may

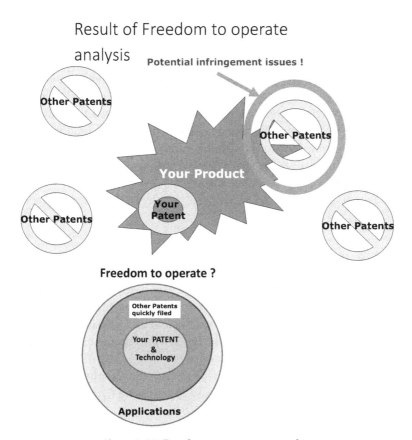

Figure 2.26 Freedom to operate examples.

find that it is not always easy to enforce patent rights even if they are entitled to compensation.

If an individual or organisation infringes a patent by selling and marketing a solution, there are no policing bodies dedicated to protecting the grounds on which a patent is held. It is also the responsibility of the patent owners to secure that they are not infringing someone else's patent. Even after a patent has been granted, under the jurisdiction of certain countries, competitors can challenge the validity of a newly issued patent for a period of up to 9 months. Importantly, a patent does not automatically provide the right to produce or sell a product. Legislation or regulation may prevent commercial exploitation of the IPR acquired or a situation may arise in which other patents dominate your rights.

A patent may not always be enforceable. For example, if another company independently makes the same invention and starts using it before the original patent owner applied for the patent, then in many jurisdictions, the first company will be allowed to continue using the invention. Furthermore, the legal rights conferred by patents do not extend to acts done privately and for non-commercial purposes or acts done for sole experimental purposes relating to the subject matter of the patented invention.

Patent rights can be transferred, e.g. by selling, licensing or donating the patent.

2.18.8 IPR Infringement

IPR or patent infringement cases can be very costly, especially in the USA. Besides demanding licence fees and infringement damages, the patent holder can forbid the production and distribution of all the products covered by the patent, but can only secure enforcement via court order and litigation.

Some statistics from recent years on the number of court proceedings on patent infringement (approximate figures only) are as follows:

- USA: >1000/year
- Germany: 600/year
- France: 300/year
- UK: 70/year
- Netherlands: 50/year

The average cost for patent infringement and associated court proceedings (excluding the resulting licence fees and indemnification for the patent owner) is about €125,000 in the UK and about €25,000 in Germany. The exact amount largely depends on the values at stake. Some insurance companies offer insurance to cover the cost of court proceedings, but only if the client has in place a reasonable patent monitoring process. There are instances where the exercise of patent rights conflicts with competition law, e.g. if a large company uses its intellectual property to secure a monopoly.

Apart from the direct costs associated with a potential patent infringement, a conflict may also damage a well-planned business strategy or funding process. Litigation is not only costly but also a lengthy process, during which uncertainty over the litigation outcome can grow. This uncertainty is perceived by investors as an unwelcome risk.

It is not uncommon for companies to use the uncertainty created in patent conflicts to damage their competitors' sales. For example, a competitor who is suing you for patent infringement could tell your customers that "they are free to buy and use your product, but if the patent litigation case is won, they will either have to pay a royalty to the competitor or be unable to use the product". In these instances, maintaining a strong sales pipeline becomes an up-hill battle.

Despite this, patent rights are often respected and not challenged. Sometimes competitors may even have an interest in supporting their competitors' patent rights and associated first mover position, in particular if the patent owner is willing to offer a cross-licence. Overall, careful strategic thought is required before progressing with a patent application, even if the indications are that an invention is able to be IPR protected.

If a potential IPR infringement situation is looming, no matter if you risk infringing the patent of someone, or someone is infringing your IPR, there is a need for strategic *business and legal considerations.*

Among the key questions to consider are:

- What are the strengths of the patents involved?
- What is the value of the potential revenue stream protected by the patents?
- What are the costs associated with fighting the case?
- What are the chances of winning and when?
- Can you avoid a conflict by taking the initiative to offer a courtesy payment and get a royalty free licence? (Actually this method often works.)
- What is the likelihood of having costs and losses refunded by the other party?

- Are there alternative ways to settle the dispute, e.g. develop a new "win–win" solution for both parties?
- Have both parties' interests and options been analysed?
- What are the relative financial strengths of the parties involved?
- Do you have the intelligence network and financial strength to enforce efficient policing?

It can be beneficial to conduct a structured analysis of both parties' positions and interests before deciding which route to follow. This requires an understanding of the "hot buttons", or most relevant and important issues and decisions which confront each business. These will vary from company to company and from situation to situation.

2.19 Patenting as a Business Strategic Decision

A decision to protect a technology or business via patents or other types of IPR should primarily be a strategic decision, rather than a technical (can it be patented or not?) or financial decision. And the reason to enter the patenting process should also be clear to potential investors.

It is necessary to closely examine the degree and values of the protection potentially achieved and mirror this value against all the costs of obtaining, maintaining and policing the protection. It is my experience that of the many entrepreneurs looking for financing and who want to get their "world-class technology" IP protected, only a few have fully analysed if the technology can also lead to a "world-class business". Good technology and IP protection are only a small (but important) part of a successful business. Production capabilities, sales and marketing skills, selection of the right business model, the existence of a large market and experienced management skills are often more important criteria to achieve business success. Isaac Singer knew it and put his trust in an innovative business model.

In many situations, it is very difficult to assess the strategic value of a patent protection. However, as the cost of the first part of the patenting process, the initial filing of a patent, is not very high, it is often advisable to file the patent application in order to obtain an early priority date. The filing process provides a period where the strategic situation can be better assessed and the value of the protection can be analysed. The value of other strategic advantages may likewise be identified. These values should then be mirrored against the IPR cost.

Before entering into the full and costly patent process, it is important to analyse the whole strategic situation, including how the new business is going to be financed. If VC is one of the sources of funding, the value of the patent *protection* can also be seen from a different angle, namely, that of the investor.

Investors, in general, are interested in good patent protection but often for different reasons than the inventor. Issued patents show the investor that the area of technology has been searched and that a third-party patent suddenly preventing the sales of products protected under the patent is unlikely. Issued patents also provide the investment target with bargaining power to get access to licences to other companies' IPR. From an investor's point of view, it should always be the company and not the inventor who should own the patent. This prevents the entrepreneur/inventor from leaving the company to establish his own production and taking the IPR along. In this way, some of the risks which an investor always fears are reduced.

2.19.1 Patenting or Not?

There some key questions to ask when deciding on whether or not to patent an invention:

- What are the strengths of the patent?
- How can it be policed?
- Which revenue stream is potentially being protected by a patent?
- What are the costs associated with patenting and policing?
- Are potential returns greater than the costs? (Patenting should be progressed only if expected revenues are greater than cost, and if funds are available to pay for all the cost in advance of revenues being generated).
- Do you have the intelligence network and financial strength to enforce efficient policing?

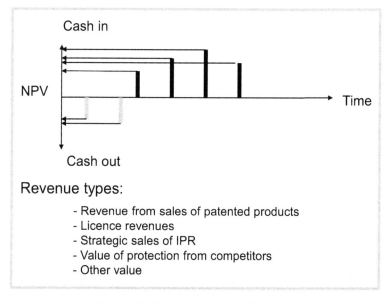

Figure 2.27 Net present value calculation.

The Net Present Value (NPV) of all costs associated with the patenting process and its policing must be calculated and compared to the NPV of the protected potential revenue stream. In Fig. 2.27, only the costs are easy to estimate, but revenue projection is much less certain. Even in cases where the NPV is very positive, it might not be possible to complete the patenting process or successfully win upcoming litigation cases, if the liquidity does not allow for it.

To conclude, *a patent in itself does not have any value.* The value is connected to the revenue stream the invention/technology might generate or the strategic value the protection provides. If it does not generate revenue or create strategic value, or the protection is not needed, the patent has, in principle, no value. However, if a patent can prevent a competitor from entering the market, then the patent might be valuable for the company. Thus, formulating the company's IPR policy should be an integrated part of the strategic thinking of the company; otherwise, the company risks spending money on a patent activity which has no impact on revenue generation. To make the decision on a patent possibility, it is not enough to consult a patent attorney to ask whether a technology can be patented or not;

Figure 2.28 A trademark dispute in Denmark.

it should also be thoroughly analysed whether the protection brings additional revenue/value to compensate for the patenting costs.

Trademarks are distinctive signs identifying and distinguishing the commercial source of goods or services. As long as trademarks are used and the fee is paid, the trademark protection is valid.

Another type of intellectual property is **registered designs** which protect the external appearance of a product. Like a patent, a trademark or a registered design does not have a value in itself. The value is in the customer loyalty or product quality recognition it is protecting. Therefore, the "freedom to operate" analysis is also fully relevant to conduct with respect to product names, domain names, trademarks designs and other IP rights.

Not only dispute about patents can be costly and complicated, this also goes for disputes about trademarks and designs which can result in lengthy and costly litigation.

How far reaching a trademark protection goes can be illustrated by a dispute from 2014 between a successful Danish family steak restaurant chain and a successful restaurant in a small provincial town in Denmark, which specialised in serving fish.

The steak restaurant chain "Jensen Steak House" with restaurants all over Denmark has a profile of being a place for families to go for a good beef. The local fish restaurant was profiling its excellence in serving fish under the name and logo "Jensen Fish restaurant". The dispute was not about beef or fish, but the combined use of the family name "Jensen" and menu specialties. The dispute did not find a solution until the case went to the Supreme Court of Denmark.

Both restaurants were established by clever entrepreneurs from the food business. The problem was that the founders happened to have the same family name "Jensen", which by the way is one of the most common family names in Denmark. Palle Jensen (Steak) argued that the name and logo of the fish restaurant owned by Jacob Jensen (Fish) violated his established and registered trade name and logo. To cut a long and complicated legal dispute in short, Jensen (Steak) won the case and Jensen (Fish) had to change name and logo. To win or lose this type of litigation is often a matter of refined legal conditions and arguments, which few entrepreneurs can normally see through. It has been argued that had Jensen (Fish) personally owned the fish restaurant, and not via his 100% owned private fish-processing company, Jensen (Steak) would have lost. The argument goes that you can always (in Denmark) use your family name as part of your company name. However, McDonald disputed this issue a few years back when a sausage street vendor with a family name McDonald would call his street boot "McDonald Sausages". After a lot of negative publicity and fall in sales, McDonald stopped the litigation. Jensen (Steak) also experienced a substantial fall in sales during the case as his regular customers disapproved his behaviour.

The cases illustrate the potential risk a business faces if it does not carry out its "freedom to operate" analysis in a proper way. That a company can operate freely in its national territory with a special product name and logo is no guarantee that it can operate under the same name and logo internationally. Hence, a successful and costly product, logo and trademark profiling locally, which has created a strong local brand name and lots of satisfied reference customers, may be worthless in an international sales and marketing campaign.

Most companies with strong and valuable names and trademarks, e.g. McDonald, Starbucks, iPad, Toyota, Coca-Cola, Lego, B&O and many others, will fiercely defend the trademark, design and name wherever it is registered. Not necessarily because a small individual name, trademark or design violation threatened its business, but because if one clear violation is tolerated, how can they defend their rights next time if precedence for tolerance has been created. This was most probably the real reasoning behind McDonald's fight with the sausage vendor McDonald in Aalborg.

Investors know about these challenges from bitter experiences and will, therefore, ask for assurance that the "freedom to operate" analysis has been conducted and that there is a next to 100% guarantee that this type of barriers will not prevent a planned international expansion of the company.

2.20 Certification and Regulatory Compliance

When a product or service is ready to be launched in the market, there may still be barriers to cross, even if the feedback from test customers is positive and the market analysis confirms a large lucrative market. In many sectors, products and services need to be approved by public authorities or need to be certified in one way or the other. Or special labour market conditions may apply. Also on this subject, investors will ask for a clear and facts-substantiated presentation. It is definitely not a satisfactory answer to "assume" there is a need to "know".

There can easily be local labour market conditions which may prevent some business models. An example is the conflict in 2015 between the Irish low-cost carrier Ryanair and the Danish Flight Personnel Union, an affiliate of the Danish Labour Market Services Union.

Ryanair announced in 2015 that it would set up an airbase in Copenhagen Airport to complement the base it had in smaller Danish provincial airport for years. The Flight Personnel Union had concluded collective agreements with other Copenhagen airlines with bases in the Copenhagen Airport. Now they also wanted to conclude a collective agreement with Ryanair "to ensure decent conditions for pilots and cabin crew on Ryanair bases in Denmark". If Ryanair would not sign a collective agreement, the Union threatened with a blockade of all services to Ryanair flights landing in Copenhagen. After a lengthy legal dispute involving the Danish Labour Market Court, the blockade was ruled legal. As it is part of Ryanair's business model not to sign collective agreements for their employees, Ryanair decided, when faced with the risk of getting all its flights to and from Denmark being blockaded, to close all its bases in Denmark a few days before the blockade would become effective. Now it serves Danish destinations without a local base with its own staff.

It does not come as a surprise that new medicine and drugs need to be approved before being sold and used to patient treatment, but it might be more surprising that many other products or services also need to be certified or approved before they can be put into the market. It is evident that this book cannot present a comprehensive guide to all potential certification and approval processes and requirements. I can give a few examples and illustrate the importance of certification and regulation in your "freedom to operate" analysis.

There are, in principle, two major problems connected to certification and regulatory approval. One is obvious; without approval, you are not allowed to trade. The other is, however, also important. It can take time, lots of time to get the required approval. If the time factor is not imbedded in the budgets, it may cause severe liquidity problems and may even kill the business. In particular, with respect to the approval process for medicine and drugs, the process costs hundred millions of euros and takes years.

Again investors know about these problems and the implication for a realistic budget. They will ask if the approval process has been taken into account for all potential markets, and if not, they may quickly lose interest in the venture.

Before all the current EU rules about free movement of goods and services were fully implemented, a family owned Danish producer of electronic weights for the food industry fought with the French metric standardisation authorities for years before they got the certification needed and were allowed to sell their weights to the French food-processing industry. The case is interesting because the weights were sold without any problems on many other European and international markets. Hence, local or national certification requirements can still present at least temporary barriers for trade. This needs to be examined as part of any national or international sales and marketing process.

Certification need not be considered a barrier as it can be a useful tool to add credibility to a product or service and demonstrate that a product or service meets the expectations of the customers. For some industries, certification is a legal or contractual requirement.

ISO certification is one of the most well-known certifications/ approvals or mandatory markings of products.

Internationally, the ISO certification is a widely recognised standard. At the International Standard Organization, they develop international standards, such as ISO 9001 and ISO 14001. ISO is not involved in product certification and does not issue certificates. Thus, a company or organisation cannot be certified by ISO. However, ISO's Committee on Conformity Assessment (CASCO) has produced a number of standards related to the certification process, which again is used by certification bodies. The actual certification is conducted by external certification bodies or companies. A well-known certification organisation is Norske Veritas.

In countries which are members of ISO, there are one or more accredited organisations which offer customers both to influence the development of European and international standards and to provide services for standards, certification, standardisation and best practices. There are standards for a wide range of products and services. For example, there exists an ecolabel "the Flower" and "the Swan", which can only be applied to products which are produced under certain eco standards.

A larger number of industrial products are ISO certified. This means not only that the production and the production process follow specific standards, but also that compliance with these standards is regularly checked by the certification accredited consultant. This ISO certification also means that supplies from third-party suppliers which goes into the product need to confirm with the required ISO standards.

Hence, in our example with the "embedded product", the heat sink or the micro-battery, if the producer of the laptop or the hearing aid wants to sell his or her technology or product to a customer, who is ISO certified, then his or her own production process needs to follow an ISO standard and needs to be certified.

If potential investors think that the product from a potential new venture requires ISO certification, they will examine if it is likely that the process to acquire the requested ISO certification can be brought in place. They will also examine if the organisation is fit for ISO standard processes, as living up to ISO-certified processes is not straightforward and often requires both organisational and decision process adaptations.

Entrepreneurs and young management teams, therefore, need to include cost and structural organisational adaptation of the entire production setup in their initial planning and budgeting to comply with standardisation requirements.

Another type of certification widely known is the "FDA approval". The US Food and Drug Administration (FDA) examines, tests and approves a wide range of items for medical use, including drugs and medical appliances. In the simplest terms, "FDA approval" means that the FDA has decided the benefits of the approved item outweigh the potential risks for the item's planned use. The FDA uses a three-tier screening process to decide whether or not a medical device will require approval and how hard the FDA needs to look at the medical device before approving it. For "high-risk" devices, including medical implants and devices unlike anything currently on the market, the FDA applies its highest level of evaluation. For "moderate-risk" devices, including devices "substantially similar" to things already approved by the FDA, the FDA gives the item a summary screening under section 510(k). For "low-risk" devices such as adhesive bandages and many other items sold over the counter, the FDA does not require approval at all.

The "CE mark" is a mandatory conformity marking for certain products sold within the European Economic Area (EEA) since 1985. The CE marking is also found on products sold outside the EEA, which are manufactured in or designed to be sold in the EEA. This makes the CE marking recognisable worldwide even to people who are not familiar with the EEA. It consists of the CE logo and, if applicable, the four-digit identification number of the notified body involved in the conformity assessment procedure.

As the CE marking is the manufacturer's declaration that the product meets the requirements of the applicable EC directives, it is not like the FDA system, an "approval system", but is not either a "free ride". The manufacturer of a product which affixes the CE marking to it has to take certain obligatory steps before the product can bear CE marking. The manufacturer must carry out a conformity assessment, set up a technical file and sign a declaration stipulated by the leading legislation for the product. The documentation has to be made available to authorities on request. By affixing the CE marking on a product, a manufacturer is declaring, at its sole responsibility, conformity with all the legal requirements to achieve CE marking, which allows free movement and sale of the product throughout the EEA. Hence, if the product does not conform to the legal requirement to achieve the CE marking, the company runs a high liability risk, and also risks, if its products are found on the market, to be exposed for litigation and ban on sales.

For example, most electrical products must comply with the Low Voltage Directive and the Electromagnetic Compatibility (EMC) Directive; toys must comply with the Toy Safety Directive. The marking does not indicate that the producer is an EEA manufacture. It implies that the manufacturer of the CE-marked goods has verified that the product complies with all applicable EU requirements, such as safety, health and environmental protection, and if stipulated in any EU product legislation, has had them examined by a notified body or produces according to a certified production quality system.

Not all products need CE marking to be traded in the EEA; only product categories subject to relevant directives or regulations are required (and allowed) to bear CE marking. Most CE-marked products can be placed on the market subject only to an internal production control by the manufacturer with no independent check of conformity of the product with EU legislation. Often retailers refer to products as "CE approved" while forgetting that the mark does not actually signify approval. Certain categories of products require type testing by an independent body to ensure conformity with relevant technical standards, but CE marking in itself does not certify that this has been done.

Many industry sectors have their own certification/approval standards. Some are built on the ISO processes, others on other similar processes as mentioned above.

But it is not only products which need "certification". Many professions also require that the owner or all employees in an organisation conform to some professional standard, often represented by having passed an exam and got a diploma. The fulfilment of the requirement can be controlled by an official public entity or been entirely left to the local organisation of professionals. In the "old days", the control was often made by the Guild. The purpose was arguably always to secure high and uniform quality; however, in many cases, it was also used to limit competition and prevent newcomers to enter the market. In some countries, the "old days" system has survived. Therefore, it is not evident that a recognised diploma in one country or state is recognised in a different country or state.

To summarise, before a product or service is ready to be launched into the market, you need to check if there are regulatory barriers to cross or certification requirements to be fulfilled. The investors will ask for this type of assurance, and if these special types of potential barriers have not been checked, the investors will associate even more risk (lower value) to the potential venture.

In other words, it may cost lots of money not to be prepared!

2.21 Agreements

The documents which constitute the basis for the investment negotiation and eventually the investment have different names in different countries and under different jurisdictions, but the purpose and impact are more or less the same. In this book, we will use the standard English terminology.

2.21.1 Term Sheet

It is the working document which will be drafted during the contract negotiation. It basically outlines the general conditions for the deal, including conditions for exit. It is, in principle, legally binding, but it normally includes a lot of "escape routes" for the investors.

- Typical number of pages: 3–5
- Non-public/private document

2.21.2 Shareholders Agreement

The term sheet does not cover all the details in a formal investment agreement. It, therefore, needs to be converted into a detailed legally binding shareholders agreement.

* Typical number of pages: 20–40
* Non-public/private document

2.21.3 Subscription Agreement

This is the agreement about how the money will be paid and released.

* Typical number of pages: 1–2
* Non-public/private document

2.21.4 Articles of Association

It is normally a public accessible document which is filed with the national company register. It is, therefore, normally known to the outside world.

Typical number of pages: varies according to the legal system
                           Public document

2.21.5 Rules of Procedures for Board of Directors

In many countries, a public accessible document and known to the outside world.

* Typical number of pages: varies according to the legal system

In Chapter 3, we will deal in greater details with all these elements and terms. In Annexure 4, you will find the famous "Rosetta term sheet", which many investors use as a template.

Although term sheets and shareholders' agreements obviously vary enormously between different countries and different commercial fields, a characteristic term sheet and a shareholders' agreement would normally be expected to regulate the following matters.

In addition, the agreements will often make provision for the following:

* The nature and amount of initial contribution (whether capital contribution or other) to the company

---

- Regulating the ownership and voting rights of the <u>shares</u> in the company, including
  - <u>Lock-down provisions</u>
  - Restrictions on transferring shares, or granting <u>security interests</u> over shares
  - <u>Pre-emption rights</u> and <u>rights of first refusal</u> in relation to any shares issued by the company (often called a *buy–sell agreement*)
  - "<u>Tag-along</u>" and "<u>drag-along</u>" rights
  - Minority protection provisions
  - Anti dilutions provisions

- Control and management of the company, which may include
  - Power for certain shareholders to designate individual for election to the <u>board of directors</u>
  - Imposing super-majority voting requirements for "reserved matters" which are of key importance to the parties
  - Imposing requirements to provide shareholders with accounts or other information that they might not otherwise be entitled to by law

- Making provision for the resolution of any future disputes between shareholders, including
  - <u>Deadlock provisions</u>
  - <u>Dispute resolution</u> provisions

- Protecting the competitive interests of the company which may include
  - Restrictions on a shareholder's ability to be involved in a competing business to the company
  - Restrictions on a shareholder's ability to poach key employees of the company
  - Key terms with suppliers or customers who are also shareholders

---

Figure 2.29 Typical items to be covered in a term sheet/shareholders agreement.

- The proposed nature of the business
- How future capital contributions or financing arrangements are to be made
- The governing law of the shareholders agreement
- Ethical practices or environmental practices
- Allocation of key roles or responsibilities

2.21.6 Decision Making

Decision-making in companies with third-party investors changes dramatically from the time when one man owned the entire company and could act in the dual position of being owner and manager. After the company becomes funded by private equity, three decision levels are often instituted. Actually, the same normally applies for public-listed companies. The formal rules and requirement varies from country to country. The actual power and roles of the different decision levels are normally described in detail in the shareholders agreement.

Often the following system applies:

- **Management** runs the daily business of the company based on a strategy approved by the board of directors.

- **Board of directors** appoints the management, oversees the general business activities and plays a role in formulating the business strategy.

  » Meeting frequency varies from company to company, but in general, the board as a minimum approves the yearly budget and also approves the annual account. However, in most cases, for young companies, the board also functions as a valuable sparring partner for the management with monthly or by-monthly meetings.

  » Members of the board can both be executive directors and non-executive directors.

- **Shareholders meetings** are often held once a year. It normally selects the board of directors and formally approves the annual account. The role of shareholders meeting differs from country to country.

In Chapter 3, we will deal with "the art" of negotiating with investors and keeping them committed all the way until an investment is made.

Chapter 3

Ready to Meet with Investors and Accept Their Investments and Conditions?

This chapter focuses on the funding challenges and investors' priorities. It uses a number of "real-life" examples to illustrate many of the issues connected to finding and negotiating with investors and which cannot be put in "formulas" or schematic forms. The examples have been selected to illustrate that all cases are different, and that even the best textbooks cannot replace "real-life experience".

3.1 Funding, Liquidity and Investors

Although money is in the focus, when we talk about investors, all other issues mentioned in the previous chapters are the decisive factors behind a yes or no from investors. In reality, the investors convert all the information about the business, products or services, market and trends, competitors, entrepreneur and the entire organisation into an answer to the questions:

- Do I believe in what I have been told?
- If I invest, can I exit from the investment and make a profit?

How to Attract Investors: A Personal Guide to Understanding Their Mindset and Requirements
Uffe Bundgaard-Jørgensen
Copyright © 2017 Pan Stanford Publishing Pte. Ltd.
ISBN 978-981-4745-20-8 (Hardcover), 978-981-4745-21-5 (eBook)
www.panstanford.com

They will also ask themselves or their partners:

- Which other opportunities do I miss by placing money on this venture? (also called: opportunity cost).

The investors always have the possibility to move their money to other investment opportunities, while the entrepreneur seldom has the choice of a whole range of potential investors. Most often the situation for the entrepreneur becomes:

- Take it or leave it, which means to start the process over from scratch, if the ends do not meet.

The investors are not making this analysis alone on an excel spread sheet. It is the close analysis of the budget numbers and their underlying assumptions that combined with impressions from meetings with the team help structure the analysis.

For the entrepreneur, the budget is the answer book, where he or she compiles and converts the result of all the assumptions made about business activities, innovation, production, sales and marketing, certification, organisation and much more into one and the same denomination: "money". In this way, all these elements are expressed in money terms and in costs and revenues. From this, he or she can construct a budget for each coming month or years. This budget will hopefully in the end show potential profit, but most importantly, it will also show the liquidity requirement.

A complied cost budget could look like Fig. 3.1, which illustrates cost per month for the first 2 years of commercial operation of a small software company North Sensor. In principle, anybody can make this combined but very simple excel spreadsheet, and fill it in with assumptions about the business activities, as they have been analysed in the business plan puzzle exercise. As previously explained, it is smart to make the budget on a monthly basis for the first 2 years of operation, but also try to make the next 3–5-year budget on yearly basis. If it is possible to make credible forecast for a longer period, it is fine. But do not expect the numbers for year 3 or 5 to materialise as shown in the forecast. Investors know this; you should also be realistic about uncertainty about the future.

North Sensor A/S

Cost Projections (in 1000 EUR)	jan-01	feb-01	mar-01	apr-01	maj-01	apr-03	maj-03	jun-03	jul-03	aug-03	sep-03	okt-03	nov-03	dec-03	year 1 - 3 total
Staff	30	30	30	30	30	120	120	140	150	150	150	160	160	160	2.930
Total Personnel	**30**	**30**	**30**	**30**	**30**	**120**	**120**	**140**	**150**	**150**	**150**	**160**	**160**	**160**	**2.930**
Rent	5	5	5	5	5	5	5	5	5	5	5	5	5	5	180
Total Rent & related	**5**	**5**	**5**	**5**	**5**	**5**	**5**	**5**	**5**	**5**	**5**	**5**	**5**	**5**	**180**
Office supplies	5	5	5	5	5	20	20	20	20	20	20	20	20	20	450
Software Licenses	1	1	1	1	1	1	1	1	1	1	1	1	1	1	36
Material						225	235	245	255	265	275	285	295	305	4.810
Total administrative costs	**6**	**6**	**6**	**6**	**6**	**246**	**256**	**266**	**276**	**286**	**296**	**306**	**316**	**326**	**5.296**
travel	2	2	2	2	2	6	6	6	6	6	6	6	6	6	168
Conference participation											5				15
Exhibitions															15
Total marketing costs	**2**	**2**	**2**	**2**	**2**	**6**	**6**	**6**	**6**	**6**	**11**	**6**	**6**	**6**	**198**
Other, material & production	13	13	13	13	18	90	100	110	120	130	140	150	160	170	1.547
Overhead total costs						**467**	**487**	**527**	**557**	**577**	**602**	**627**	**647**	**667**	**7.221**
Legal	3	3	3	3	3	3	3	3	3	3	3	3	3	3	84
Consultants	3	3	3	3	5	5	5	5	5	5					88
Total External Advisory	**6**	**6**	**6**	**6**	**8**	**8**	**8**	**8**	**8**	**8**	**3**	**3**	**3**	**3**	**172**
Total operating expenses	*49*	*46*	*49*	*43*	*56*	*475*	*495*	*535*	*565*	*585*	*605*	*630*	*650*	*670*	*10.323*
Development/Investment	10	30	40	40	50	20	20	20	20	20	20	20	20	20	2.200
Patents				5							20				60
Total development/investment	**10**	**30**	**40**	**45**	**50**	**20**	**20**	**20**	**20**	**20**	**40**	**20**	**20**	**20**	**2.260**
Total Costs	**59**	**76**	**89**	**88**	**106**	**495**	**515**	**555**	**585**	**605**	**645**	**650**	**670**	**690**	**12.583**

North Sensor A/S

Revenue Projections (in 1000 EUR)	jan-01	feb-01	mar-01	apr-01	maj-01	jun-01	maj-03	jun-03	jul-03	aug-03	sep-03	okt-03	nov-03	dec-03	0 - 3 Year
Product 1	-	-	-	-	-	-	310	400	600	700	700	750	850	900	7.970
Product 2							600	550	500	500	550	600	750	800	8.217
Product 3							300	300	400	450	450	500	550	550	5.570
Other sales related revenue	-	-	-	-	-	-									-
Pre-payment and Gross cost claims	-	-	-	-	-	-	**1.210**	**1.250**	**1.500**	**1.600**	**1.700**	**1.850**	**2.150**	**2.250**	**21.757**
Commision							121	125	150	160	170	185	215	225	2.176
Fees							182	188	225	240	255	278	323	338	3.264
Sales cost							**303**	**313**	**375**	**400**	**425**	**463**	**538**	**563**	**5.439**
Net payment/grant							**908**	**938**	**1.125**	**1.200**	**1.275**	**1.388**	**1.613**	**1.688**	**16.318**

Figure 3.1 Monthly cost and revenue budget—an example.

I have many times asked the entrepreneur, when being presented with sales forecasts for year 3 or 5: "how many customers do you have in year 3 or 5?" The answer is often "how could I know?" The next question is then: "how did you then make the year 3 and 5 sales forecast, without knowing how many customers you would have?" This is always a good starting point for a discussion about risk and uncertainty, and an excellent opportunity to make an assessment about the quality and experience of the entrepreneur or his team.

Even if the numbers are not carved in solid rock, they can give an indication about the expectations about future profit and potential liquidity gaps, which need to be covered by some funding sources, which could come from an investor.

These two fundamental budget elements, costs and revenues, are the basis for the profit and loss account, the income statement and the liquidity analysis, which is illustrated in Fig. 3.2.

When making the first budget exercise, it is wise to make an initial assessment if the business case has a chance to attract investors. This means that based on your own, until now, unchallenged assumptions, you should evaluate the business case seen through the eyes of an investor. In other words, can the investor make money by investing in your venture? In order to do so, you need to estimate how much money is needed and how large percentage ownership you are willing to offer to the investors, and for that amount of investment money. In the example illustrated in Fig. 3.2 the company North Sensor starts with a cash position of €1.000,000, but it will already need additional funding in month 9. As normal investor search processes take between 6 and 12 months, the investor search has to start now if we assume we are now in January year 1.

If we had also shown the 3 year budget for North Sensor it would have shown a continued need for funding as illustrated graphically in Fig. 3.3. The liquidity analysis would indicate that the liquidity gap increased until a maximum close to €4,000,000 was reached. This would mean that eventual investor negotiations need to be completed before substantial sales have taken place, which means that the investors really need to believe in the "story", as there are no solid customer reactions to base sales forecast assumption on. All in all, a difficult funding exercise for the North Sensor entrepreneur.

North Sensor A/S

Income Statement (in 1000 DKK)	jan	feb	mar ---	sept	oct	nov	dec	Year
Net Earnings	-	-	-	(8)	(5)	3	11	34
Personnel cost	*2ff*	*3ff*	*3ff*	*5ff*	*5f*	*5f*	*ff*	427
Overhead cost	*12V*	*33*	*21*	*4f*	*4f*	*ff*	*2V*	468
External Advisory cost	*f*	*f*	*f*	*ff*	*f*	*f*	*f*	101
Operating expenses	*f4f*	*ff*	*5f*	*ff*	*ff*	*5f*	*ff*	*ffff*
EBITD	(149)	(68)	(56)	(95)	(94)	(56)	(65)	(962)
EBITD. Net Net Earnings	*^^*	*^^*	*^^*	*^^*	*^^*	*ff*	*ff*	*ff*
Depreciation	-	-	-	5	6	7	8	39
EBIT	(149)	(68)	(56)	(100)	(100)	(63)	(73)	**###**
EBIT. Net Net Earnings	*^^*	*^^*	*^^*	*^^*	*^^*	*ffff*	*ff*	*ffff*
Financial income								-
Interest expenses								-
Profit Before Tax	(149)	(68)	(56)	(100)	(100)	(63)	(73)	**###**
Taxes								-
Net Profit	(149)	(68)	(56)	(100)	(100)	(63)	(73)	**###**

(Depreciation 20%, Taxes 30%)

North Sensor A/S

Balance sheet (in 1000 DKK)	previous period	jan	feb	mar ---.	sept	oct	nov	dec	Year
ASSETS									
Cash	1.000	851	783	727	(67)	(201)	(312)	(417)	(417)
Development/Investment		-	-	-	320	360	415	455	455
Accumulated Depreciation		-	-	-	18	24	31	39	39
Receivables									
Total Assets		1.000	851	783	727	235	135	72	(1)	(1)
LIABILITIES&EQUITY									
Short-Term Debt									-
Long-Term Debt									-
Payables									-
Total Liabilities		-	-	-	-	-	-	-	-	-
Liabilities is Net Total theory		*ff*	*ff*	*ff*	*ff*	*ff*	*ff*	*ff*	*^^*	*^^*
Share Capital		1.000	1.000	1.000	1.000	1.000	1.000	1.000	1.000	1.000
Reserves									-
Accumulated Profit/Loss		(149)	(217)	(273)	(765)	(865)	(928)	(1.001)	(1.001)
Total Equity		1.000	851	783	727	235	135	72	(1)	(1)
Total Liabilities and Equity		1.000	851	783	727	235	135	72	(1)	(1)

North Sensor A/S

Liquidity (in 1000 DKK)	previous period	jan	feb	mar ---	sept	oct	nov	dec	Year
Beginning of period		1.000	851	783	68	(67)	(201)	(312)	1.000
Plus P/L from current period		(149)	(68)	(56)	(100)	(100)	(63)	(73)	
Less Development/Investment costs		-	-	-	(40)	(40)	(55)	(40)	
Plus Depreciation		-	-	-	5	6	7	8	
Plus Increases in Payables		-	-	-	-	-	-	-	
Less Increases in Receivables		-	-	-	-	-	-	-	
Plus New Debt/Less Repaid Debt		-	-	-	-	-	-	-	
Plus New Equity Contributions		-	-	-	-	-	-	-	
End of period		1.000	851	783	727	(67)	(201)	(312)	(417)	(417)

Figure 3.2 Income statement, balance sheet and liquidity.

If the entrepreneur can make investors believe that the budgeted sales figures continue to rise and with the indicated growth rate in the coming years, it may be possible to make a first assessment of the future value of the company. However, to make these sales numbers become a reality, the liquidity gap needs to be filled. With no track record, he or she can forget about bank loans, but investors might be interested if an agreement on "pre-money"[1] valuation (or ownership percentage) with investors can be reached.

---

[1]Pre-money valuation: the value of the company before the investment is made.

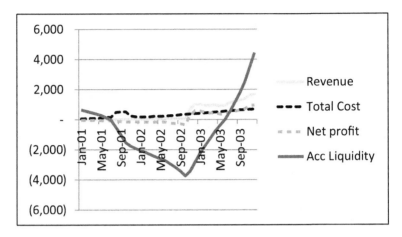

Figure 3.3 The liquidity gap.

It all boils down to the problems of using the budget to calculate the expected return on investment (ROI),[2] which can be estimated using the budgets, if they are trustworthy. To calculate the ROI, the benefit (or return) of an investment is divided by the cost of the investment, and the result is expressed as a percentage or a ratio:

$$ROI = \frac{(\text{Gain from Investment} - \text{Cost of Investment})}{\text{Cost of Investment}}$$

and estimating the risk-adjusted ROI.

Alternatively, the internal rate of return (IRR)[3] can be calculated. However, these calculations put focus on both the budget numbers, but not on the risk factors.

There are many ways of estimating the future value of the company and converting this estimated value into NPV.[4] A standard

---

[2]The ROI tells "how many times you get your money back". However, it does not take into account the time dimension. Today €100 has a higher value to you than €100 in 5 years. Therefore, also the internal rate of return (IRR) term is often used as a yardstick. However IRR and ROI are directly connected. An ROI of 5 calculated on "money back" in 5 years equals an IRR of close to 40%. See more about financial calculations in Annexure 5.

[3]See Annexure 5 for more information about financial calculations.

[4]Net present value means the discounted net value of all future cost and revenues. See Annexure 5 for definition and calculations.

way of doing it is using a discounted cash flow analysis. Another often used method is to estimate the value of the company in the year when the investor potentially can exit from the investment by using the PE[5] factor. There are many other ways of doing it. However, even the most sophisticated mathematical models cannot remove the underlying uncertainty about future revenues, costs, competitors, their reaction and market conditions. Also mathematical models cannot remove the fact that if the data in the budget are "garbage in", then even the best economic model creates "garbage out", no matter however sophisticated analytical models are used.

Actually, the only thing which is certain is that the budgeted numbers in, e.g. year 3 or 5 will not be the numbers to be realised and appear in the annual account for year 3 or 5! But still making a series of well-thought thorough budget simulations on different scenarios, or making structured sensitivity analysis of "what if" types, is a bit better than "flipping the coin".

In principle, all projects are confronted with at least two types of risks:

- **Controllable risks** (CR), which can be addressed to some extent through planning and knowledge
- **Uncontrollable risks** (UCR) from the "outside world", which cannot be removed or reduced via planning. Good contingency plans may reduce the impact.

It is, therefore, always the expected "risk-adjusted" ROI which must be attractive to the investor.

What the investor therefore tries to estimate is the risk-adjusted ROI, which in principle is calculated by multiplying the ROI with the assumed risk factors. In an oversimplified way, this can be expressed as:

Risk-adjusted ROI = ROI × (Controllable risk × Uncontrollable risk)

---

[5]PE: The price-to-earnings ratio, or PE ratio, is an equity valuation multiple. It is defined as market price per share divided by annual earnings per share.

When the investors make an estimate of the ROI and the risk-adjusted ROI, they will look at the budget and make a major effort to understand the entire business concept, the quality of people behind and how the "outside" world will influence the business case, and the associated risks, as they see them!

Estimating the two risk factors is more a question of using your own experience and common sense than using sophisticated probability models. However, if you are the type of person who really believes in results calculated from risk formulas connected to business development, you are probably also among the few people who have a firm belief in the 3-week weather forecast, and use these forecasts for setting sails and destination for your next sailing trip, but also you are in for surprises!

Many investors are like the people who have doubt even about the 1-day weather forecast and always carry an umbrella. This means they also associate large potential uncertainty to budgets and budget forecasts. If the result of the different scenarios gives the potential investor an IRR indication far below the IRR "benchmark" 30–40%,[6] it is a good idea to reconsider the assumptions behind the budget. It will be a good idea to consider how cost savings can be made, how sales can be moved forward or even that the investor should be offered a bigger "slice of the pie".

If the IRR numbers are really far below the benchmark, it is wise to reconsider the entire business case and consider alternative business models. The entrepreneur cannot fully simulate how the individual investors will assess the case and the associated risks, but by doing his or her own simulations, he or she gets an idea of how the investment case can look from an investor's point of view. This is always a good starting point for any qualified discussion.

Although I have put a lot of emphasis on budgets and budget simulations, the meetings with investors normally do not quickly focus on the budget and the potential exit value for the investor. It is the business case and the assumptions behind which are the focus of the discussion. However, the budget and its underlying detailed assumptions always help structure the business case discussion. The more the investors like the assumptions and buy into these

---

[6]See Chapter 1.

assumptions, the smoother the discussion about the business case. This, however, does not signal an eventual agreement about the "pre-money valuation".[7] It is just the starting point for the discussion.

Very often the first step to make the investors interested in a potential deal is to let them see the value offered and when they fully understand the value they are being offered, then price discussion can start. Putting a price tag on the deal before the investor interest is created might easily make the investor leave the discussion. Any price on a deal which you do not fully understand is always "too high".

Although the money discussion has structured most part of the reasoning, money is not all. Before an investment is ever being made, there needs to be an agreement about the pre-money valuation and an agreement on the general investment deal conditions. In particular, the investors are not only interested in the conditions for making the investment, their interest is equally focused on how they eventually can "exit" from the investment. A large part of a shareholders' agreement is actually focused on the challenges connected to exit.

Many things can go wrong in this negotiation process, even if an agreement about valuation has been reached. The two parties in the negotiation actually have two different focus points. The entrepreneur is focused on getting his or her venture funded and to get on with technology and product development or increase sales effort. The investors are focused on how life with this entrepreneur will materialise, from the investment is made and until they can eventually exit from the investment, hopefully with a serious capital gain.

Therefore, the entrepreneur should understand that in principle the agreement with the investors will cover the three phases, where only the first one is about getting access to investor money.

- The pre-investment or negotiation phase
- The "live together" or "project monitoring" phase after the investment has taken place

---

[7]Pre-money valuation defines the value of the company before the investment is made. Meaning, if you invest €1 million and the "pre-money" is €1 million, you will get a 50% ownership, while if the "pre-money" was €4 million, you would only get 20% ownership for your investment.

- The "exit phase" where the investor want to sell his shares and become liquid.

In the first of the three phases, the "investment phase", the normal primary interest of the entrepreneur is to achieve as high a "pre-money" evaluation as possible, while the investors, besides the interest in a low "pre-money", also have their focus on securing an agreement which reflects all the risks associated with the investment and secure optimal conditions for their eventual exit.

In the next phase, the "project monitoring phase", the interests of the two parties should be aligned in securing the maximum growth in value of the company, but there are also many conflict points, which we will deal with in this chapter.

In the final phase, the "exit" phase, the two parties' interests may again differ. The investors will normally want to optimise their exit value, while the entrepreneur's focus is on further business development.

3.2 Investors' Interest

Investors are interested in having a strong quality deal flowing from where they can pick and choose the most promising deals. However, dealing with a strong deal flow is both a "blessing" and a "challenge". The nice thing about a strong deal flow is that it gives a lot of opportunities to pick from and it also gives a good feeling about the market and development in technology trends. The challenge is how to minimise the time and resources spent on materials which do not bring either:

- Valuable knowledge about market and technology
- Relevant investment opportunities

Investors often spend time looking at projects in which they have no intention to invest in. They do it if it brings valuable competitive information about the market and new technologies. They get the information for free and may gain from the knowledge acquired. However, they prefer to allocate their best resources to projects which represent realistic investment opportunities. The management challenge for a venture capital (VC) team is both securing the optimal allocation of funds to the different projects they are involved in and optimising the allocation of the investor's management resources to screen incoming deals, monitor the actual portfolio and secure the optimal exit opportunities.

From an investor's point of view, he or she should only allocate time to analyse a new project if the time is not better spent on monitoring and supporting the existing portfolio or supporting the exit process. This means that a new project arriving at the desk of an investor not only competes for the attention with the other new projects arriving during the same period, but also competes for the attention, which could otherwise have been allocated to the existing portfolio. The first contact with an investor is, therefore, crucial. If it is not obvious that time spent on the new project is not better spent on the existing portfolio or on other activities, why bother to take a closer look? This is also one of the reasons why so many projects get rejected only after a very superficial analysis. The more prior experience and knowledge an investor has with a technology or a market, the easier it is for him or her to make the decision. The easiest decision is to say no; no cost is involved, and the investor only risks losing a potential upside in a single investment.

Therefore, entrepreneurs looking for funding should conduct a thorough screening of potential investors before the first contact is made. Besides having a top of the class "investment summary" and business plan to forward to prospective investors, they also need to contact only a few investors to whom it is likely that this opportunity will appeal.

When an investor decides to spend time on a new project, let alone invest, they take into consideration not only the money they will be investing in the project, but also the time and human resource it would take to move the investment forward to a profitable exit.

As previously mentioned, basically the whole process falls into three different stages as illustrated in Fig. 3.4.

In order to get to the point where a meeting with investors is set up, there is a need to find the right investors, make them interested in a meeting, and then prepare for the meeting.

In the previous chapters, we have discussed how to make a few checks which will give an indication if an investment proposal

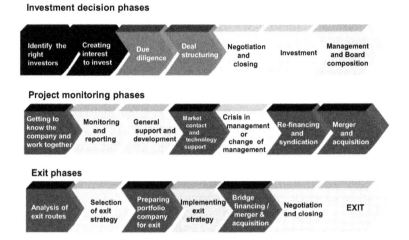

Figure 3.4 Phases of the investment process.

could be of interest to particular investors from a pure financial point of view. Investors, however, not only look at numbers but also prefer to invest in projects which they have a certain background to understand and evaluate. This is a way for the investors to conceptually reduce the risk factors. In many cases, they also prefer business opportunities which they have personal interest in seeing developed.

A strategy for multiple "blind" approaches to several investors and hoping in this way to make the "jackpot" is not a good idea, as we illustrated by the "deal funnel".[8] The best way is to approach investors, where it can be expected that it is easy to create an interest for this particular investment opportunity. The best chances are where it fits the profile of the investors or the profile of their current project portfolio. In particular, VC funds often have a smaller or larger portfolio of companies, which they show on their website. Therefore, it is always good advice to consult the websites of potential investors before approaching them. They might also have invested in your worst competitor, so why serve valuable competitor information on a plate.

---

[8]See Fig. 1.2, Section 1.2, Chapter 1.

The other criterion for selecting the right investor is about "money available for investments". If the management team of the VC fund is only managing "old" funds, the appetite for investing in new projects is minimal. However, they might still welcome new investment opportunities but will not tell that new projects will serve more in their own fundraising effort by demonstrating a strong deal flow, than as an investment opportunity right now.

Any investor wants to be sure that he or she has access to a strong quality deal flow. Therefore, professional investors often offer well-structured and appealing websites, where they present their investment preferences and also provide indication as to which elements in a business plan they put special emphasis on. The purpose is to attract the best possible deals and then apply an efficient screening process to ensure that they only spend their scarce resources on the deals which they feel are potentially attractive investment opportunities.

Some of the selection criteria of investors are:

- Technology or industry focus
- Stage of development (start-up/seed/early stage/later stage/development)
- Expected size of investment
- Location of investment target
- Market and growth expectation
- Product unique selling proposition (USP)
- Management experiences
- Intellectual property rights (IPR) strength
- And many other

However, a quick look at various VC directories and VC websites indicates that the selection criteria are defined very broadly—why? Despite all the formulated "focus principles", most investors also behave opportunistic and invest with the objective to make a profit. Hence, by presenting too narrow defined selection criteria, the investors might scare away a top project they would love to invest, even if its business focus is outside the described investment focus. It is a complicated world, and as a consequence, many projects sent to investors are doomed to be rejected, not because of lack of quality, but because of "lack of fit".

Access to business angels is, in many cases, only possible via the business angel network manager, who has the task of selecting investment opportunities for the next network meeting. Using a personal network to facilitate this approach is excellent, provided your personal network happens to include relevant business angels or someone who knows them.

VC funds are easy to find. Just go to the national VC association website and take a look at the websites of all the funds. Alternatively, go to international VC associations, such as the European Venture Capital Association (EVCA), and do the same. Business angels are best found via the business angel networks, which are often organised in national or international business angels network associations, such as European Business Angel Network (EBAN). Pick up the phone and ask your way to find the right person to speak with.

Alternatively, use an advisor as a guide. In many countries, some advisors are funded by public sources (e.g. "tech trans officers" at universities or officers at chambers of commerce). Their advice is often for free, and they have a large relevant network to draw upon. Others are commercial advisors. Large investment banker houses, international accountant houses, individual consultants or brokering houses provide this type of service. The role is to help in finding and negotiating with investors. Also the local bank or lawyers might have a large and relevant network.

Another way of identifying the relevant investors is to participate in venture forums or similar conferences, where potential investors are expected to be present. Participation in business plan competition can also be a way to get visibility. However, some of these contests have developed to be more a beauty contest, than a serious selection of solid promising business plans. Being visible at exhibitions and at conferences might also help investors "finding you". High visibility can also be achieved if a project becomes funded via the EU-initiated H2020 SME Instrument funding. The EU Commission is promoting companies they co-fund to the investor community, in order to make it easy for investors to find you. They have even introduced a "Seal of Excellence", which will be awarded to companies which passes the qualification "threshold" to get funded, but which do not get funded because of limited funding resources at the Commission level. The value of the "Seal of Excellence" remains to be seen.

Figure 3.5 Beneficiaries of EU H2020 SME instrument funding.

Excellent innovative businesses which have received funding from the Horizon 2020 SME Instrument, which was introduced by the EU Commission in 2014, get automatically a lot of valuable visibility, particularly via the interactive map the EU Commission has made, which it updates four times a year. More and more investors take a look at the national or local champion companies displayed here to see what is "moving" in the industry and sometimes also to find investment targets for themselves or to find partners for their existing portfolio of companies.

Irrespective of how much visibility is achieved, e.g. from the EU H2020 Map or via a personal network, it is a good idea to retain an advisor, both for the final investor identification and contact phase, and to act as a coach in the negotiation process. Investors do this type of investment transactions regularly, while it is a "once in your lifetime" or "first-time" experience for many entrepreneurs. Also investors appreciate if the entrepreneur teams up with a good and qualified advisor. This often leads to more, at least perceived, balanced and fair deals.

If a professional advisor is retained, it is important that the financial service agreement to be signed with him is fair and easy to understand. A success fee (no-cure-no pay) agreement might be tempting; it costs nothing if no results are achieved. However, sometimes it is the entrepreneur who pays the bill, and not the company which signed the service agreement and which will receive the investment money. I have experienced many cases where the investors do not accept that this particular advisor bill will be paid by the company after the investors become co-owners. The investors will argue that their money "should not be used to pay for being invited to invest"! A success fees can be high, and it can be a very unpleasant bill to pay for the entrepreneur. Pure success fee transactions can also be an invitation to an imposter acting as an advisor, as the following real world case illustrates.

If you have read the aforementioned case, you will understand that even while entering into a very "favourable" success fee agreement with an advisor for the funding process, there is a need to check his or her credentials. You also need to secure that if you have to pay, the money is due only if the work is actually done as expected, and the services have been provided as promised.

Years back, when I was active in the VC business, I had frequent visits from a Mr. Gooddee (name disguised) from California, USA. He also visited the headquarters of major banks in Copenhagen. According to his CV, which he had presented at our first meeting in Copenhagen, he had a PhD in finance from Berkeley and a background as funding consultant for Stanford University and a few other West Coast universities. What he offered was his large US network of business angels and VC funds, which could be potential investors in our portfolio companies. He made the same presentation to many of the Danish banks. He offered his services on a pure success fee basis. During all these years, we got to know each other well (I thought), and he created a good trust relation. He had never asked for anything, just talked and provided "free of charge" information about the US private capital market and about his personal impressive network.

At one point of time, one of our portfolio companies was looking for US funding. I contacted him, and he sent me a draft financial service agreement, which spelled out the type of services he would offer in details. The agreement was fully "no cure no pay". His office was in Los Angeles, and we could meet whenever I was on the West Coast. At that time, I was often in the States, also on the West Coast. I tried to arrange meetings with him in his office a number of times. Sometimes he was travelling, and at other times, it turned out to be more convenient, according to him, that we met at my hotel or downtown.

One day, after such a meeting at my hotel, I had lunch with the Danish consul in Los Angeles. I mentioned Mr. Gooddee and his good connections with Danish banks. I suggested that the consulate could use his contacts. The Danish consul got a copy of his business card and noted down a few key elements from his CV. Next day, I got a phone call from the consul, who told me that there had never been a Mr. Gooddee getting his PhD from Berkeley; actually the name did not figure on their student alumni lists. Furthermore, Stanford had informed him that a Mr. Gooddee had never worked as funding consultant or in any other consulting functions for Stanford. The consul also told me that there were quite a few financial "advisors" who offered their services on a "no cure no pay" basis. However, they also did almost nothing for the client, but made their money by following the funding process of all their "clients" and then, when the funding was secured, they sent their "success fee bill". If you did not pay, they would sue you. In most cases, as law suits in the USA are extremely costly, and in order to get "on with your life", a settlement was agreed upon. Leaving you pay for a service you had never got!

It turned out to be a valuable lunch with the Danish consul. I had become wiser and found another way to secure funding for the company.

Sometimes a fixed fee agreement with specific milestones may be a better way of securing a good and professional service combined with an incentive success fee.

3.3 Contacting Investors

It is often a good idea to make the first contact with relevant investors by phone, at a meeting or via mail before any material is sent. And when the material is sent, it is a good idea not to send the entire business plan. Start sending an investment summary or something similar, but always following KISS principle

3.3.1 Business Plan

In principle, a business plan needs to encapsulate all the elements of the business plan puzzle. It should be the roadmap for the company to grow and develop its business. It is also the document to be discussed with the board of directors, when the business strategy is being discussed, and it serves well to impress the bank and get all the leading staff members aligned with the business strategy of the company. However, it is not necessarily meant to be an easy-to-read introduction to what an investment in the company has to offer investors. Its purpose is to outline a strategy for the development of the business, of which funding is only a part. In many books, it is recommended to structure the business plan as illustrated in Fig. 3.3.

- Product and services
- Technology and business concept
- including business plan
- IPR
- Business model
- Price and Customers
- The market
- Competitors
- Sales & marketing
- Management
- The company
- Budget and financial
- Funding requirements
- Investor considerations

Figure 3.6 Business plan: typical list of content.

However, this list of content or the order in which it is listed may definitely not be right for all types of projects or businesses.

Irrespective of how the business plan is structured, I would always recommend a short introduction, which really describes the "problem being solved", "why" it is a business opportunity, "who" the customers are and the "value" your solution brings to the customers. This is a nice setting for an introduction, also for your staff, if they are ever going to read the business plan.

For a business venture, which is primarily market focused and where the key enabler for success is a "blue ocean" strategy, the reader needs to understand why this business model will lead to success. Therefore, in this case, I would start explaining the market and the business model, and why it is unique and "why" and "how" it will work. However, if the venture is based on a new technology solution, I would start with the "problem solved" and "why this technology solves the problem". Other business proposals might benefit from starting by describing the current markets and the products or solutions, and then describing why this business venture will change "the rules of the game" in this particular market. Therefore, the "list of content", from the many books about business plans, should only be regarded as a checklist, securing that all relevant elements are encapsulated in the business plan. The way the document should finally be structured should be defined by the importance and relevance of the different sections.

The "business plan" could also just be a number of separate sections in a binder, which can be read as separate documents. Each document can cover one or more of the individual elements in the business plan puzzle. This signals that the business plan is a "work in progress" document, which is constantly updated and, in essence, also serves daily management objectives. Some investors will be appealed by this approach, but not all.

Irrespective of how the business plan document is structured, you need to make a short executive summary, which can be used for an introductory explanation about the business to banks, partners and other interested parties. Many entrepreneurs make the mistake that the executive summary from the business plan is also sent to investors.

My general advice is to write a special "investment summary" targeting the needs and special interests of investors. This should be an easy-to-read and appealing document, which should create the first investor interest. The purpose of the investment summary is to explain how the investors can make money while the company prospers. The business plan should tell how the company can make money.

The main differences between the three documents are as follows:

- *Investment summary* caters to the investors' needs by describing and listing the core reasons "why this excellent business idea offers a good investment opportunity to the investors".
- *Executive summary* summarises the management's roadmap for business development and "how the company can make money".
- *Business plan* is a detailed roadmap for business development and also a useful document for the due diligence process.

3.3.2 Investment Summary

The investment summary serves to shift the focus away from the business and direct the focus towards the needs of the investor, thus getting the investor into the right frame of mind. The key elements and arguments in the investment summary should also be found in the business plan, but the investment summary serves as a teaser presentation, and must primarily meet all of the investors' criteria of choice and adhere to the KISS (Keep it Short and Simple) principle.

The objective of the investment summary is twofold: First to create curiosity and interest, and second to secure that the company gets on the investors' shortlist and stays on their list of possible investment opportunities. This shortlist diminishes after every round of screening and selection process. Being precise and concise cannot be stressed enough. If that criterion is not met, punishment comes swiftly in the form of early rejection.

The investors have little tolerance with long unclear and woolly sentences, which do not accurately describe the business proposal. So to avoid ending in the investors' already overfilled dustbin, the investment summary should give a short description of the proposed investment opportunity, why the investor can make money from the investment, the current capital requirement, previous funding rounds and the specific purpose of this funding round and the likely timing of an exit for the investor.

Furthermore, the investors should be able to find in the first 3–5 pages of the investment summary:

- A short but accurate description of the company, its products and/or services.
- The market in which the company is intended to operate or is already operating, including information covering market size and penetration.
- The main USPs listed in order of priority.
- Introduction to the business model and how it will generate revenue.
- Proof of concept (particularly if no actual sales yet).
- Overview of any IPR which may protect the company against competition.
- The team, references and acknowledgements.
- Budgets covering the most important financials, including EBITDA (earnings before interest tax and depreciation and amortisation) for the current year, plus 3–5 coming years, enabling the investors

to make their own return on investment (ROI) calculations and evaluate the potential profitability of their investment.

• Overview of the current capitalisation and rounds of funding.
• The likely timeframe for the investment and a clear indication of the likely route to exit for the investors.

When the final version of the investment summary has been completed, the search for investors can start. In many cases, it is useful to have, already when writing the investment summary, a shortlist of potential investors, so that the wording of the investment summary is tailored to their needs.

Before sending an investment summary or a business plan to an investor, there is often a delicate discussion about the need for the investors to sign a non-disclosure agreement (NDA). Some investors refuse by principle to sign an NDA, while others would not hesitate to sign. It is a hard choice if the investors say "no", and there is a good reason to insist. A solution can be to remove sensitive information and let the investors start their due diligence. If they then get enthusiastic about the project, their attitude might shift, or trust has been built between the entrepreneur and the investors that the issue is no longer relevant. To insist on an NDA signature in front of an investor who, by principle, says "no" has a very simple consequence: new investors need to be contacted!

3.3.3 First Investor Approach

There are various ways and self-assessment tests which can be used to find out if an entrepreneur is "ready to meet with investors", but a good advisor, coach or mentor can also make a good and neutral assessment. However, entrepreneurs are normally not rational in their approach to this challenge. They have not chosen to become an entrepreneur unless they have a strong belief in themselves and confidence in their invention or business idea. Particularly in Europe, there is no tradition among entrepreneurs to use advisors for this part of the process. Actually this attitude is ironic, as most entrepreneurs will find it normal to seek advice from auditors, lawyers and patent lawyers on accounting, tax, legal and IPR issues. However, seeking advice from investment professionals, when it comes to the funding process, is less common.

There is no point in having conceived a good idea if you are the only one who sees the ingenuity of it. Unless it is possible to communicate the idea in the right way, the entrepreneur will be alone with his or her vision! Not all entrepreneurs fully understand that a good business concept is only the first step in the right direction. In the end, it is the combination of a well-formulated business case, the connected strategy and the personal impression of the entrepreneur and his or her team which will determine whether it will be possible to attract funding. Simply getting a good business plan written does not satisfy the "job application". What remains is to present and defend the case, which is a far bigger challenge than most people imagine. In this respect, it is my experience that an "investor readiness competence test"[9] is a good instrument to identify the weaknesses and strengths of an entrepreneurial team. Investors, in general, accept that not all qualifications and experiences need to be present from the start. However, they hate to meet teams which think they are "the champion league", and then after a few probing questions, it becomes evident that they are not.

Investors find again and again that entrepreneurs leave too much to chance when it comes to presenting their ideas. Often investors receive unintelligent emails with one or more attached files representing the investment case, and it is left with the recipient who then has to establish the logical sequence of these documents. In most cases, because the entrepreneurs do not fully understand the challenge and the way investors make a living, they will not get their project funded. Too many entrepreneurs underestimate the risk of being turned away at the door of the investor because of a minor issue with the presentation or a small "foot fault" with respect to, e.g. valuation.

Whether the task is to describe the investment opportunity (or the company) orally or in writing, it has to be done by getting to the point in a brief and concise way. If the overall concept is relatively complex and comprehensive, there is still a need to communicate it in an easy-to-grasp manner. In most cases, those who will be willing to read or listen to a presentation only have limited time to spend, and if the message cannot be communicated quickly and in a well-

---

[9]InvestorNet-gate2growth has developed an easy to use "investor readiness" test. For more information, contact the author.

structured manner, the audience will be lost. The problem is simple: On average, a venture investor or business angel will not spend more than an initial 5–10 minutes reading a summary or listening to a first phone call. So the message has to be clear cut.

Especially when it comes to personal contacts, it is important to remember the KISS principle. Mastering the art of simplicity often requires practice, a lot more than most people imagine. Some people are born communicators, capable of selling sand in Sahara, but they are few and far between. Most entrepreneurs by far will do themselves a favour if they practice communicating their business idea to advisors, associates, friends and other social connections. Practicing may be quite frustrating at first, when people react with total lack of comprehension. But it is worth the effort.

Timing is another vital factor. Investors see too many presentations of companies or business ideas, where it is evident that the presenter did not time and plan his or her presentation in detail. In these situations, the investors will find themselves leaning back in their chairs while their thoughts are wandering and lost! The more prepared the presentation, the better the result. Even born actors do a lot of preparation and rehearsal before going on stage

3.4 Negotiation with Investors

Before embarking on the formal due diligence[10] process, which is a costly process for the investors, they need to have a good "guts feeling" about the investment opportunity. In principle, they should feel that unless the due diligence reveals negative surprises, it is actually worth an investment. This means that the "investment summary" needs to give confidence and encourage the investors to spend time reading the full business plan and meet with the team. The meeting and the reading of the full business plan hopefully will confirm that there is a solid business model behind the project, and

---

[10]Due diligence is the process through which a potential investor evaluates a target company or its assets. The due diligence process contributes to informed decision-making by ensuring that all relevant information is systematically used to deliberate in a reflexive manner on the decision at hand and all its costs, benefits and risks.

the terms offered will indicate that here is an interesting investment opportunity.

The investors know that they are facing an asymmetrical negotiation. Despite their financial bargaining power, it is the entrepreneur who knows more about the project, its risks and opportunities. The investors, therefore, need to have their "guts feeling" confirmed through a few phone calls to their private "network". If these feedbacks confirm their "gut feeling", then the decision to embark on the due diligence process is made. Today, many investors, as a routine, also "Google you".

It is also a good idea to "Google" yourself, your company and your products to see what the investors are likely to see when they "Google you". If surprises pop up, then it is better to be prepared to explain these "surprises", perhaps even send the investor a polite forewarning or heads up.

3.4.1 Due Diligence

The purpose of the due diligence process is not to convince the investors about the opportunity, but to clarify the risk elements which could change a "go" decision to a "no-go" decision. During the due diligence process, the investors look for reasons "not to invest", not the opposite. However, the due diligence process might give the investors a special insight into the business and business strategy, and they might come up with ideas as how to improve it even if the funding requirements then increase. If you experience this reaction, it is a good sign of an involved and active investor, and also a good starting point for the negotiation.

The aim of due diligence is not only control but also to bring the investors closer to the information level of the entrepreneur. Sometimes the results from a due diligence process redefine the funding requirements and often to a higher level. This might also lead to the conclusion that more than one investor is needed to fund the company.

After the conclusion of the due diligence process, the investors have a much better impression of the growth potential of the deal offered, the actual capital requirement, need for planned follow-up funding and the type and significance of risks associated to the deal.

Therefore, many due diligence processes start with an identified disagreement about both funding requirement and pre-money valuation, but also an agreement to let these issues remain pending for further negotiations.

The due diligence process covers a thorough examination of all elements in the business plan, including checking all the material assumptions on which it is built. The process normally takes from a few weeks to a couple of months. It is a stressful period of time for the entrepreneur as it requires substantial input from him or her. The investors expect instant replies to their many questions, and the entrepreneur should be prepared to give these answers at short notice.

It is rare for a due diligence process to proceed smoothly. Many unexpected issues will pop up along the way. How the management addresses these issues makes all the difference. It is normal for the investors to put the management to the test by stressing them and seeing how they deal with being put under pressure during negotiations and with the added workload. There are many good reasons why investors put so much emphasis on the quality of management. One of these is very simple: "A really good management team would probably not be associated with a second rate project". So indirectly the management reactions provide input for the first steps in the due diligence process. Investors know that after the investment has taken place, the quality and robustness of the management is of paramount importance if the company is going to develop successfully. So better test how the management reacts under stress before the investing!

Consequently, many due diligence processes result in a "no thanks" from the investors, no matter how good the project looks. In many cases, it is solely due to management failure. A "strong management team" can handle weaknesses and unexpected events, while a "weak management team" is doomed to fail under stress or when confronted with unexpected changes and conditions.

If the business plan puzzle has been completed, and the business plan is thoroughly worked out and is coherent and accurate down to the smallest detail with no unfounded representations, entrepreneurs should be well prepared for the due diligence process and have nothing to fear. It is, therefore, important to anticipate all the due diligence questions which are likely to be raised and be prepared to answer these questions without any delay.

Therefore, due diligence is definitely not a formality; in practice, if it leads to a positive result, it is a beginning of learning to work together. As the time spent on due diligence and the costs for the investors' advisors represent a substantial cost for the investors, they feel they are running a big risk if the entrepreneur, during the process, "walks away with a better offer". Therefore, they will often want to tie in the entrepreneur with a term sheet, which will commit the entrepreneur more than them. They are willing to take the cost, even if the outcome is negative and they will not invest. If the outcome of the due diligence is positive, the bird shall not have flown.

Investors normally use very structured methods with clear "go/ no-go" milestones while screening and selecting among the incoming projects, also in the due diligence process. In the end, only the very few projects selected for investment will be thoroughly analysed via a full due diligence process.

If a project requires many rounds of financing, investors commanding smaller funds and operating in the early stage market segment may decline even the most promising investment opportunity which, by all other criteria, looks promising. They perceive the risk of dilution[11] during the planned subsequent rounds of financing as being too big.

3.4.2 Term Sheet and Shareholders Agreement

The term sheet is a legally binding document which constitutes a draft of all the material issues and terms later to be found in the shareholders agreement. It is normally drafted prior to the completion of the due diligence process. The term sheet resembles a pre-nuptial agreement entered into before becoming husband and wife and regulates how duties and benefits are shared if it should be executed. Normally, the term sheet includes so many escape routes in particular for the investors that the "legally binding" term overstates the hold the entrepreneur has on the investors.

---

[11]See Section 3.5.

The entrepreneur should prepare for what goes into the shareholders agreement by outlining all these issues in the term sheet. The final term sheet might differ substantially from the first draft, as it develops during the negotiation phase with the investors. However, if the entrepreneur has created the original structure, the possibilities to influence the final document, and thereby also the shareholders agreement are enhanced. In this respect, it is also important that the post-money phase is well thought through and that the term sheet covers the conditions for the exit.

I would normally recommend that the entrepreneurs together with their advisor take the initiative of shaping the term sheet. Not only will it ensure that they have familiarised themselves with all the important terms before actual negotiations with the investors take place, but by being proactive, they are also the one who can direct the focus of issues which need to be addressed and emphasise areas of great importance to them. Through this process, the entrepreneurs should end up with a pretty clear idea about the price they can accept and what other terms they will find acceptable. I find it is important that they know their own tolerance thresholds and are able to come up with quick answers, as the negotiations with the investors' progress, and the various conditions find their way into the term sheet.

Important parts of the terms sheet addresses the amount of money being sought (the investment) and the share of company ownership this money will give the investors title to.

Therefore, an important term, "pre-money" valuation, now comes into play:

- It is a measure of the value of the company before the new investment comes in.
- It is a formula and you can always calculate it.
- It reflects directly the ownership percentage the new investors get.

It is calculated using the following formula:

$$\text{Pre Money Value} = \frac{\text{New Investment} \times (1 - \text{Ownership\%})}{\text{Ownership\%}}$$

New investment	Owner %	Pre-Money	Post-Money
€ 1,000,000	50%	€ 1,000,000	€ 2,000,000
€ 1,000,000	18%	€ 4,555,556	€ 5,555,556
€ 1,500,000	40%	€ 2,250,000	€ 3,750,000
€ 750,000	15%	€ 4,250,000	€ 5,000,000

Figure 3.7 Example of pre-money valuation calculations.

Figure 3.7 illustrates the implication of the pre-money valuation. If an investor invests €1 million in a company and the "pre-money" value is €1 million, then he or she will get 50% ownership. After the investment is made the "post-money" is €2 million, however, if he or she is offered only 18% ownership, the "pre-money" value can be calculated to be €4,555,556. In both cases, the entrepreneur needs to be able to explain how he or she arrived at this valuation.

Many entrepreneurs have been surprised by being asked by investors, when asking for €1 million in investment and offering, e.g. an 18% ownership in the company, "why do you consider that your company today is worth €4,555,556?" Many entrepreneurs forget the pre-money formula and cannot answer the questions. They had just decided on the ownership share of 18%, and that it would be fair!

Closely related to "pre-money" valuation (and ownership percentage) is the budget and business growth requirement. The ROI (expressed in IRR) the investors can estimate from the budgets is closely related to the ownership percentage offered. This is illustrated in Fig. 3.8.

The graph illustrates the required exit value of the company in year 5 if an investor has invested €1 million in year 1, and if offered different ownership percentage. If the investors' benchmark required ROI is, e.g. 40%, then the value of the company, according to the budgets in year 5, needs to be about €12 million, provided that the investors, at that time (fully diluted[12]), own 33% of the company. However, the future value only needs to be about €7–8 million if the entrepreneur had given the investors a 50% ownership. Hence, the

---

[12]Fully diluted: see Section 2.19.

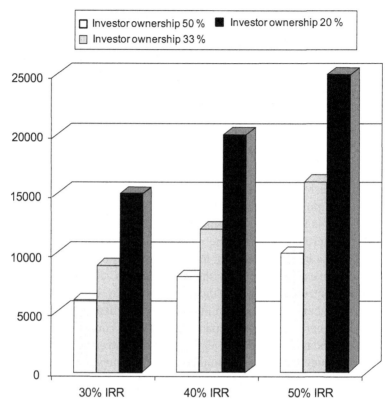

Figure 3.8 Ownership and value growth requirements (ordinate axis shall explain € 1000).

same budget on which the investors are making their ROI calculation may fail to meet their benchmark ROI target if the offering on the table is a 33% ownership, but may look okay and attractive if the offer on the table is a 50% ownership.

It is a prudent move for the entrepreneur or the management team to make a series of calculation about how much an investor can be expected to make as ROI or IRR depending on different pre-money valuations and different exit scenarios. The analysis can be combined with different scenarios of funding structure and timing of rounds of investment. It has a substantial impact on the investors' ROI or IRR if the investment can be phased in when needed. Many entrepreneurs like to have "it all in" from the start, disregarding that

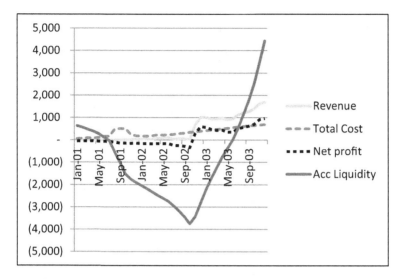

Figure 3.9 Liquidity requirements.

the more investment transferred from the investors to the company early on, the more pressure is put on the required business growth rate. A few examples can illustrate the problem.

3.4.3 Negotiating the Funding Plan and Structure

In the following example, the company in question is in need of funding to secure liquidity for a relatively short period of time. In principle, the total estimated funding requirement is €4 million. However, all the money need not be available on day 1, and the liquidity actually permits a certain repayment already late in year 3 or at least beginning year 4.

For simplicity, we assume that the entrepreneur offers the investors 40% ownership and that the two of them agree that a potential exit value of €25 million in year 5 could not be unrealistic if the investors provide the requested funding. At least three different funding scenarios can be envisaged, all of which cover the liquidity gap:

1. A one-time investment of €4 million combined with a 40% shareholding.

2. A milestones-dependent stepwise investment of €4 million combined with a 40% shareholding.

3. A one-time investment of €2 million and two times milestones-dependent convertible loans, which become repaid as soon as liquidity permits, or converted to shares if not repaid. Still combined with a 40% shareholding, although the actual investment in shares is only €2 million, but the total commitment is €4 million.

All three examples secure the company the requested funding. However, investor Example 2 and 3 offer three advantages. The first one is that in both scenarios "fresh" money is only released, when a milestone is passed, which reduces the risk associated to the next investment. The second advantage is that the money is out of the investors' pocket for a shorter period of time. This improves

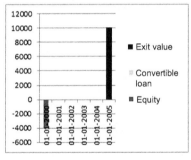

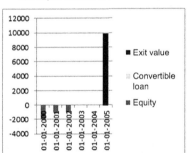

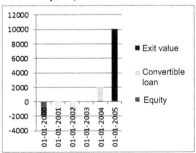

Figure 3.10 Funding strategies.

their ROI measured in IRR. The third advantage is connected to the combination of equity investment and loans. In Example 3, the investors disperse their money as in Example 2, but €2 million of the €4 million is paid back by the company 1 year before the anticipated time of exit.

Furthermore, the investors have the option to convert the loans into shares and giving them a larger ownership percentage if milestones are not passed.

To illustrate the difference between the investment examples, we assume that the total number of shares after investment is 1000, of which the investors get 400 shares. We can then calculate the price per share the investors have paid in Example 1 and 2 to €10,000 per share.

In the third example, the same total funding is provided by the investors, although partly in equity and partly in the form of a convertible loan. It is, therefore, reasonable to assume that the investors still get 400 shares; however, now they have only paid €5,000 per share. In this type of investment cases, it is often requested that the conversion rate for the convertible loans is the same as for equity, if the loans are not repaid in a timely manner.

If the liquidity does not permit timely repayment of the loans, the investors can choose to convert the loans into equity and get shares in return. By converting loans into equity, the total capital of the company increases and so does the number of shares. In our case, the investors get additional 400 shares in the company, which

Table 3.1 The IRR result of the three examples

Example	Investment	Ownership in per cent	Calculated IRR
1	€4 million invested one time	40%	20%
2	€4 million invested in three phases depending on milestone	40%	24%
3	€2 million invested and €2 million convertible loans being repaid in time	40%	30%
3b	€2 million and €2 million convertible loans converted into shares	57%	34%

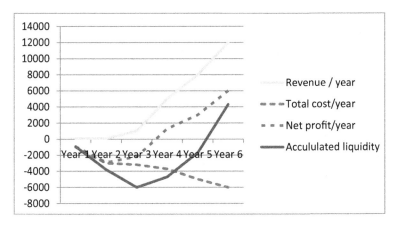

Figure 3.11 The five-year investment example.

changes their ownership percentage from 40% to 57% (the new number of shares is 1400 and the investors now hold 800 shares). If the exit value in year 5 is still €25 million, the investors will now get €14 million instead of the €10 million and experience an IRR of 34%. Or if the delays which prevented the repayment of the loans have caused a reduced exit value or postponed it a few months, they can still get their benchmark 30% IRR even if the total exit value drops from €25 million to €22 million.

In the next example (Fig. 3.11), the total funding requirement is €6 million, and the funding is required for a longer period. It is, therefore, not likely that a solution with convertible loans will provide much help.

Let us look at this example in more details. The entrepreneurs have in year 0 created and incorporated the company with an infusion of €500,000 of their own money, issued themselves 500 shares (nominal value/Series A share = €1000). At incorporation, they own the company 100%. Irrespective of how many new rounds of funding, they will still own 500 shares; however, their ownership percentage will change.

We have anticipated a two-round investment plan. In the first round of investment, a new investor will invest €4 million (Series B shares) as part of the total capital requirement. This investment takes place before sales begin and at a pre-money valuation of €4 million. It is of interest for both the entrepreneurs and the first investors that the anticipated second round of funding (Series C shares) is realised at a higher pre-money evaluation than the first round. The optimal timing would be when the sales begin to take off and a "proof of concept" has been realised by actual market participants (customers).

As illustrated earlier, the maximum liquidity requirement is about €6 million, and revenues are expected to really "take off" in year 3. Hence, the real "proof of concept" via customer reactions is 2 years from the first infusion of external funding. After year 3, the company is assumed to have a smooth ride with steadily increasing sales and positive cash flow.

Let us assume that there is a common understanding between the first investor and entrepreneurs that it could be realistic to realise an exit in year 6 at a value about €30 million via a trade sales to a large international corporation. The exit value is estimated based on the budget and by using a PE 6 factor on the budgeted net profit in year 6; an assumption which should not be unreasonable if the sale has developed as budgeted.

The entrepreneurs' "dream scenario", which also gives them critical voting rights, could be summarised as follows: The first external round secures an investment of €4 million in the beginning of year 1 at a pre-money valuation of €4 million. The price per share is €8,000, giving the investor 500 shares and an ownership of 50%. The next round is planned to take place at the beginning of year 3 and should raise €2 million in Series C shares. At that time, sales are assumed to "take off" and a higher "pre-money" valuation can be realised. If we assume that a pre-money of now €10 million can be achieved, this will give a price per share of €10,000 and give the new Series C shareholder 16.7% ownership. The Series B shareholders' ownership drops from 50% to 41.6%; the same will happen for the entrepreneur.

An analysis of the anticipated exit situation of this case in year 6 shows that the Series B shareholder (the first investor) can expect an IRR of 20% and the Series C shareholder (the second investor) can expect an IRR well below 20%. This result is hardly good enough to satisfy the investors. And if the entrepreneurs also fully exit (sell all their shares) in year 6, they would pocket a capital gain of about €12

Financing rounds and shareholders

EUR	Year of first round = Year 1						
Pre money:	4,000,000						
Post money:	8,000,000						
Number of shares after investment:	1,000						
	Amount invested	Price/share	Number of shares before	Number of new shares allocated	Total number of shares	Ownership % from new investment	Resulting ownership %
Total amount in this round	4,000,000	8,000				50.00%	100.00%
Accumulated invested	4,000,000						
Shareholders:							
Entr. Series A	0	Allocated	500	0	500	0.00%	50.00%
Series B	4,000,000	8,000	0	500	500	50.00%	50.00%

Figure 3.12 *Continue.*

EUR	Year of first round = Year 3						
Pre money:							10,000,000
Post money:							12,000,000
Number of shares after investment:							1,200
	Amount invested	Price/share	Number of shares before	Number of new shares allocated	Total number of shares	Ownership % from new investment	Resulting ownership %
Total amount in this round	2,000,000	10,000				16.67%	100.00%
Accumulated invested	6,000,000						
Shareholders:							
Entr. Series A	0	10,000	500	0	500	0.00%	41.67%
Series B	0	10,000	500	0	500	0.00%	41.67%
Series C	2,000,000	10,000	0	200	200	16.67%	16.67%

Figure 3.12 Entrepreneur "dream scenario".

million or an ROI measured in IRR of more than 70%, which will not be considered reasonable by the investors.

If, however, we adjust the example to a more "investor acceptable" scenario (Fig. 3.13), the Series B shareholder could invest €4 million at a pre-money valuation of €1 million. In this case, the Series B investor would get 2000 shares, and until the next investor comes on board, he or she would hold an ownership of 80%. The series C shareholder could make an acceptable deal by providing a €2 million funding[13] of which €1 million is invested at a pre-money of €12.5 million, and get 400 shares and 14% ownership. The remaining €1 million should come as convertible loan being repaid during year 5. If we continue to assume that the total exit value is €30 million, the Series B investor will get about 31% IRR and the Series C shareholder (and convertible loan provider) would get about 28%.

In this scenario, the 17% final ownership still provides the entrepreneurs an interesting outcome of the venture plus the salary they have earned during the project period. If this result is enough to incentivise an entrepreneur is another question.

Table 3.2 IRR in two rounds of funding after exit (fully diluted)

Investor	Investment	Ownership in %	Calculated IRR
Entrepreneur	€500,000 invested at incorporation	17.2%	20%
Series B	€4 million invested in year 1	69%	31%
Series C	€1 million invested and €1 million convertible loans being repaid in time	13.8%	28%

The entrepreneurs might also feel that "giving away" 80% ownership of the company is the same as losing control. However, if this is a key stumbling block, a solution could be to allocate more voting rights to the Series A shares than to Series B and subsequently Series C shares. In this way, the same voting right situation as in

---

[13]In Fig. 3.12, the entire funding from the Series C investor is for calculation reasons only, registered as "investment" although 50% is in equity and 50% in convertible loan.

Financing rounds and shareholders

EUR	Year of first round = Year 1					
Pre money:						1,000,000
Post money:						5,000,000
Number of shares after investment:						2,500
	Amount invested	Price/share	Number of shares before	Number of new shares allocated	Total number of shares	Ownership % from new investment	Resulting ownership %
Total amount in this round	4,000,000	2,000				80.00%	100.00%
Accumulated invested	4,000,000						
Shareholders:						
Entr. Series A	0	Allocated	500	0	500	0.00%	20.00%
Series B	4,000,000	2,000	0	2,000	2,000	80.00%	80.00%

Figure 3.13 *Continue.*

EUR	Year of first round = Year 3						
Pre money:							12,500,000
Post money:							14,500,000
Number of shares after investment:							2,900
	Amount invested	Price/share	Number of shares before	Number of new shares allocated	Total number of shares	Ownership % from new investment	Resulting ownership %
Total amount in this round	2,000,000	5,000				13.79%	100.00%
Accumulated invested	6,000,000						
Shareholders:							
Entr. Series A	0	5,000	500	0	500	0.00%	17.24%
Series B	0	5,000	2,000	0	2,000	0.00%	68.97%
Series C	2,000,000	5,000	0	400	400	13.79%	13.79%

Figure 3.13 Two more realistic rounds of investments.

the "dream scenario" can be established if an agreement with the investors can be made.

Although the reasoning and the investment simulations might appear complicated to follow, I have tried, with these two examples, to illustrate the wide range of possibilities which exist to reach an agreement if both sides are reasonable and understand the other parties' priorities and concerns. However, I hope also to have illustrated that this "game" is not suited for first-time negotiators, which is often the case for many entrepreneurs. Lack of negotiation skills and experience can easily kill an otherwise promising deal.

If in the end, the division of the eventual "spoils" of an investment is considered fair and attractive by the investors, a final condition for a sealed deal is the proved substance of the business case, its realistic potential, and not the least that alternative investment possibilities for the investors are considered less attractive than your deal.

Besides general business failure, the success for the investors of a chosen investment strategy depends, to a large extent, on the possibility to raise the next round of funding at a fair and higher valuation. If the Series C investor is unwilling to accept the proposed deal, and if the Series B investor does not have funds to cover the "missing" €2 million, then there is a risk that the funding round for Series C shares needs to be realised at a much lower valuation. This can lead to a severe dilution[14] of the Series B shareholder.

Although these considerations seem to be solely seen from the investors' point of view, they are important for the entrepreneurs to fully understand. If the only potential investor finds that the risk is too high, the offered pre-money valuation is too high and the expected IRR is too low, the entrepreneurs need to be creative. They need to understand the concerns of the investors and try to present solutions which address these concerns. The investors always have alternative investments possibilities, which include keeping the money in a bank. The entrepreneurs, however, seldom have many alternative funding sources which can step in if a deal goes sour.

Flexible financial solutions can lead to agreements which are satisfactory for both the investors and the management team or the entrepreneurs. Finding this type of solution requires good insight

---

[14]See Section 3.5.

into financial thinking and in the mindset of investors. If the team which negotiates with the investor demonstrates flexible attitude to alternative financial solutions, it will often soften the negotiation atmosphere and bring forward creative solutions from the investors' side.

It is my experience that a number of difficult deals in which I have been part became funded solely because both parties demonstrated flexibility on the funding solutions, combined with good demonstrated willingness to find acceptable solutions to unforeseen situations in the future. It also needs to be remembered that during the last part of the heated valuation negotiation, the parties do not sit with their computers and models only. They discuss which solutions they find fair and reasonable. Agreements are never reached unless all parties have a good understanding of what it means to "give away" or "request" on, e.g. pre-money valuation.

When a solution to the funding requirement has been hammered out and entered into the draft term sheet, we have actually only covered the ownership percentage and investment size part of the term sheet, in other words only the very first part of the agreement. All other elements mentioned previously also need to be discussed before the draft term sheet is ready to be signed. This negotiation often continues until the due diligence process becomes serious.

When the due diligence process has been concluded with an acceptable result, there is often a need to revise the term sheet and renegotiate some of the previously agreed terms. When a revised term sheet has been finalised, the work of converting the conditions in the term sheet into a legally binding shareholders agreement can start. For this job, a qualified lawyer is required. Although the term sheet, in principle, should be easy to convert into a shareholders agreement, you will, in practice, be surprised how many loose ends have to be tied in and which can require heart-breaking negotiations. When it comes to legal agreements, "the devil lies in the details".

3.4.4 Milestone Payment Solutions

Funding solutions which are built on a milestones-dependent funding plan are often well suited to create the bridge over concerns about risk and other types of uncertainty. However, there is also a backside of the coin, as these types of solutions also have their own built-in complexity and uncertainty.

First, a milestones-dependent payment needs to be scheduled in such a way that the milestones planned to be met have a date well in advance of the moment where the company gets to the bottom of its liquidity. In practice, from the moment a milestone is met and until a board meeting can be scheduled, where officially it is agreed that "the milestone xyz has been met", it can take weeks if not months. It also often happens that not all the elements in the milestone are met or that market or technology conditions have changed, making it meaningless to meet this milestone. In many cases and over time, another solution or milestone than originally anticipated is now the only sensible way to go. When these situations occur, formally the milestone payments are no longer a legal obligation for the investors. It now becomes up to the investors to decide if they refrain from providing the planned funding and let the company file for bankruptcy, or provide the required funding but renegotiate some of the terms.

I recently reviewed a sample of more than 30 investment cases in which I have been directly involved as investor or advisor. *In none of the cases, the pre-anticipated funding plans were executed as foreseen.* In many cases, the company structure was changed in an unforeseen way and even over a short period. In other cases, new investors were brought in; none of them had been on the "radar screen" when the original investment was made. In other cases, international daughter companies were created to accomplish internationalisation, and the funding was secured via foreign investors, who lived under different tax systems, and therefore "our Danish funding and company models" did not work. Unplanned convertible bridge loans were offered to the companies in order to secure survival during transition periods. Through these unplanned loans, the companies survived and could meet new milestones, which again, when passed, could open for new investors to be brought on board. Following all these changes of the "never to be changed" shareholders agreement, we soon worked with version 5 or 6. To keep track of the different shareholders position and compare it to the original ownership, and explain who got how much diluted or the opposite and why, became a nightmare and led to long fruitless discussions both at the board level and at shareholders meetings.

All in all, the complicated and very emotional discussion about ownership and company valuation when the first investment is made is, in reality, a heated discussion at blurred vision, which seldom materialises as foreseen. Therefore, the most important element in the negotiation strategy is to secure that the agreements which are being made have room for flexibility and leave little room for individual parties to stop changes via a veto and holding the other parties at ransom. If changes are to be made in the structure or in the agreements, it is important that all parties see an interest in reaching out for a compromise. Compromises are so difficult to reach if one party can wave the "veto flag".

It is often seen that compromises are difficult to find when one investor in a syndicate is low in cash and cannot participate in a capital increase. Then the "veto card" is played to force the other parties into a compromise, almost as holding someone at ransom. It is also often difficult to find a "fair" and acceptable solution when an investor cannot honour his or her milestone payment obligation. What happens then? Often a process for finding new investors need to be initiated, and if the investment has been provided via syndication, then a discussion needs to be started on whether some of the other members of the syndicate can step in and on which conditions.

When these situations occur, you really understand deeper meaning of the sentence by the Danish poet Piet Hein: "thing takes time".

It can take weeks, if not months, to find a solution, and you will also often experience that the more lukewarm partners in the syndicate will use the occasion to also step out of their obligations. It is, therefore, important that milestones are placed well in advance of critical liquidity flex points. Otherwise, there is not enough room for negotiation and finding solutions. If liquidity pressure becomes a limiting factor, it can often lead to wrong decisions. It is easier under pressure to say "here we stop" than "ok, we provide more funding".

The presentation of some of the negotiation challenges has been explained using rational terms and formal calculations. In real life, decision-making is not a fully rational process; it is strongly influenced by emotions, irrational behaviour, biased behaviour to both risk and opportunities, cultural background and actual experiences from previous investments or rumours.

3.4.5 An Unhealthy Grant-Optimising Strategy from Real Life

A few years ago I became involved in a "simple" case which turned out to be rather complicated, although the sequences of decision were fully logical, when it all started.

The business case concerned the establishment of a pilot plant for a biomass refinery. The pilot plant had a possibility to be easily converted to normal production capacity. The original company (a biomass refinery) and funding structure looked like Fig. 3.13, unfortunately only in the beginning. Two entrepreneurs funded via their private means a 50/50 owned holding company CO1. An international investor was invited to participate in the creation of NewCo DK Development, and the ownership distribution ended 51% to CO1 and 49% to the investor. The funding from the investor was partially equity partial convertible loans, both with two instalments.

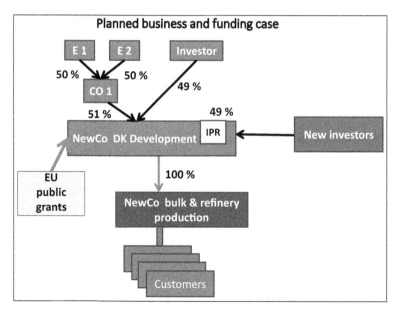

Figure 3.14 Structure of concrete business case as it was planned.

It was planned in 2 years' time, after having completed the pilot plant, to invite new investors to invest directly in NewCo DK Development. The investment was expected to take place at a higher pre-money valuation. The company had also attracted substantial EU funding in the form of a large grant, which actually was one of the reasons that the first investors accepted to invest.

Based on this investment strategy, it was possible to simulate how the ownership for the different parties would evolve depending on how the pre-money valuation of the company would be at different future rounds of planned funding. The general conclusion was that even with a conservative estimated pre-money valuation, when new investors would be invited to invest, it would leave the entrepreneurs with a total shareholding between 30% and 40%, or in other words a qualified minority shareholding.

However, 1 year into the pilot plant development phase, the investor found out that an additional and substantial national public grant could be obtained if a NewCo International could be created as a separate entity in the country of his residence. The challenge was that EU funding could not be combined with other public money funding for the same project. Hence, the entrepreneurs and the investor decided, in order to optimise the amount of public grants, to form a NewCo International in the country of residence of the investor. As a condition to obtain the new public grant, it was important that the new company became independent in its own right. NewCo International was, therefore, funded by diverting the investor's second instalment from NewCo DK Development. Had it not been for the public grant-optimising strategy, the refinery activities now in "NewCo International" should have been located in a 100% owned "daughter" to the NewCo DK Development, as illustrated in Fig. 3.15. This "daughter" would operate both bulk and refinery activities. In the new structure, however, NewCo International was only related to the original company by a licence agreement, and would only undertake all refinery services after the development phase.

In Chapter 4, we will discuss if the grant-optimising strategy was a lucky choice and if the convertible loans from the investor became a "burden" or a "blessing".

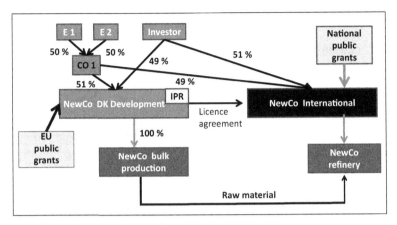

Figure 3.15 Structure of concrete business case, as it developed.

3.4.6 Investors Are Only "Visiting Guests"

During the entire funding negotiation process, it is important that the entrepreneurs have considered what should happen post funding, not only in a rational way but also emotionally, and have confronted themselves with what lies ahead: the post-investment phase. In this phase, they will cooperate with the investors, where the funding will be put to good use, where the business will be developed and hopefully also the milestones are achieved. This period might be lengthy and last until the time of exit, where conflicting interests between the entrepreneur and the investor are likely to reappear.

Basically the investment by the investors is a "visiting investment". At some stage (often sooner rather than later), the investors typically feel that enough value has been created, so that they can sell their shares with a profit, or they feel that they and the entrepreneurs have grown apart and that they want "a divorce" or an "exit".

It is important that the entrepreneurs prepare for the exit right from the start, whether the exit is caused by successful wealth creation, disagreements about the future development or a potential financial failure. Being proactive is critical. Also in this phase, an advisor can be of great help, as typically the entrepreneurs feel the conditions around the exit more emotionally than at the original investment.

3.5 Negotiating the Terms of Investment

The entrepreneurs should realise that the investors have been through many negotiations with other entrepreneurs. In fact, they do it for a living. Experience means everything here, and the entrepreneurs should take care, listen carefully and seek advice.

It is also worth to remember that cash is king! That phrase is a cliché often heard; however, here it rings especially true: Some unethical investors have proceeded with a deal, gone deep into the due diligence process, only to change conditions offered or threaten to pull out just before signing the shareholders agreement, as they realised that the entrepreneurs are running out of money and do not have the liquidity to start a new investor search and negotiation round. Faced with such conditions, many entrepreneurs feel that they are forced to accept unreasonable and weak terms, as the alternative is "close shop".

It is my personal experience that deals concluded on terms where one of the parties feels being "run over by a large truck" create mistrust and negative sentiments. Mutual mistrust is not a good way of starting a close relationship, although it can be removed over time. However, there are no solid statistics demonstrating that deals build on "fear" have a failure rate different from deals where both parties were happy with the initial deal. But there is evidence of a lot of unhappiness and frustration being created.

When the due diligence process has been completed with a positive outcome, and the right group of investors (if more than one is needed) have been brought together, then starts the detailed discussion of the structure of financing. It has become more and more frequent that financing by a consortium turns out to be a combination of pure equity investment combined with convertible loans. A carefully planned investment in more phases can substantially improve the anticipated IRR for the investors. However, this solution also carries along potential problems if business or development does not develop as anticipated.

Different share classes (often with different voting rights and anti-dilution provisions) are often part of the deal if more rounds of financing are anticipated. When all these elements are in place, the famous shareholders agreement can be hammered out in the final details and the deal is closed.

The shareholders agreement is normally built on the term sheet which was negotiated prior to starting the formal due diligence process. However, it is often seen that the due diligence process results in changes in the term sheet, seldom to a higher valuation of the opportunity and more often to a lower valuation, but also from time to time a higher than planned investment!

Regulation of the ownership and voting rights on the shares are often some of the major and most difficult issues to reach an agreement on. Hence, very often the starting point for investment negotiations is to reach an "in-principle" agreement about:

- The funding required (loan, equity or grants) on the short term (next 12–24 months) and on the longer perspective.
- Ownership percentage of the company for the equity provider.
- Influence on decision-making.

The company which is requesting the equity investment needs to make its own calculation of how the deal will look like through the eyes of an investor. There is no need to indicate any precise expected "pre-money" valuation from the start of the negotiations, but you should be ready to provide a rough idea about the pre-money valuation if pressed by the investors to come forward with an indication. Use the budget, which has been presented to the investors, as the basis for this benchmark calculation. It is important that the indication will give an "interesting ROI" for the investors if they use the same budget to make their calculations. Therefore, it is important to get to know beforehand the investors' ROI "flex point", between "potentially interesting deal" and "no interest". The examples given in the previous pages should fully illustrate how important it is that the "deal" is interesting also from an investors' point of view.

If the investors see that a fair deal is presented, it is much easier later on in the negotiations to reach an agreement about what should be the consequences if real life turns out to be very different from what has been budgeted. The business case may change structure, as in the example with "NewCo Development".

Most investors have two concerns when entering into an investment negotiation. One is about having an *ownership* percentage which (when fully diluted) will provide an acceptable ROI for the investors, when they eventually exit from the investment. The other is about *influence* on decision-making. Although the ownership percentage can be used to argue for a lower pre-money valuation (higher ownership percentage for same investment), these concerns need not be met exclusively through a high ownership percentage for the investors. The "influence" part can be regulated via the shareholders agreement, and by issuing some shares without voting rights, or with double voting rights. Hence, it is a good idea from the start of the negotiation to deal with these two concerns separately.

As mentioned before, in real life, the situation for the company and the general business environment 2–3 years ahead will never look like what assumed in the budgets for year 2 or 3. Actually the discussion of the "pre-money" valuation is, in reality, a discussion about what we believe will be the value of the company many years into the future or more precisely, during the period from the investment is made and until the investors expect to exit from the investment. Hence, instead of losing the deal because an agreement on a fixed pre-money value cannot be reached, the budget could be used as an agreed benchmark. Deviation from this benchmark could then be managed by combined incentive and uncertainty regulation mechanism in the agreement.

There is often an advantage in separating the "influence" discussion from the "value" discussion. If possible, it can be wise to conduct this negotiation in two separate unrelated discussions. By decoupling "influence" from "value", more flexible mechanisms can be included for solving the valuation disagreement conflict.

My preferred solution to the "value" disagreement question is to go a long way to accept the investors' wish for a low pre-money valuation, but introduce a share transfer mechanism in favour of the founders of the company, if the company's performance is in accordance or better than budgeted. In that case, the investors would be required to "sell" a predefined number of shares to the founders at a price which is only a small percentage of the price paid per share at investment time. In practice, this transaction is a post-regulation of the pre-money valuation. If the company does not perform as foreseen, nothing happens. This mechanism can also be executed the other way: the founders transfer shares to the investors if the performance does not live up to expectations. However, from a psychological point of view, the former method is to be preferred, because the founders/entrepreneurs are "punished" twice via the second method, i.e. they get depressed because of the non-performance and at the same time they lose their shares. Although the end result can be the same, the impact on "company mood" differs.

There are many other tips and tricks for reaching a fair and balanced agreement available to the experienced negotiators. However, advanced regulation mechanisms also have their limitation, as they can make the agreement very difficult to read and understand. They may also be difficult to implement in practice if a disagreement about interpretation pops up. Solving this type of problems via arbitration or in court is not a good idea. It should be avoided. It is costly, and what is worse is that reaching a final verdict often takes many months, if not years. Business-related conflicts need to be solved quickly; left unsolved for a longer time, they can kill even the best company.

When an agreement of the total investment is made and the "pre-money" valuation issue is settled, even only partially, there might also be a need for an agreement about what happens if planned or unplanned further investment is needed, e.g. to reach the business objectives. In the event that unplanned further investment takes place at a lower share price than what the first investors paid, the first investors become "diluted". Therefore, investors will often ask for special provision for "valuation compensation", or "anti-dilution clauses".

A provision for "valuation compensation" is also often connected to situations where planned milestones are not reached. If the deal is made via a combination of shares and convertible loans, investors will often ask to have some of these loans converted into shares in the case of non-performance. Depending on how severe the diversion from milestones is, the conversion rate into shares can be very low, and hence dilute the entrepreneur's ownership percentage significantly. When faced with this type of requests, the entrepreneurs can request to have clauses inserted which favour him if the performance exceeds what is planned. In that case, the original "pre-money" has, in theory, been too low, and the agreement can include provisions such as the "share transfer" mechanism described above.

There are numerous ways of designing solutions to "what if" situations, resulting in sometimes too complicated agreements. It can really be a valuable move in these complicated negotiations to have a neutral advisor, who can ensure that the final agreement does not become a complicated stumbling block for future seamless cooperation or subsequent rounds of funding.

I was once the chief negotiator for the Danish regional natural gas distribution companies, when they negotiated a 30-year natural gas contract with the state-owned Natural Gas Company (DONG). The gas contract was not only a gas purchase contract; it should also form the basis for the regional gas companies' investment in an entirely new gas distribution system. In essence, the contract was about introduction of natural gas in Denmark for the first time in history. It was historical as it also created, besides the 30-year natural gas purchases agreement, the basis for gas-pipeline investments of billions of euros. Hence, a lot of uncertainty and risk was associated to the contract, which included hundreds of provision for "what if" situations. The contract was much more than 100 pages plus annexures, included substantial force major conditions, including the famous "Acts of God" clause. Over the many years since the contract was signed, a lot of unforeseen situations occurred; however, none of these had been foreseen in the contract. And almost none of the foreseen "what if" situations ever occurred. And it was for these situations we had inserted long and complicated clauses to provide solutions if that or that happened.

3.5.1 Lessons Learned (from This and Other Cases)

Accept that unforeseen situations will occur; this is why they are unforeseen. It is better to focus on processes to handle unforeseen situations than to try to foresee the unforeseen and write solutions beforehand.

3.5.2 Other Standard Clauses in Term Sheets and Shareholders Agreements

The term sheet or shareholders agreement also normally include "pre-emption rights" provision. This means that the shareholders cannot sell their shares to any third party unless the shares have first been offered to other shareholders. We often also see provisions that secure that the entrepreneur is fully "locked up" until the investors have got their money back.

Normal agreements also include "tag-along" and "drag-along" clauses. The purpose of these clauses is to protect other shareholders if one of the shareholders wants to sell to a third party and the other shareholders do not have the funds to buy the shares offered. With this clause, they get the right to sell their shares also to this third party. Sometimes a third party, e.g. a competitor, comes to the table with an offer to buy the company, provided he or she can buy 100% of the shares. The "drag along" clause allows, under certain minimum price conditions, that the group of shareholders who want to use this opportunity to cash in on their investment can force all the other shareholders also to sell at the same price and conditions.

Normally "minority shareholders" who are not directly part of the management team are protected by special provisions taking care of their legitimate minority interest.

The discussion about the term sheet and the later discussions about the shareholders agreement will also cover provisions about how to control and support the management, and what power certain investors will have when appointed to the board and the management. The agreement will also normally include provisions regarding potential competition from companies in which the shareholders might also have a financial interest, and various provisions for solving potential conflicts which might occur.

These and a number of similar provisions are complicated to write from a legal standpoint and may even be difficult to understand for the untrained eye, but they do seldom create conflict of interest.

Many investors meet the entrepreneurs with "standard" term sheet and standard shareholders agreements which, as they often say, "will make it much easier for all of us, as we just need to fill in the numbers". A few years ago, a number of investors pooled their experiences and created a "standard term sheet" (the Rosetta term sheet),[15] which could be used as an easy general standard for upcoming deals. It is my impression that this document is slightly more aligned with solving investor concerns than addressing the concerns of the investee company and its owner(s). However, a lot of the standard clauses can be picked directly from this document with no harms done. It also can serve well as references to be sure that all normal items are included in the actual agreements being negotiated.

However, if it is used as a rigid standard, it may fit the individual investment case as well as a standard army uniforms sown to fit the average size of new recruits will fit the individual soldier.

The shareholders agreement describes how and when the money is transferred from the investors to the company. To secure that no problems occur between the signature of the shareholders agreement and the time when the money resides at the bank account of the target company, it is wise to make a "subscription agreement" which also takes care of the situation where not all investors in the end comply with the payment provisions laid down in the shareholders agreement. If the deal is made with a group of business angels, it has occurred that one of the business angels died or went bankrupt before the payment process was closed. The subscription agreement should take care of such "unlikely" but still very unpleasant situations, including dead angels.

3.6 Risk of Dilution

While discussion about many of the technical clauses normally goes smoothly, it is an entirely different matter when it comes to the so-called "anti-dilution" provisions. Here often a heated discussion gets started, and definitely no standard solution can be made. However, the individual tailored solutions can be greatly inspired by the way similar conflict of interest has been solved.

When the term "dilution" is used in this book, it means "value dilution". When new investors invest, new shares are issued, and the original ownership percentage of the "old" shareholders drops. That

---

[15]See Annexure 4.

is not dilution, and the number of shares the individual shareholders had before the new investors came on board remains unchanged. However, the value of the "old" shares may shift, depending on the price per share the new investor paid or, in other words, depending on the "pre-money" valuation term for the new investor.

Numerous books have been written about the business risk connected with investing in high-growth/high-tech SMEs. There is no need to repeat all this accumulated wisdom. One can safely assume that the business risks facing business angels and venture funds are the same, but as VC funds in general have "deeper pockets" than business angels, the "dilution risk" impacts the two types of investors differently.

A successful and even profitable SME growing in excess of 20% per annum is typically unable to sustain growth with retained earnings and cash flow. Usually, the credit constraints are due to an inadequate capital base. So in order to sustain the growth, more financing is needed via selling of equity. For a growth company not yet profitable, the situation is worse. The more rapid the growth of the company, the more severe the finance and cash flow problems normally become. Hence, there is also often a need for subsequent funding rounds even for successful growth companies.

It is normally assumed that along with the development of the company and realised sales, the perceived risk associated with the company is reduced, in particular, compared to the situation when the first investments took place. Along with risk reduction, normally "up goes the valuation". Therefore, it is considered wise not to raise all the money the company needs when valuation is low but plan for a series of capital expansion alongside the expected increase in company valuation.

These subsequent rounds of funding are often called round B, round C, round D ... While the incorporation funding round for the company is often just called the founding round, the shares are often called A shares. The shares issued in connection to the next rounds are called Series B, Series C, Series D ... shares. The different series of shares can have different rights associated, such as power to appoint board members, voting rights, liquidation preferences and anti-dilution clauses.

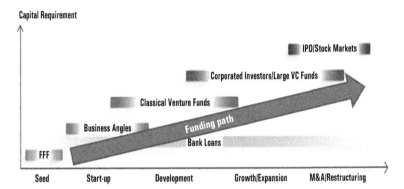

Figure 3.16 Investment process and the associated type of investors.

Often the path to funding is (Fig. 3.16) a smooth process where one type of investors replaces the next along with the development of the company. However, the "funding path" is, in reality, more "bumpy", as illustrated in Fig. 3.17.

Figure 3.17 describes the traditional perception in the investment process. First you start with the FFF (family, friends and fools) investors. Then as the capital requirement and the value of the company increase, business angels come in. Later, the classical venture funds arrive on the scene. Eventually, you move into the "late stage market" and so on until the final initial public offering (IPO). Because each round of financing has taken place at still higher valuation levels, everybody is smiling and happy—the first FFF and business angel investors. Some "bridge financing" might come in the form of a credit line from a bank.

The early investors, typically the 3F's, business angels and the small seed funds, should in principle be those to be rewarded the highest IRR when exiting to compensate for the high risk they have been running and the losses they may have endured from the failures with other investments. However, due to limited funds available, business angels and small seed funds are, in general, more exposed to an additional and different kind of risk: "the dilution risk". This risk is not alone associated to the success or failure of the target company in which the investment is made. It is ironically associated to its success and the risk of not being able to fully harvest the ripe fruit of a success.

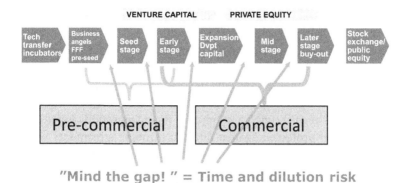

"Mind the gap! " = Time and dilution risk

Figure 3.17 Funding of a growth company may require a number of rounds of financing.

The "risk of dilution" is a risk which occurs during the following rounds of funding: In principle, if an original investor can co-invest with new investors and maintain his or her ownership percentage during each subsequent round of financing, this investor is, in principle, indifferent about the pre-money valuation for each new rounds of financing. However, if he cannot or will not follow up, he will be facing dilution in case the following rounds are not completed at steady higher valuations of the company.

If an early investor does not have "deep pockets" enough to participate in the later rounds of financing, the value of his or her shares in the total company might get severely diluted. In the ideal world, the valuation of the company and the share price increase for each new round of financing, thus securing Series A and B investors against dilution when Series C, D and E rounds of financing take place. However, the world is seldom ideal. In the real world, subsequent pre-valuations might actually go down.

For each round of financing, there is a risk that "money runs out" before a new round of funding has been secured, and even if money is secured, the pre-money valuation might be lower than the pre-money valuation for the pre-seeding round of funding. It is, therefore, important to understand the expression "mind the gap". If the process of securing the next rounds of planned funding becomes too long, the company risks being exposed to the deadly "liquidity trap". Running into a liquidity trap is a far more severe situation than encountering an unexpected deficit on the annual account. Next year might bring the expected profit, but if the liquidity does not permit survival until then, the company will not experience the profit situation!

This is one of the reasons why the "rational" business angel with limited financial resources will often not invest in companies which are expected to go through a number of financing rounds unless he or she is well protected against dilution through agreements with the entrepreneur. This is also one of the reasons why we often see business angels investing in service-oriented businesses with a more limited capital requirement.

The golden rule, which is often forgotten, is that for each new investment round, all conditions are negotiable or can be forced to be so, particularly if the liquidity trap is looming. If the company is up against the wall and is in desperate need of a funding, which the current investors cannot or will not provide, the early investors are often willing to waive many of the dearly bought rights associated to their shares. In particular, if the alternative is to accept harsh conditions for the next round of funding is a liquidation of the company, where they lose all.

At each round of financing, the valuation of the company and the price per share are determined partly by the performance and the prospect of the company and partly by the strength of the current shareholders to negotiate a good deal. In most of these cases, strength is measured by "deep pocket". This means being able to neglect offers from new investors, if the valuation is too low or is connected to other disadvantageous conditions, because it is possible to continue funding the company without the new investors. Alternatively, secure enough liquidity in the company via temporary funding (e.g. convertible loans) and willingness to wait for other investors who will accept a more fair valuation.

Many early stage investors wrongly assume that the interest of entrepreneurs to avoid dilution is aligned with their interest. However, the dilution problem, which the early investors and apparently also the entrepreneur are facing, can be easily solved for the entrepreneur. The new investors in the subsequent rounds of financing can fully compensate the dilution the entrepreneur has experienced through the issue of warrants, if they can get control of enough voting shares.

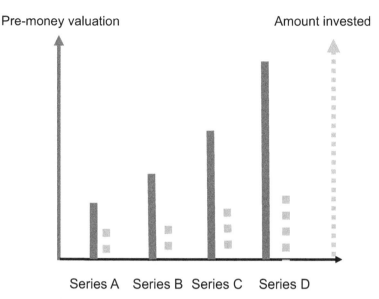

Pre-money valuation   Amount invested

Series A   Series B   Series C   Series D

Figure 3.18 Planned fundraising process and expected development in valuation.

No matter what is written in a shareholders agreement, it should always be remembered that "all is up for negotiation" if a company is facing a liquidity crisis. The early investors, therefore, risk losing out during the later rounds of financing. They even risk getting diluted to such an extent that they are not able to fully benefit from a successful exit from the initial investment or even recover their initial investment.

Figure 3.18 illustrates the ideal traditional funding process with numerous rounds of financing, where the pre-money valuation increases from each round of financing to the next. (Series A = FFF investors/business angels, Series B = business angels, Series C = classical VC funds, Series D = later stage VC funds).

However, nothing prevents the situation from developing as shown in Fig. 3.19. The unfortunate slow development in pre-money valuation does not necessarily reflect poor performance by the company. It might reflect changes in market conditions (e.g. right after the bubble burst in 2000, valuations dropped dramatically) or a weak negotiation position by the current investors (e.g. not enough deep pockets).

Pre-money valuation   Amount invested

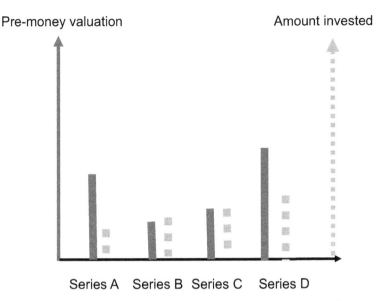

Series A   Series B   Series C   Series D

Figure 3.19 Funding rounds not reflected in increase in pre-money valuation.

Poor performance or overoptimistic assumptions regarding market penetration combined with a lack of financial strength of Series A and B shareholders can also result in a drop in the share price and pre-money valuation. The Secretary General of the EVCA, at a recent meeting with the EU Commission, stated: "The terms for any Venture Capital Fund investment is a result of a negotiation—not a result of an objective calculation!"

No matter what the background for the slow or unfortunate development in the pre-money valuation might be, in the example Series A and B investors are suffering substantial dilution. However, Series C investors are in for a substantial gain reflected in the significant increase in the pre-money valuation prior to Series D round of financing.

This can also be illustrated as shown in Fig. 3.20. Here we have compared two investment cases. Let us look more closely at the two scenarios, each describing an investment case over four rounds and a total investment of €5,000,000. Exit price in both cases is €10,000,000. In the first case, the share prices increase during each round, and in the second case, there is a drop after the second round.

Exit Price					10.000.000
Round number	1	2	3	4	exit
Year	2000	2001	2004	2006	2007
Price / share	40,00	40,00	10,00	25,00	31,90

Total investment	201.000	500.000	2.000.000	2.400.000	5.101.000
Accumulate number of shares	5.025	17.525	217.525	313.525	

Exit Price					10.000.000
Round number	1	2	3	4	exit
Year	2000	2001	2004	2006	2007
Price / share	40,00	50,00	60,00	70,00	121,00

Total investment	201.000	500.000	2.000.000	2.400.000	5.101.000
Accumulate number of shares	5.025	15.025	48.358	82.644	

Figure 3.20 Two different investment cases.

Increase in share price			Decrease in share price NO FOLLOW UP			Decrease in share price FOLLOW UP		
Investor	IRR	Accumulated investment	Investor	IRR	Accumulated investment	Investor	IRR	Accumulated investment
Entrepreneur	594,24%	1.000	Entrepreneur	421,31%	1.000	Entrepreneur	421,31%	1.000
BA 1	23,46%	200.000	BA 1	-7,30%	200.000	BA 1	17,26%	725.000
BA 2	22,95%	500.000	BA 2	-8,61%	500.000	BA 2	19,16%	875.000
VC 1	25,08%	1.200.000	VC 1	68,90%	1.200.000	VC 1	68,09%	975.000
VC 2	25,08%	1.200.000	VC 2	68,90%	1.200.000	VC 2	68,09%	975.000
VC 3	32,74%	1.000.000	VC 3	18,17%	1.000.000	VC 3	18,17%	775.000
VC 4	32,74%	1.000.000	VC 4	18,17%	1.000.000	VC 4	18,17%	775.000

Figure 3.21 Three investment scenarios.

In particular, it is important to take note of the number of shares issued in the two cases. In the first case, the total number of shares is 82,644, while in the second case, the number of shares is 313,525, because the price per share in rounds 2, 3 and 4 is lower than that in the first case. This also means that although the first investors hold the same number of shares in both cases, the selling price per share in the exit situation is much lower, even if the assumed exit price in the two cases is the same.

Figure 3.21 illustrates the result for the different investors. In the left scenario, the share price increases from one round to the next. The middle scenario illustrates the situation for the investors if the share price does not increase, and what happens if an investor cannot follow up with his proportional part of the new investment round. In the scenario to the right, it is assumed that the early investors follow up and secure their original ownership percentage. The example highlights the problem for the early investors with limited financial resources. In the case of "no follow-up", the two business angels even receive a negative IRR! The investor who really "makes the pot" is the investor who joins right before the exit; not surprisingly many VC funds have transferred their investment focus to this market segment!

The example illustrates one of the reasons why the "rational" business angel with limited financial resources would be inclined not to invest in companies which are expected to go through a number of financing rounds unless he or she is well protected against dilution through agreements with the co-shareholders and the entrepreneur.

For the business angel with an appetite for the more capital-intensive projects, however, there are several tools which can reduce the dilution problem. Among these are put and call options related to later rounds of financing. These terms should be negotiated between the business angel and the entrepreneur as part of the conditions for the Series A investment. Other tools are also available.

An alternative investment strategy has recently been pursued by some business angels. They have formed small dedicated closed-end funds through which they pool their resources. These pooled resources, together with a very prudent investment strategy and project monitoring, provide enough "staying power" to avoid a too severe dilution in case a portfolio company becomes successful and needs follow-up financing. Alternative structures for this activity have also been observed, and some have been connected to the new funding phenomenon called "crowdfunding". These alternative investment structures are simultaneously trying to protect against dilution, optimise tax benefits and pool resources for both screening, selecting and due diligence, as well as the task associated to company coaching and exit.

The optimal strategy for the venture capital is to invest "at the tail" of a constant pre-money valuation round, right before the final round where a substantially higher pre-money valuation could materialise. Many venture capitals have made tons of money by going in late before an IPO, and then benefited from the sharp rise in stock price when the shares got listed.

Negotiation talent and experience are required for both the entrepreneur and the Series A investor to hammer out such agreements. However, it is also important that the initial agreement is regarded as a reasonable agreement by the investors joining in the later rounds of financing. This "balance" is important because if a reasonable balance is not reflected in the initial agreement, then such agreements are often pre-conditionally cancelled as a condition for, e.g. Series C investments. The Series A investors or the entrepreneur can always refuse to do so, but if that makes the new investment deal "go south", the speed of the underlying business development will be affected adversely, possibly with disastrous consequences!

No matter what is written in a shareholders agreement, it has to be remembered that even the best formulated agreement is a negotiable piece of paper if a company is facing a liquidity crisis. The

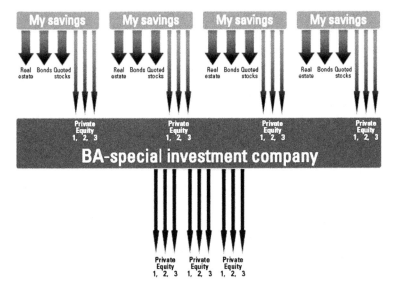

Figure 3.22 Business angels pooling resources into a special investment vehicle.

early investors, therefore, risk losing out during the later rounds of financing.

Worldwide, the business angels represent a considerable risk-taking investment potential, which can provide hitherto untapped funding opportunities for SMEs in Europe and elsewhere. Taking into account the already significant size of the business angel market, it is surprising that no more formal methods and support schemes have been developed to assist the business angels in their investment decisions and to bring the funding-seeking SME in better contact with the business angels.

In Chapter 1, an illustration of how a combination of public grants and early business angel investments can mitigate the risk of dilution for the early investors is provided. If public grants are used in a clever way, a combination of public grants and business angel investments can also provide a good way of securing a higher interest among business angels to invest in the more capital-intensive young companies, where normally the dilution risk is highest. Entrepreneurs who are looking for funding should secure, when discussion with their funding investors, that also this opportunity (if available in your country) is actively explored.

The examples also illustrate that investing in these types of projects is not a "beginner's game", neither for the investor nor for the entrepreneur/management team. Support to newcomers of how to choose the right way to "play the game" might untie substantial financial resources for the greater good of innovative entrepreneurs and thus society. For entrepreneurs and SME management teams, the financial "jungle" is an area where you can easily get lost if not guided by a professional hand.

In reality, it is ironic that a general political fear of "supporting the rich" (business angels and VC funds) in many European countries reduces the impact from a number of public initiatives launched by both the EU and many national governments with the aim of supporting the creation of high-growth SMEs. This was very concretely illustrated by the reaction from senior European Commission staff members when I, as chairman of the H2020 SME Innovation Advisory Group to the EU Commission, in connection to a conference on the new Horizon 2020 SME Instrument, pointed out that the SME instrument also represented an interesting opportunity for investors to reduce their risk exposure in portfolio companies. The "automat" reaction from the EU officials was: "No, you are wrong, the SME instrument funding has been created to support SMEs, not investors". This reaction illustrates how difficult it is for public servants or politicians to understand how risk and risk perception play a critical role in the investment decision process.

In some European countries, however, serious steps have been taken to encourage the funding by business angels, either through favourable tax schemes or by direct co-investment schemes such as the Seed and Venture Capital Scheme, the UK Enterprise Capital Fund (incentives through tax breaks) and Scottish Co Investment Fund. The Horizon 2020 SME Instrument created by the European Commission includes, beside direct funding opportunities for SMEs, initiatives and financial measures aimed at invigorating both the VC and business angel segment in Europe, and special guarantee instruments aimed at the banking sector.

3.7 Investment, Management and Board

Normally a board of directors should be formed right after the investment has been made. It is, therefore, important particularly for the entrepreneurs to consider whom they would appoint. The person they appoint should be a quality match with the experienced board members the investors will appoint. If the entrepreneur is also the CEO, then why insist on taking up a board position? The CEO normally participates in board meeting. My advice is that the entrepreneur should use the power of appointing his or her own board members to secure a loyal and competent board, which will have the stature and experience also to take over as chairperson of the board and, at any rate, be a strong match to the other investor-appointed board members.

However, sometimes the shareholders agreement has different solutions, which could have been avoided if the "cards had been played in the right way" during the negotiations. A solution, which I have often supported, is to secure that the chairperson of the board is appointed by both the entrepreneur and the investors and both sides have the right of veto.

Normally, the board should consist of an unequal number; however, one of my CEO friends said one day that three members, he felt, were too many! But in most cases, three to five members are good, in particular if they complement each other with respect to competence and insight in the particular business of the company.

Lots of discussions precede the final clauses in the shareholders agreement about voting rights and the identifying of items for decisions, which require not only majority but qualified majority vote. Sometimes the investors request a veto right on certain decisions in order to protect their special financial interest in the business. It is wise to secure that all these issues have found a solution before the shareholders agreement is signed, and do not leave those types of questions for a fight in the board of directors.

Piles of books have been written on these subject: shareholders agreements and the functioning of a board. My personal experience is that a board should, as a golden rule, always try to reach agreements, and decisions should be taken without voting. It makes the work in the board more constructive and pleasant. On top, it also means that all board members become responsible for all decisions. It is a way to avoid the "what did I say" situation when one or two board members are voting "no" to a particular decision which eventually turns out to be wrong. It leads to a much more constructive board discussion about "how to get out of the mess" when all feel that they are responsible, and you have no "back benchers".

If the work in the board gets into the habit that the majority always is voting the minority out, the board does not function any more as the sounding board for the management it is meant to be. Furthermore, wise decisions might not anymore be made when not all board members over time feel equally responsible for the decisions made at the board meeting.

However, as this is not a book about good board governance, it is advised to consult many books on this subject if in doubt about proper good board governance.

Formally the individual board members have equal rights and influence in the board. Competence and experience might tilt the influence, but in particular the board members who directly or indirectly sit on the mandate of the investors have a special (hidden) power. They have direct access to the money if suddenly the company needs further funding, be it a short bridge financing to cover a short-term liquidity problem if, e.g. a customer is late in payment or to secure bridge funding while waiting for more permanent funding solutions. This means that you need to carefully listen to their points of view and priorities in situations where liquidity concerns, sooner or later, are at the top of the board agenda.

As we will see in Chapter 4, the investor-representative board members' informal strong influence can have a sometimes unhealthy influence on day-to-day business decisions and choice of business models. Also often the investors' board members have the final say about the fulfilment of a milestone and the release of a milestone payment. If these board members are rigid in their interpretation of the milestone description, they can create serious barriers for the adaptation of new business strategies as a response to unforeseen market trends or market reactions, not to mention reaction to unforeseen technology challenges.

For this reason, the entrepreneur's appointed board members and the chairman of the board must have adequate business experience and time to interact with the company, its management and the other board members. It is important that these board members have courage to confront the management with problems and challenges to be discussed at board meetings. It is their obligation to secure that the management strategies presented at board meetings are adequate and balanced in a way that it becomes credible, that the management is able, through its proposed actions, to overcome these problems or challenges. If well prepared, it is often possible to convince even the investor appointed board members that those initiatives are sound solutions and merit acceptance of changes in milestone description.

3.8 Do It Yourself (DIY) or Get Help from an Advisor

To illustrate some of the challenges connected to the investor search and negotiation process, let us, as an example, look at the imaginary entrepreneur Mr. H. Ighhope, who is looking for funding for his young company, which has developed a new implantable hearing aid.

For whatever reason, Mr. Ighhope has come to the conclusion that his company needs external funding if his growth and development ambitions are to be fulfilled. Typically, the situation is that he, as many other entrepreneurs in the same situation, has already exhausted other sources of finance. He has funded the start of the company himself by "bootstrapping". He has also followed the principle of proximity by visiting the "3F s" (family, friends and fools) and got some money. He now sees that in the short run, the growth of the company cannot be ensured through the feeble revenues generated by the company. He may also have been discussing the business project with his long-time banking partner, who turned him down because of lack of security.

He now faces an entirely different situation from anything previous: He now has to go and ask for funding from professional private equity investors, who have a totally different set of values than him. They want to buy part of his company as an investment in return for providing the funding. He, on the contrary, wants to give up as little ownership of the company as possible. In other words, he is trying to get a high price for the shares he intends to sell. The opposing set of values seems quite apparent, and there is initially little understanding for the points of view of the other party's interest and concerns. Mr. Ighhope is now considering if he really needs the assistance from a professional advisor to help him, or whether he should try to wing it on his own.

For him the best known sources of funding are VC companies or business angels, but he knows that getting their attention is like "getting a camel through the eye of a needle". He is not familiar with all the financial terms, nor does he fully understand investor reasoning.

3.8.1 Should He "DIY" or Find an Advisor?

Many of the failures in obtaining financing from private sources can be related to the lack of understanding of simple market mechanisms and the special behaviour and requirements of investors operating in the private equity segment of the financial market. Most entrepreneurs are brave hearted, dismissing all the obstacles and setting out to conquer the obstacles all on their own. Sometimes, this can be the right decision and they get funded, but more often it is not. However, our Mr. Ighhope is a prudent fellow and wants to know: Can I do it myself or is it preferable to seek advice from a professional?

The choice is also a choice about the cost of getting good advice, namely, is there a reasonable balance between the costs and benefits? Also in the world of advisors, the saying is often true: "if you feed peanuts, you get monkeys".

On being invited into the investment process with the objective to secure that the minds of entrepreneurs and investors meet, the investment professional often finds that both sides lack fundamental understanding of the other party's point of view and there is very little common ground. This is more often true when entrepreneurs meet VC teams than when they meet business angels. But business angels also sometimes forget how they and the world looked like before they pocketed the first million euro or USD.

3.8.2 Ideal Role of the Innovation Professional

The role of an advisor is to ensure that the entrepreneur gets the required funding and on acceptable terms. "Acceptable terms" in this case mean terms which are reasonable and fair for both the entrepreneur and the investors. The role of good professional advisors is not like that of real estate agents: to get the best price at any cost. Their role is to secure a balanced price and agreement for both parties. This is because an investment is the starting point for a close and years long relation between the investor and the entrepreneur. This relationship does not end until a full exit is realised. If this relationship from the start is unbalanced, hell might break out early on.

With respect to the aforementioned principles, the advisor should, on a best effort basis, try to secure the best possible terms for the entrepreneur who has hired him or her, but should also secure terms which the investors feel comfortable with. The advisors' network of potential investors and their knowledge of their investment preferences should enable them to direct the contact to those investors most likely to be interested in the company and its technology. Furthermore, they can assist the entrepreneur in getting his or her business and business plan investor ready, so that the investors can quickly assess the quality and the opportunities connected to the deal offered. A good advisor knows that investors do not waste time to look at deals that are difficult to understand; therefore, structuring the offering in a way which fits investor preferences is essential, not only to create interest but also to get the right terms.

The specific role of the advisors may change during the various stages of the investment process. Sometimes they play a leading role, and sometimes they step into the background. Then they shift to a mentor's role, only to change into being a sounding board. No matter what, they are there to help the entrepreneur follow the most advantageous route towards the investors, while avoiding the many pitfalls that present themselves along the way.

The search for funding and the investment process progress more or less sequentially through the following stages:

1. Adjust misconceptions and manage expectations.
2. Align the chosen business model to the type of investor search initiated.
3. Get the entrepreneur investor ready.
4. Establish fair valuation principles and levels.
5. Find suitable and relevant interested investors.
6. Secure an investor-friendly presentation.
7. If need be, structure an investor consortium.

8. Assist in drafting and negotiate a balanced the term sheet.
9. Support during the due diligence process.
10. Assist in the negotiation of the final shareholders agreement with the investors.
11. Closing the deal; secure that in the end a shareholders agreement is signed.
12. Advice both parties in defining selection criteria for board of directors.

3.8.3 Adjusting Misconceptions and Expectations

- Many entrepreneurs expect that their business proposal is so important to investors that the investors are prepared to give them endless amounts of undivided attention and spend lots of time studying their business plans: **Not true**
  - » **The fact**: It is simply not going to happen. The investors do not have enough time to go into in-depth analysis of long business plans. If they did, they would not be able to screen enough deals from which to choose their investments. As illustrated in Figure 1.2, Chapter 1, a lot of potential deals are quickly screened by investors. Only a few make it through to finally convince the investors to make an investment.
  - » **The bad news**: Most business proposals forwarded to private equity investors, be it VC funds, corporate VC funds (CVCs) or business angels, get rejected and only a very small percentage finds funding from the first investors they approach and many run out of steam before they finally find an interested investor.
- Making the workload of investors less burdensome should remain a high priority for any entrepreneur seeking funding. Many entrepreneurs say: "Getting my company and myself 'investor ready' takes no time and effort; we just have to send the business plan to the investors." **Not true!**
  - » It typically takes several weeks if not months to get to the stage where the company and the investment opportunity can be presented to investors without quickly being taken apart during the due diligence work undertaken by the investors.
- Many entrepreneurs believe that if they are invited to the second meeting with investors, "money is just around the corner". **Not true!**

» The sad experience is that on average it takes between 6 and 12 months or more to get to the stage where the investment is secured. In particular, if we calculate from the moment the process is started and until the shareholders agreement is signed, it often takes a few additional weeks or months before the money appears on the bank account! If the company runs into liquidity trouble because of the long process, the trouble is not caused by lack of capital or investor willingness; the reason is that the process was started too late!

The investment process is sequential by nature, and many of the stages cannot be commenced without the former being completed, and "Things take time", as so nicely expressed by the Danish poet Piet Hein.

This short list of typical misconceptions among entrepreneurs should make the need for professional advice obvious. If an entrepreneur is a victim of just one of these misconceptions, he or she should seek a trusted advisor or partner with experience and relevant contacts. Rightly chosen, a great deal of time can be saved if all the typical entrepreneurial misconceptions are cleared away early on. If the advisor is working closely with the entrepreneur during this process, it also provides him or her with a good understanding of the entrepreneur's business, concerns and ambitions, thereby paving the way ahead, so that suitable solutions can be found.

Entrepreneurs coming from universities and other public research institutions can often get substantial support from the technology transfer officers (TTO) from the university. However, not all TTOs have intimate knowledge, experience or adequate contacts in the financial world, while they are often experts in IPR and licensing strategies. Therefore, it goes without saying that choosing an advisor also requires a type of "due diligence" on the background and track record of the advisor.

Chapter 4

Life with Investors

This chapter digs into aspects of the mindset of investors, which is often difficult to understand. It also, via examples, illustrates the importance of building the required mutual trust, which will be needed when a crisis occurs—not "if" but "when". All companies will sooner or later be facing unforeseen challenges, and it is the ability to tackle unforeseen challenges or real crisis which makes the difference between success and failure.

4.1 Introduction

A business case seldom develops as planned, and "sound" decisions made early in the business development process may in hindsight turn out to be unwise. In the previous "public grant optimizing" case described in the previous chapter, both the management and the investors tried to minimise the need for "private money" by structuring the business for obtaining a maximum of public grants (soft money). The total value of the public grants obtained amounted to more than €10 million compared to the total private funding of €7.2 million (equity and loans combined). The company structure with Danish and an international entity had always been the ultimate plan, but in the original plan, the international entity should have been a 100% daughter of the mother company, and not

How to Attract Investors: A Personal Guide to Understanding Their Mindset and Requirements
Uffe Bundgaard-Jørgensen
Copyright © 2017 Pan Stanford Publishing Pte. Ltd.
ISBN 978-981-4745-20-8 (Hardcover), 978-981-4745-21-5 (eBook)
www.panstanford.com

a separate entity fully separated shareholder wise from the Danish mother company. However, after the "grant optimising" strategy had been implemented, the Danish company should now besides its own business activity deliver raw materials to its "step daughter". From a pure operational point of view this solution could make good technical, business and marketing sense, and the public grant situation had been optimised, as depicted in the left graph in Fig. 4.1.

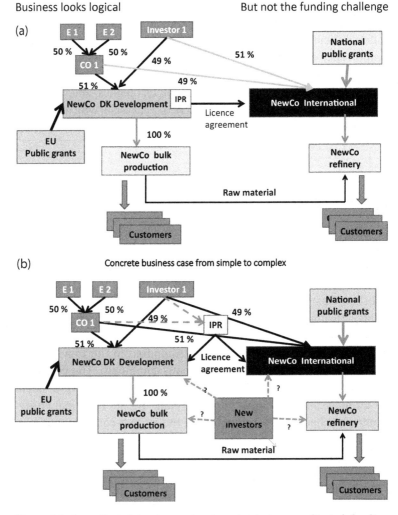

Figure 4.1 Complicated business structure leads to complicated funding challenge.

But when the next round of funding was about to take place, this company structure was not well suited for new investors. It was difficult for the investors to determine in which of the legal entities the real value would be created, and where the optimal exit value would reside.

The situation became further complicated when the original external investor suddenly wanted a quick exit from his investment in both companies. To put pressure, he requested, as a condition for accepting the changes in the shareholders agreement which were needed to allow new investors to invest, that the intellectual property rights (IPR) should be carved out from NewCo Development and put in a special IPR company, from which he then could exit. This situation is illustrated in Fig. 4.1(b). If this was not accepted he would convert his loans and take full control. A full conversion of the loans would give him a 65% ownership in both companies.

Suddenly the loans moved from being a blessing to become a burden. Although a conversion of the loans would not solve this investor's exit objective, it would put him in absolute control, a situation which the entrepreneurs feared. The alternative, a separate IPR company, would in principle support the investor's exit objective but leave NewCo DK Development without its own IPR. This solution would substantially reduce the pre-money valuation in connection to any new round of funding. It now became a serious problem to reach an agreement about where and how the new funding should take place, and how to get acceptance to needed changes in the shareholders agreements. In principle, the company was brought into a deadlock.

Creating a profitable exit situation for the entire conglomerate via trade sales or initial public offering (IPO) would take years to contemplate, and it would also need further funding and a clearer company structure. The problem with the structure was that value was created in two entities, and not in one entity (the mother company). The logical grant optimising company structure had turned out to be a liability and not an asset.

After lengthy negotiations with the new investors, they agreed to invest €10 million in NewCo DK Development, and the IPR remained there. NewCo DK Development would then invest directly in NewCo International. NewCo DK Development in reality now became the

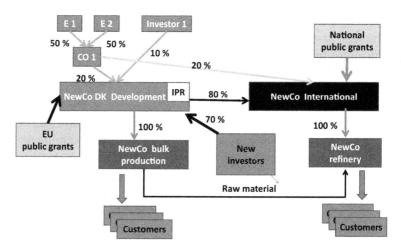

Figure 4.2 Final solution (before eventual conversion of loans).

mother company from which an eventual exit could take place. The new investors took over the convertible loans (including the favourable conversion right) from the first investor. Furthermore, part of the first investor's shareholding was bought by the new investors, securing his partial exit. The new investors became 70% majority shareholders in NewCo DK Development. If they exercised the conversion rights for the loans they had taken over, they would control more than 90% of the company.

The entrepreneurs' combined ownership dropped to 20% (before an eventual loan conversion), which was far less than foreseen in the original plan. The company survived, and the "grant optimising" strategy had really "backfired" and turned out to be an expensive strategy for the entrepreneurs.

The lesson learned from this case is: Any rational business solution needs to be mirrored with a longsighted funding strategy and an eye fixed on the exit strategy. This is often overlooked during the hunt to cheap and easy money.

Although the case might sound complicated, the case was not more complicated than many of the other business development cases I have witnessed. Actually, when I reviewed both a number of investment cases in which my previous venture capital (VC) fund was involved, and cases where I have been involved as an advisor. It became clear to me how impossible it is at the beginning of an investment case, to imagine how the funding structure and funding challenges would evolve over time. Even the most elaborated budget simulations and contingency plans had seldom captured the unforeseen situations which confronted the companies "down the road". That is why it is called "unforeseen".

4.2 The Limit to Rational Decisions

The previous "grant optimising" example reflects, in principle, what we would normally call "economic rational behaviour". That the strategy eventually turned out not to be well chosen was not caused by irrational behaviour. It was primarily caused by miscalculation of how the chosen solution influenced subsequent funding rounds. Also an element of "greed" did play a role in the decision objective: The more "soft non diluting money" the better, or let someone else (public money) take the risk! However, when chasing "cheap public money" in the form of a substantial grant, there is a risk that it distorts otherwise clear business objectives.

It is, therefore, relevant also to look at the general assumption of transparent and rational behaviour.

In the previous sections, we have primarily dealt with investment decisions and negotiations based on the assumption of rational and transparent behaviour from both the investors and the entrepreneur. This "rationality" and "transparency" assumption makes it easy to develop analytical models or predict and analyse decision processes. Unfortunately, real-life decisions are not always rational or transparent and involve many other aspects than what can be converted into numbers and calculation.

Rational and transparent behaviour is, in principle, based on a simple assumption that if a person prefers solution A compared to solution B and also prefers solution B compared to solution C, then he or she will also prefer A compared to C, or

$$\text{If } A > B \text{ and } B > C, \text{ then } A > C$$

However, in real life, this rational behaviour is not always what governs our decisions not necessarily because persons act in irrational way, but because a lot of factors other than those that can be captured in "A", "B" and "C" influence the final preferences. Other elements which influence the decision, such as "anchoring effect", should not be forgotten.

The well-known naturalist Konrad Lorentz, some decades ago, discovered that goslings, upon breaking out of their eggs, became attached to the first moving object they encounter (normally their mother). Lorenz knew this because in one experiment, he became the first thing goslings saw and they followed him loyally until adolescence. Investors are not goslings, but like any normal human being, they become influenced in their investment decision by the "first impression" or "similar previous impressions". This is often called the anchoring effect. Professional psychologists have impressive names for it, such as "negative reinforcement".

The anchoring effect has also been demonstrated by the father of behavioural economics, Daniel Kahneman, in his research.[1] If the first impression is good, there is a tendency to see "good elements" in the entire business case, while if the first impression is bad, the same business case would be looked upon through darker glasses.

Other psychological elements such as "fear", "greed" and "lust" also influence our otherwise "rational" behaviour.

If you visit many international airports nowadays, you often meet eager "smart car" lottery sales staff. They stand in front of glittering Ferraris, Porsches or Lamborghinis and offer expensive lottery tickets of which "only" 1000 tickets are for sale and a draw is made each month. Here the "greed or lust" factor often plays a trick by convincing the weak soul that the chance is high and with the "bait" in front of your eyes, you focus on the "high chance" of success, compared to other lotteries, where the chance might be 1/1,000,000. Subconsciously your brain converts the 1/1000 probability into a "high" chance to win compared to other lotteries and because you really want this car for "only" €150.

The same brain works in the opposite way when confronted with a "risk" connected to something you really want. This could be parachute jumping, jumpy jump or scuba diving with sharks. If you really want it, the risk is "only" 1/1000 and your brain converts it to "no risk".

---

[1]Daniel Kahneman won the Nobel Prize in economics in 2002.

You also consider a risk to be bigger when the situation is "out of control" compared to when you are in control. Travellers are often more nervous of flying[2] although it is one of the safest means of transport, particularly compared to the risk you are exposed to when taking a taxi from the airport to the hotel. In many cities, it is actually a high-risk adventure. However, you are used to sit in a taxi, and you feel to be in control to some extent and do not consider your trip to be dangerous. Actually people use their seat belts more often in private cars than in taxis!

Although economists will hate to admit, money and all the other objective elements discussed in Chapters 1–3 are only part of the final criteria behind any investment decision. Even if A, B and C could symbolise all relevant elements in the final decision, human beings are also influenced by personal experiences and by the strange ways our brain works. In his book *Thinking Fast and Slow*,[3] Kahneman has provided an interesting insight into why some decisions do not fulfil Bernoulli's well-known utility function.

Kahneman describes it as our brains' "automatic response system" and its "effortful system". For simplicity, the first is called "System 1" and the second surprisingly "System 2", which he has adopted from the psychologists Keith Stanovich and Richard West. Kahneman describes the two "systems" in the following way:

- System 1 operates automatically and quickly, with little or no effort and no sense of voluntary control.
- System 2 allocates attention to the effortful mental activities that demand it, including complex computation. The operations of System 2 are often associated with the subjective experience of agency, choice and concentration.

If you are an entrepreneur, you will effortlessly recognise Fig. 4.3(a) and perhaps also make an association to the "no" you often get from investors, while the drawing in the middle will be met with disbelief.

---

[2]This is often called subconscious depression and is said to be generated from the many times we see detailed description of aircraft crashes and our reaction is "this could have been me".
[3]*Thinking Fast and Slow*, Daniel Kahneman, Penguin Books, 2011.

Figure 4.3 The "no" (© CartoonStock Ltd. 2016).

If you happen to be an investor or have a background as advisor who often meets enthusiastic entrepreneurs with great ideas and business dreams, the drawing to the right might effortlessly give you an association.

However, if you are exposed to the question below, you will most probably need some effort to find the result, and it will be difficult to do so, e.g. while driving through a roundabout in rush hour traffic.

$$17 \times 187.5 = ?$$

Kahneman further explains that although the mental effort associated to System 2 should overrule the "quick and un-reflected" reaction of System 1, it still often prevails. A typical example is the comparison of the two lines in Fig. 4.4.

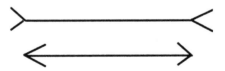

Figure 4.4 Two lines.

Which line is longer: upper or lower? It is easy to use a ruler and find out that the two lines are of equal length, but even with this factual knowledge (obtained using all your System 2 brain power), your "automatic" System 1 will still try to overrule your "factual" System 2 knowledge and indicate "different length". If two simple straight lines can trick your brain, how about more complicated decision situation? Therefore, it is reasonable to assume that decision-making about investments is influenced by both System 1 and System 2 reactions and interactions.

Investment behaviour in the case of System 2 always has a cognitive[4] content, or a set of specific cognitions. Cognitions might be either interiorised or formed on the basis of past experience (most often, strong emotional experience). Some of the cognitions might be conscious, while some of them might be subconscious/unconscious.

An example of a set of cognitions favourable for signing a contract: "I am clever as an investor, and the decision I make is a clever decision." Or "I must take a chance, because I can make it happen and I will gain". However, it is my experience that an investor with this self-perception also often reacts strongly when proven wrong about his "self-perception". In his self-perception, he will consider that he was not wrong, but it was entirely the fault of the entrepreneur that the business ran into troubles. Often the investor will, therefore, quickly revert to a "cut your losses" strategy and refuse to participate in any rescue operation. If he exceptionally chooses to participate with additional funding, he is typically very firm in securing an adjustment of his ownership position in order to be compensated against an eventual lower pre-money valuation or lower anticipated exit value.

The reasoning of others can follow this line: "This team seems trustworthy, and they are serial entrepreneurs who have shown that they can make it happen, so I trust the team even if not all in the business plan make sense". If this trust is damaged, e.g. if crucial information is not shared with the investors, working with this type of investors becomes very difficult, because the trust is lost. If one of the key reasons for making the investment is "trust" and this trust is broken, it takes months, if not years, to rebuild a broken trust. And "trust" is not rebuilt by offering the investor more shares as compensation.

Some fund managers will also be attracted to a management team when they can conclude: "They have high moral standards and high energy level. They are organised, constructive, experienced, seeking for excellence. This project is innovative and contributing to the welfare of society. Ethical people invest in projects which are contributing to the society. If we invest, we prove to be an ethical

---

[4]Cognitions (schemas, beliefs, attitudes, expectations, anticipations, stereotypes, automatic thoughts, conscious meanings, values—"things you tell yourself" about self, life, others, future) of the investor are the key element explaining most of investors' decision-making (System 2).

fund". These investors' reaction to unforeseen situations also differs from the previous ones, as the motivation behind the investment decision had a different dimension. However, here unethical behaviour will course troubles.

It is, therefore, important to understand that the personality of an investor can have an impact on the investment behaviour of the investor. Narcissistic investors would usually have a schema "I am the best". They might also falsely believe that their decisions are always right. Even if sometimes it turned out not to be true, they will tend to "forget" (repress) the failure immediately. Having this type of personalities directly represented in a board can be a real challenge. Depressive investors might be motivated to take various unnecessary precautions. It can be a nightmare to negotiate a contract with them. They would also have the negative expectations or a nihilistic view of the future. Bipolar investors would have "dichotomous thinking", which might be expressed through a schema "now or never". It is my experience that they will often refuse to participate in unplanned follow-up investments.

Hippomanic investors would indiscriminately attribute positive values to their past, unrealistically expect favourable results from their endeavours and exaggerate their success in the future. If they have had great successes, they strongly believe that the next investment will also be a success. This behaviour can lead to personal bankruptcy, as I have seen over the past years a few times with very high-profile business angels.

Paranoid investors would assume that other people will start deliberately abusing them or interfere with their objectives or have access to information that they do not have. I encountered this personality when I was chairman of the board of an ICT company a few years ago. This type of investors could send a mail to the entrepreneur saying:

> "I am not the one who was bull scrapping everyone in sight for three whole years; you and your voiceless buddy were, by constantly misinforming me."

Traits of this type of personalities and behaviour can easily be identified in some of the cases which will be discussed in the following sections. However, not being an expert in psychology, I will refrain from making any diagnosis.

Also the personalities of the entrepreneurs differ as much as that of investors, and actually merit an entire book. However, in this book, the focus is on understanding the mindset of investors. Research shows that investors prefer collaborating with entrepreneurs who are not depressive, but open to experience and extrovert. Sadly, as previously described, there are many records of cases when investors have trusted imposters (or psychopaths) when they succeeded in creating socially attractive self-image.

In the book *Predictably Irrational*, Dan Ariely,[5] who is a professor of behavioural economics at Duke University, outlines other flaws in the general assumption behind traditional rational behaviour on which so much decision theory is based. In Annexure 6, you will find a series of scientific abstracts, which further support the view that it is not the economists' "rational" and "economic" man which best describes investor behaviour.[6]

I have not been arguing that investors make irrational investment decision, although some decisions look alike. We just have to recognise that many other factors than those which can be described in a business plan, in a budget and in a financial analysis play an important role. All these elements are factored in when the final decision is made. This includes the investor's personality and personal experiences from previous investments and events in life (the anchoring factor). Some of them may overrule the conclusion drawn from all the formal financial analysis like System 1 which still plays a trick with your brain in the two-line example. Those are all elements influencing the investor's final decision and making it difficult for an outsider to predict the outcome.

I have had a very concrete experience of the influence of the "anchoring effect". It was connected to the final phase of a second-round funding negotiation with a large VC fund from Holland. It was a "sure deal" which was lost in the last minute. In this case, a long negotiation had finally come to an end, all documents had been

---

[5]*Predictably Irrational: The Hidden Forces That Shape Our Decisions*, Dan Ariely, HarperCollins, 2009.
[6]This reference is kindly provided by Dr. Aistë Dirzyté, from the Psychological Well Being Research Laboratory, Vilnius, Lithuania.

drafted, all conditions had been agreed upon with three of the four VC fund partners and the final approval "just" needed the okay from the last partner, who had been travelling the last three weeks on a safari in South Africa. As his approval was assumed to be a small formality, the signature meeting and following dinner was planned next week. Then one evening I got a phone call from the senior partner of the fund, explaining with regret that the last partner had returned and had unexpectedly vetoed the deal "because he would never again accept that the fund invested in anything related to the retail industry, because he had personally not only lost money but he had been cheated in connection to investment in the retail industry". The partner was firm in his attitude, and as all partners in the fund had a right of veto, the deal was off the table. This was a very concrete example of the "anchoring effect". The "no" was not related to the concrete business case; the reason was that the case was related to a sector where the partner had bad experiences.

Before being carried away to thinking that planning and budgeting are useless, it has to be remembered that the factual information contained in the business plan and the budgets still plays an important role in giving the investors an impression of the business case and the team behind.

But the final investment decision is based on a sort of "holistic" (or "lean back and test your guts feeling") assessment of the opportunity:

- Do I believe in what I am told?
- Do I understand it and can I trust them?
- Is it realistic?
- Can they make it?
- Is this opportunity better for me than all the other opportunities available?

We included this "holistic" element in the H2020 SME evaluation criteria, when I a few years ago worked as an advisor to the EU Commission: We recommended that project evaluators should add a special "lean back and take a holistic view of the application" criteria. These criteria should complement the traditional quality scoring of specific elements (excellence, impact and implementation). It was not easy to get a "non-factual" element included in the EU evaluation system, but after some fight, the "lean back" elements became included in the H2020 SME evaluation system.

In the end, all the formal analysis and calculations are made to support the final decision, not to make it. It is like the drunkard leaning at the lamppost; it is more for support than for enlighten. You can also formulate it in a different way: If all the "facts" which are presented in the business case, in the associated budgets and the financial calculations indicate that it is not a convincing business and investment case, it is not likely that it can attract investor interest. However, even if all the "facts" indicate, on all criteria, an interesting business and investment case, you may still be a long way from having convinced the investors to invest.

Is it fair? No, but life is not designed to be fair, and in the end, there is a big difference from being "investor ready" to be "investor attractive".

The entrepreneurs should be conscious of the many "soft" decision factors which determine an investment decision and should not forget the importance of making a good "first impression". If the first impression makes an investor to put on the "dark glasses", he may be unconsciously influenced to focus on the irreversible risks associated with any business venture rather than on the opportunities. This will influence the final calculations and thereby support the first (negative) impression (subconsciously chances are turned into risk). However, if the first impression is excellent and stirs "lust and greed", an opposite association mechanism is set in motion and subconsciously "risks" suddenly become "chances or opportunities".

Investors know that although no investment decision is made "if in doubt", many "wise" decisions turn out to be "wrong" decisions, which should never had been made. This is why investors are so focused on the exceptional "upside" in any deal. These exceptional upsides need to materialise to cover the loss from "wise" decisions which turned out to be wrong decisions.

Unfortunately, it is not possible to put weights on how much the "hard" analysis compared to the "soft" elements eventually influences the final decision. This also varies from investor to investor and is influenced by the individual investors' risk adverseness, subconscious anchoring effects and personal experiences or a strong need for a dramatic success.

4.3 Right or Wrong Decisions?

As mentioned in the previous sections, there is a world of difference between getting financed via bank loans or via private equity (investments). The bank does not interfere with the business, but they attach their hope for repayment to the value of the collateral and a sound budget. An investor becomes co-owner, and the individual investors are very different with respect to how much involvement they want to have on day-to-day activities of the company. There is also a big difference in their decision behaviour, but that does not make the individual decisions more or less "rational", just different.

The business angels invest their own money and behave accordingly. Their behaviour varies substantially depending on how dependent they are on the financial outcome of the investment, and their individual "deep pocket" level. Business angels are private individuals; therefore, they are exposed to all the traditional human risks such as personal financial disasters with other investments, disease, divorce or death, all factors which can suddenly change their behaviour and preferences. If the "deep pocket" of a business angel becomes empty because of failure of some of his or her other investments, the "innocent" portfolio company may suffer.

Many entrepreneurs have experienced that following a change in financial status of a business angel, even milestone payments contractually carved in rock were not paid according to contractual requirements. In a few cases, this pushed the company funded by the business angel into deep financial troubles and sometimes bankruptcy.

In contrast, VC funds are normally financially stable (during their lifetime). They invest other people's money, but the managers work under a higher performance pressure than the business angels, whose responsibility is only to themselves and perhaps their family. As you may recall, a venture fund is just a "large bank account" made available by a group of professional investors with "deep pockets".[7] It is normally governed by a management company with partners and investment managers. Their objective is to find business cases to invest and to support the development of different business cases and eventually sell the shares with a profit.

---

[7]Typically, the investors are pension funds, mutual funds, insurance companies, banks and sometimes large companies.

The objective is clearly financial, but decision-making is in the end also influenced by a large array of non-financial elements, including the selfish interest of the management team to be "staying in business" for a longer time than the maturity of the fund they are currently managing. Also the VC fund in Holland, with the partner who did not like the retail industry, was a large and very professional and successful fund.

Although the management of a fund normally receives a fixed fee of between 1% and 2% of the "fund under administration", they are also often incentivised via "over-performance premium". This could be formulated as follows: The investors in the fund first get their investment back with accumulated interest calculated on a "benchmark" rate of return. If, thereafter, there is a surplus, this could be divided between the investors and the management with an 80/20 split. Most funds are closed-end funds with a maturity of 10–12 years. Therefore, they typically invest in new business opportunities the first 3–4 years, develop the portfolio the next 3–4 years, and use the remaining lifetime of the fund to sell. After 10–12 years, the balance is made up. For a fund of €100 million, the accumulated benchmark could be that the investors will first have €250 million back, before there is anything to split. If it goes well and the management has chosen good cases and sold them at high prices, the partners in the management company can "walk on water". If the end result is €350 million, the three to four partners share €20 million and can live a comfortable life for a few years. If the fund does not perform, they have proven that they cannot manage a venture fund and they may be lost forever working in this industry. This is a "fear-induced incentive" to perform and can lead to some risk adverseness, as discussed in details in Sections 1.7 and 1.8 (Chapter 1).

The management of an early stage VC fund knows very well (or should know) that on an average, only 20–30% of the investments will perform as expected or better. This means that the few successes will cover the underperformance of the remaining 70–80%. When doing the math on these numbers, all the cases in which the fund invests should have the potential to make 8–10 times increase in value over 5–7 years (as you never know who will be the champions). If the right choices are not made, the investors in the fund are not happy, and neither are the managers.

This performance pressure influences the behaviour of the VC managers.

Irrespective of whether the investor is a business angel or a venture fund, some like to take an active part in the business decisions of their portfolio companies, while others prefer a passive role. Some are calm investors who accept that not every part of a budget is "carved in rock", while others begin to scream at you after the smallest hick-up in your plans. But when they made the investment, they seriously believed that this business case would be the winner. Hence, if something goes wrong, both their individual personality—System 1 and System 2—and the anchoring effect will influence how they react to surprises and disappointments.

Although investors know the statistics, when confronted with delays in expected revenues, or development cost which exceeds the planned cost level, milestones are delayed or the company becomes in need for unplanned funding to continue operation, then they become both surprised and disappointed. The biggest problem often occurs with investors who have chosen the "sleeping" role. For them, the surprises always are an unwelcome "wake up call" on which they often react strongly, while the investors who follow the company closely often have a better understanding of why there is a need to deviate from a plan. For some of the investors, a "little worm also begins to gnaw" about the trust in the deal. This is, in particular, the case when there is a need to make the unplanned financial decision: "shall we throw good money after bad money?"

Some investors, whom I know, will never let a System 1 reaction "no more money" to be overruled by a System 2 consideration "maybe there are good reasons to prevail". They will not participate in the "rescue operation". Others governed by positive experiences from previous rescue operations might offer to provide the needed bridge financing. It is interesting, but also very complicated, in real life to chair a board when two investors, who possess the same information, make very different interpretation of the situation and display different reaction pattern.

I have experienced cases where, based on exactly the same information, one investor acted like "System 1" and the other investor like "System 2". One of the investors, whom we can call "System 1" type of investor, might have had good reasons to decline further capitalisation of the company. He or she might have reached his or her funds internal ceiling for individual investment case, or he or she might have no free liquidity, but often this is not the real reason to decline. It is simply the "anchoring effect" which prevails. He or she had experienced that when "throwing good money after bad", he or she had always lost and had seen that in most cases, it had been a good strategy to "cut losses" quickly. Irrespective of the particularity of the new situation, the "anchoring" effect now influenced his or her decisions. Just like the Dutch VC fund partner, who aborted a sure deal because of "never any new retail industry investments".

The other investor ("System 2 investor") saw, in this particular situation, good reasons to secure the additional funding. But he or she would not accept that the "System 1" investor get a "free ride", while he or she should take all the additional risk. Hence, he or she requested that the pre-money valuation for the "rescue" investment became so low that he or she, also after the "rescue" investment, could expect the return of investment as originally anticipated. This would mean that the founders, the entrepreneur and the other VC investor, got severely diluted. This solution the "System 1" investor did not like.

Although we are here dealing with feelings and emotions, also money, "greed" and "fear of loss" and formal influence enter the scene. In this case, the "rescue investment" would increase the System 2 investor's investment from €0.5 million to €1 million. The cause of the liquidity problem in this case was that a down payment from an industrial customer had to be replaced by a royalty agreement. Replacing the down payment was a substantial unexpected increase in funding requirement. However, with the royalty agreement signed, the realistic exit potential of about €15 million was unaffected, although it was put 1 year further out in the future. The "rescue" investor required that the share price connected to the new investment was calculated so that his or her original expected 43% internal rate of return (IRR) was unaffected.

This resulted on the following distribution of investment, ownership and IRR.

It is seldom that the investors fully understand why their colleagues act differently, when being exposed to the same information and situation. Therefore, Investor B, with the System 1 attitude, thought that Investor A, the "System 2" investor, in reality had access to some information that he or she did not have access

Table 4.1 Rescue investment

€1000	Original planned investment			Planned and "rescue" investment		
	Total investment	Fully diluted ownership allocation	Expected IRR	Total investment	Fully diluted ownership allocation	Revised IRR
Business angel/ founders	250	16%	57%	250	8%	29%
Investor A System 2	500	34%	43%	1000	69%	43%
Investor B System 1	500	34%	43%	500	16%	17%
Entrepreneur		16%	n.a.		7%	n.a.

to. Therefore, he or she was not happy with the severe dilution, although it was his or her own unwillingness to participate in the rescue operation that caused the dilution. In this case, the board composition was also determined by the ownership distribution, Investor A would get full control of the board, and subsequent board meetings became pure hell.

Investors can often block issuing of new shares at a very low price via anti-dilution clauses, if the provisions in the shareholders agreement are not formulated wisely. The reason that this did not happen in this case was that the founders, who were the entrepreneur and the "rescue" investor, were willing to go all the way to file for bankruptcy, if an agreement was not reached. Facing this threat of losing all money, Investor B relinquished and accepted the terms.

In particular, if the investors are not familiar with working together and investing together, this type of apparent irrational situations occur. It is easy to see that situations like this can easily bring the survival of the company in danger, even if it is the System 2 investor's investment strategy which prevails in the end. A fight between investors like this might encourage the best staff members to leave the company.

It is also easy to understand that now the atmosphere among the shareholders has become poisoned and so are the working conditions in the board. All decisions which had previously been taken in mutual agreement and without voting were now presented for formal voting. And the new majority used its newly gained majority to "run the ship" against the will of the "System 1" investor. Also the entrepreneur got problems maintaining good working relations with the shareholders, who had demonstrated very different risk willingness during these difficult times. In the end, the entrepreneur lost faith in the future of the company, a trade sales was made to an industrial partner at an undisclosed price, and the entrepreneur was hired as CTO.

The final outcome of this case is not the most interesting part. What is interesting is what can be learned about how different professional investors can react to the same situation and how non-financial elements influence the human decision behaviour and can influence the future of a business. Not all cases where unexpected follow-up financing is required turn out as horror stories, but some do, particularly when the investors are not used to working together and do not have an interest in establishing or maintaining a long-lasting business relationship.

For entrepreneurs, it is important to take also these aspects into consideration when an investment consortium is to be formed in order to secure the required funding. It is absolutely relevant that the investors know each other and share the same business ethics and objectives.

This is seldom the case in crowdfunding cases and could be a sort of warning about potential pitfalls connected to this increasingly more popular way to secure funding for new small enterprises.

4.4 Relationship with Investors

Inviting investors into your business is like getting married. Never do it because of the money or because of a striking beauty! If you do not really like and understand each other, better stay single and hope for a bank loan! Many investors and entrepreneurs should never have made the deals they made. Therefore, it is relevant to provide insight into some of the pitfalls which both investors and entrepreneurs may fall into.

The previous section discussed challenges connected to unforeseen developments which require an unplanned funding action and how investors' different attitudes can create problems.

The next two examples should tell how the investor behaviour "never in doubt" turns out to be "often wrong".

Both cases involved entrepreneurs who are today very successful managers of their own companies, but whom my VC fund dismissed as "not qualified" or "not possible to work with". Both names and actual companies are presented in disguise.

Let us call the first entrepreneur AEK. He is today a very successful Danish entrepreneur. He owns a thriving international business. He has his offices next to mine in the Danish Science Park "Scion DTU", and we often meet at lunch time. Let us call the other one HJ. Today he ranks high among the richest men in Denmark created through his company, which supplies technology to offshore industry.

In the 1990s, both were young entrepreneurs, each with their own promising projects in which the Danish early stage venture fund of which I was the CEO invested. It was after a brief discussion with AEK in the spring of 2013 that I began to reflect on why we, as professional investors, had made a number of decisions, which, in retrospect, we should not have made, not only with these entrepreneurs but also in other cases.

At least these two of our many investments were obviously managed by us, the "professional" investors, in the wrong way, others were also, which I will revert to in the next section.

In these two cases, the VC fund lost its entire investment. Now, almost 20 years later, it has turned out that these two entrepreneurs, whom we dismissed "because we knew better", have proven to be very successful businessmen, more or less in the same business sector which we dismissed as having no potential, at least not with them at the helm. It is, therefore, relevant to try to analyse what went wrong and why?

Could we have been part of this success if we had behaved differently, when we had the opportunity to do so? Were we too much influenced by the short-term performance expectation from our own investors in our fund, to have a clear view on potential opportunities? Did we experience misleading signal from a subconscious corporate anchoring effect combined with lack of insight in human behaviour and the driving forces in a good entrepreneur?

This is not an attempt to make contra-factual history, but an attempt to learn from real life.

Both business cases developed in a very different way than what we originally expected. We experienced substantial and frequent delays. This was not unexpected or unusual, but we also experienced substantial diversion from original plans, without having been asked for our opinion or acceptance before. Other investments also diverted from the plans, but these two cases are of particular interest. We intervened and used our majority at the board level. It was our unilateral decision which led to a demission of AEK and forced HJ into making the decision to "jump ship". It was not liquidity problems or that the funding had run out.

In both cases, we and our co-investment partners (other VC funds) had, after a few years as shareholders in the companies, simply lost trust in the business cases and in particular, we had lost trust in the entrepreneurs and their behaviour.

The VC fund which I managed had been created by leading Danish industries and financial institutions. We had a board of directors with distinguished and experienced personalities from the finest Danish innovative industries. Hence, the fund was "born" with a corporate business culture. Although it was our ambitions to be an innovative early stage VC fund, our mental expectation to our portfolio companies was "corporate" and not "entrepreneurial". Many other VC funds are managed in the same way, but the very successful are not. With these two entrepreneurs, we, therefore, experienced a clash of culture. However, influenced by the industrial or corporate anchoring effect, we did not recognise it as a "clash of culture" but as "not proper behaviour". The board and I were anchored in our perception of the innovative business culture of larger organisations. So with our perception of "good behaviour", we saw nothing wrong with the innovation culture of large innovative industries and how it was monitored. But large organisations are not like entrepreneurial start-ups!

In hindsight, we, who were primarily financial experts, did not have sufficient insight into the particular technology and the

Case 1: The dotted line moved faster than expected

The first case was managed by AEK. Here the business concept changed constantly, and as board members and investors, we felt that we were left out of all the crucial decisions. Actually as a board member, I felt that I was always informed about strategy changes after they had been implemented, never before. AEK later told me that he had given up discussing with the board about the business he was creating. From the discussions in many previous board meetings, where we focused on milestones and budget reporting, he had observed that we did not understand the dynamics in the business segment in which the company operated. The board had limited time or possibilities for direct contact with his customers and his competitors. Therefore, the board meetings provided no value to him. He felt that the board meetings turned out to be an exam where he got marks but no constructive feedback: low marks if a milestone was not passed, and high marks if it was passed, irrespective of whether this milestone was relevant or not any longer. When he proposed to have more flexibility introduced with respect to budgets and milestones, the board concluded "this would be like using an elastic as a ruler".

In this case, we experienced an unhealthy clash of cultures and "anchoring" effects. As AEK could not change the composition of the board (the investors were in majority and the board composition was defined in the shareholders agreement), he, therefore, decided to make decisions himself and inform the board afterwards. The individual board members were used to (anchoring) structured information and formal prior approval of changes in business strategy or direction of technical development (corporate anchoring). Therefore, mistrust began to grow. The board members became exposed to confusing and unstructured flow of conflicting information, and they received unfiltered feedback from customer reaction and technical challenges. As a response, they reverted in their reaction pattern to the safe home "tuff" influenced by the "corporate anchoring" effect. They requested full control and prior consultation if any change to plans was to be implemented. For obvious reasons, they did not get what they wanted. Primarily because they were not close enough to the daily business operations to fully understand the technology or the market dynamics. They could, therefore, not digest the type of information provided.

We considered any future cooperation with AEK to be fruitless. We disagreed on the constant changes in the business concept. We felt that any continued funding would just add to our potential losses. "Never throw good money after bad money" was our mantra.

A decision was made to "close the shop".

Later, AEK adjusted his business concept, refined the technology, found new investors and started a new business based on the technology and business insight which had been created via our investment. This company has become a very profitable business. Today, he is also a wealthy man, but we lost our entire investment.

dynamics of the business sector the company was operating in. At least not compared to the insight AEK had. In reality, we were unaware that we communicated with AEK at a different wavelength. Our decision to stop the project was based on "not accepting more changes in the business strategy". In reality, with the financial background and influenced by the anchoring effect from our "corporate founding history", we had not understood the dynamic and changing business environment in which the young company was operating. We could simply not see that the "dotted line"[8] had moved to the left more quickly than anticipated, and that a new business strategy was needed. We did not see or understand that the entrepreneur actually had tried to adapt the business strategy to these changes. In practice, we lost patience in the wrong moment!

In Case 2 and in hindsight, the board, the investors and the CEO of the "two-man" company, which it was 20 years back, never took the trouble to speak with HJ about anything else than technology and reporting. No one tried to fully understand who he was,

---

[8]See Fig. 2.20, Chapter 2.

Case 2: Investors' lack of interpersonal skill

In the second case, the entrepreneur HJ simply decided to "jump the ship" after we had invested more than €2.5 million in his company. It happened the evening after a large second round of financing agreement (additional about €2 million) for the company had been signed. After this capital increase had been implemented, HJ had expected finally to become managing director after having served for 3 years as CTO under a CEO appointed by us (the investors). However, we bluntly told him to continue concentrating on the technical development of his technology, while our appointed and "experienced" manager would still manage the company, and in particular secure prudent utilisation of the large new funding. We had expected HJ to be happy to have got the required additional and substantial funding into his company so that the technical development could continue unhindered. However, his impression of the situation was that the "money guys" would continue to "run the ship" and not him, the inventor. From the discussion during the dinner, where we celebrated the successful funding, he became more and more convinced that when he had succeeded with the development of the technology, the investors would sell the company and cash in on the investment. However, his ambition was not short-term cash or capital gain, but to become CEO of a world-leading company in his field of technology. It also became clear to him that we (the investors) did not see in him a strong leader.

So simply, that very evening, he walked out of the door with all his technology and knowledge. The next day the CEO met both an empty office and an empty tool warehouse when he arrived, and also all software on our computers had been wiped out.

After a lengthy process, we could retrieve both the software and the hardware, and a long unpleasant legal battle followed, which we "won", but for what use? We tried to "sail on", but we turned out to be "lousy pilots" and the "ship" went down. Without HJ, the key knowledge and innovation skills had disappeared and the company was later closed and the investment was lost.

However, this "stubborn" entrepreneur had a better understanding of the strategic value of his invention and technology for the hydrocarbon industry. He used his technical knowledge and already achieved test results, to convince a large industrial partner to fund a new start-up. The objective was to develop an international business based on this particular technology with him as the CEO. This industrial partner fully understood the potential in the new technology. They saw that when fully developed, the new technology would open exiting new business opportunities, not only for themselves, but for the entire hydrocarbon business sector. HJ is today a very wealthy man in Denmark. His fortune comes from his personally owned company built on the technology with which he walked out of the door 20 years ago.

Recently HJ has sold a part of the company to a large family owned company for hundreds of million €.

what his ambitions were and how it all could be converted to an international business. Being an introvert, HJ did not easily invite for such discussion, but this should even more have made the alarm clock ringing and initiated an open discussion. In reality, HJ was left alone with his feelings and ambitions and was only asked to get the dammed machine working!

Had the board and the investors been better to handle interpersonal relations, the investors would have been part of HJ's later impressive business success. HJ was, when we met him for the first time, right out of the technical university, a brilliant engineer only. We knew he had no practical business experience, but we did not see that he had an unmatched personal drive to convert his findings at university into a winning technology and worldwide business. We only saw him as a highly skilled engineer, not a business man. What was worse, we treated him in the same way. What should have been done was to help him get better equipped on business skills, because what he really wanted was to run a business. In a drawer in his desk, he had a world map, where he already indicated where daughter companies should be placed in the future. Had we fully understood his underlying strong business drive, we would also have understood that happiness for him was not when the machine began to function, but when customers would be queuing up to buy it. But we never sat down to discuss the future and personal feelings and ambitions with him.

Many investors make the same error!

In both cases, we had a very unpleasant time- and money-consuming fight about our decisions. Although the entrepreneurs in both cases were large co-owners in the companies, we as investors were the strong financial partner and our decisions prevailed, because we controlled the liquidity! At that time, there was no doubt in our mind that we made the right decisions. We considered ourselves as "experienced investors", and we were "never in doubt". From our point of view, the entrepreneurs were just "young inexperienced inventors" who "behaved in an irrational way", compared to our more conventional and "rational" decision processes, which nicely matched the "corporate anchoring" effects.

It is interesting that in both cases, the entrepreneurs "prevailed". They had the driving force to get their acts together and fulfil their dreams together with other investors. If we had acted differently, we could have been part in these successes.

Case 3: Inadequate business model

In a third case, we invested together with other professional VC funds in an exciting food robot technology, which was offered to us as a spin-off from a large industrial company, Carlsberg Breweries. The technology in which we invested was a continuation of the "fish bone" identifier robot described in Section 2.9 (Chapter 2). The final product was the result of a lengthy and troublesome development of an advanced food-processing robot which could both remove fish bones from fish fillets and cut fish, chicken breast and meat in predefined shape and weight. However, when the development was completed, the company moved too early and unprepared to the sales and marketing phase.

This move was strongly supported by the board members representing the investors. They were thirsty to see real sales figures after many years of waiting for the robot to work as planned, and wanted to report about sales activity to their partners in the different VC funds.

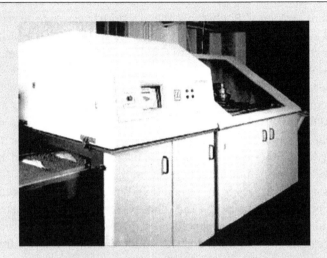

Figure 4.5 The food-processing robot.

However, this investment also failed, in this case primarily for two reasons. First, there was no direct entrepreneurial driving force behind the business. It was run by a professional "hired hand" who was really good in driving the technology forward and did also a good job in implementing a business strategy, which was largely defined by the investors. Second, because the investors became nervous about the market and wanted to see actual customer purchase decisions. We therefore urged the management to implement a business model which implied "selling" the food robots (with a buyback option). Unfortunately, this business model was implemented before the performance of the new robot had been fully tested and adjusted to the industrial environment of a food-processing factory.

To cut a long story short, it turned out that the robot technology was not fully mature when the sales started. The business model was not aligned with actual product performance and did not reflect customer interest and, in particular, customer fear.

What went wrong? When the company, after substantial delays in the development process and associated cost over runs, started to approach the market, the robot still had a few "infant problems". But because the investors began to be nervous and wanted sales results to report back to their own boards/ investment partners, the board put pressure on the management to start selling, not offering the robot for trial. A sale could be reporting in the P&L accounts and have impact on liquidity, while a demo robot installed at the customers' production facility still would be part of the company's inventory. The robot was not cheap, around €1 million. Therefore, it was a great risk for the individual food-processing plant manager to buy, if it did not work as expected or did not generate the expected savings (e.g. money back in less than 12 months). What was worse, because the processing capacity of the robot was so large, the industrial customers who would benefit most from the robot were very large food-processing industries unfortunately far away from Denmark—in Iceland or the USA.

Hence, after extended deliberations, also with respect to the choice of distributor, it was decided to sell the robot on normal commercial conditions, but also to offer the customers a free return guarantee period of 3–4 months, if the robot did not live up to expectations. A few customers actually bought the robot on these conditions and installed the robot right into their food-processing lines. The P&L account of the company at year end looked suddenly healthy, and the board was pleased.

However, the customers began to experience small irritating problems with the robot: some caused by misuse of the technology, while others caused by small mechanical or software problems connected to the robot. Now the individual plant managers, particularly in the USA, began to be nervous. Had they bought the wrong technology and could they be blamed for a wrong decision? The first machine was returned, not because it did not work, but because it was not fully as reliable as expected. By this move, the plant manager saved his skin! Now the rumours began to spread, and the next machine was returned. The liquidity of the company came under pressure, the US distributor was not pleased and the faith in the business case evaporated and eventually the company was closed down.

It is my strong belief that if we in Case 3 had adopted a different business model and offered the robots "for trial" for 4 months, provided that the test customer secured that the robot was integrated into the processing line, which would be a cost covered fully by the customer, then the plant managers' reaction would have been different. Now they should justify the cost of the test installation internally, and hence their interest to make it work would be aligned with the robot manufacturer's interest. The new robot technology would most probably have initiated small adaptation to the production process, so even a small period of "down time" could be managed. For the plant managers, a success would be needed to justify the "test installation cost" and they would probably not pay in full after 4 months. They would ask for prolongation of the trial period, but eventually they would buy.

However, in the board we were focused on getting recorded sales; we never discussed alternative business models, and the management did not present any different model primarily because the conventional wisdom prevailed: "this is the way you sell in this industry". However, when introducing new products or new technologies into conservative industries, it is often relevant to introduce new business models, even if these models go against conventional wisdom. In this case, any alternative business model would also have conflicted with the traditional business model of the of the US distributor. He also feared that his customers would request similar terms for the other products he was selling.

At that time, our imagination about advanced business models such as ESCO or others was very limited. It was years before business model books by Kim and Mauborgne and Osterwalder were published.

Analysing the three cases, it becomes obvious that the investors' losses were initiated, to a large extent, by the investors' own decisions, which were influenced by a combination of "corporate anchoring effect" and limited personal psychological skills.

Although the investors (or investor representatives) participated in all board meetings and also controlled the board, they misread the feedback they got from the management (entrepreneurs or hired), from the customers (whom they never met) and from the market. They became victims of their own perception of how a structured development should take place and had little understanding of business models. They forgot that new business plans will never be executed as written; the direction might be followed, but not the details. In the three cases, the investors deliberately took a chance, hoping to become rich, but forgot to take their own medicine and accept adaptation of business strategy to reality, also when the going got tough!

They misread signs from the management, or installed the wrong manager to take case of the wrong problems. Was the failure primarily the fault of the entrepreneur? No, because the decision power was allocated to the holders of the share majority or to those who control liquidity, namely, the investors.

The lesson learned is that the choice of investors is very important. With this I mean all investors, as in some cases the first investor might be the right one, who becomes engaged and committed to the business case like the entrepreneur. But when follow-up investment is being sought, there is a tendency to focus more on money and investment conditions than on what a new investor can bring to the table. Such a new investor might turn out to have an unpleasant anchor weight on future decisions.

In the minds of many investors, the "uncertain" business plan often becomes "carved in rock" after the investment has taken place. They seem to forget that before they invested, they had a focus on both risk and opportunities. But the risk and need for flexibility do not go away just because an investment is made. However, for many investors, any diversion from agreed plans creates mental uncertainty and is not regarded as something that opens up for new opportunities. Continued diversion from plans and milestones creates mistrust in the performance and judgement of the entrepreneur or the management.

Investors often forget that among the successes actually experienced, only very few, if any, had been achieved through the execution of the original business plan. The successful businesses have, in most cases, been adjusted to the changing world, both from a technology point of view and with respect to business concept. Luckily, in many of these cases, the changes have been executed by the management during a period where liquidity and funding issues were not on the agenda. Therefore, the investors' active involvement in the decisions was not required; often they were never told before it was being implemented.

However, in the three concrete cases mentioned earlier, the required "change in strategy" took place in connection with new funding rounds, and hence the investors became directly involved in strategy decisions of the portfolio company. In these cases, a "yes" to the change in strategy also meant more money had to be invested. So the investors became directly involved in management decisions.

It is important to understand that even if an investor is directly involved in a company via a non-executive board position, he or she will never, as a non-executive board member, via his or her participation in board meetings, get the same level of understanding of the day-to-day business operation or of the individual customers and their reaction as the management. Only if the investor really spends lots of time with the company and its customers, he or she will get this knowledge. Time constraints, however, most often prevent this type of investor involvement!

In another case, the outcome of a similar conflict between investors and the entrepreneur turned out differently because the entrepreneur took a leading role in securing investments from new investors. This young ICT company experienced similar problems as the previous cases. Although product development went well, the customers did not react as expected, unforeseen development in technology was experienced, communication bandwidth increased quicker than foreseen, and the social media revolution impacted both customer and student behaviour. Altogether it changed the rules of the game, and the money was running out. The founding investors quickly lost faith in the entrepreneur and his "excuses" and decided to close down the company.

While the founding investors saw constant erratic changes in business strategy, the company actually, and in a very able way, adjusted its business concept and technology to the actual changing needs in the market. During the few years in business, the management got a better and better knowledge about the customer preferences and the market changes. The first business concept developed by the entrepreneur was based on an "outsiders" intellectual understanding of the needs of the customers. This was the "dream" the investors invested in. The final business concept and technology were very different, but now it was tailored to meet the real needs of this market, as identified through an in-depth knowledge of this market.

In this case, the entrepreneur managed to find new investors who better understood not only the technology but also the market. The company is now operating in a different sector than originally planned. The products and solutions are completely different from those described in the original business plan, but the kernel software engine is the same. The CTO explained the need for constant market adaptation in the following way:

"When we started the company, we knew of the iPad. We all considered it as a funny toy, only few would use it—it even did not have a key-board. Today schools are providing iPad to 9 year old school children. Would our original product and business concept have survived this rapid development?"

The Danish business angel Morten Lund was one of the first who invested in the creation of Skype. He later told me:

"I really did not understand the technology or the business model, but I was convinced, that if it did not work as expected, Janus Friis and his team would come up with another solutions which would make money—and by the way I know and trust these guys"

For the investors, it often feels like a roller-coaster ride to live through rapid shift in both products and business models. The natural inclination would often be to leave, close the shop and write off the investment. However, this might not always be the right decision.

The two first cases, I have used, can serve as an illustration of some of the challenges faced by entrepreneurs whose business is funded by external investors. In these cases, it became largely the investors who made (or were ready to make) the wrong decisions. They had full control of the board, and they subsequently lost all or part of their investment. Most probably, they would have hit the jackpot had they stayed in or behaved differently.

In another case, which has previously been mentioned in this book,[9] part of this company's success was derived from active investor involvement when they captured a trophy client American Express. However, the real success which allowed the company to reach IPO was the unplanned initiative from one of the founders who, "for the sake of fun", demonstrated that the Mac solutions could easily be converted to a full Window solution. Fortunately the entrepreneur did not ask the Board before he developed the Windows solution. Many successful venture-funded companies can thank their success from supporting investors and pure luck. However, I feel it is easier to learn from errors, therefore the chosen examples.

4.5 Can We Learn?

Wise adaptation to the echoes from the real world is an important success factor, which also means that understanding of changes in smartly laid plans is as important as changing your sails and adjusting direction when the wind is changing.

All investors have experienced investment cases where a "shut down" decision was the right decision at the moment it was taken. In each case, the entrepreneurs probably questioned the investors' mental capacity! Only few investors have publicised that a "shut down" decision in retrospect was unwise, most probably because the investor would look stupid. In any case, they would not get their money back. So why expose stupidity or ignorance?

However, if there are commonalities between the cases quoted earlier, can we then learn from them? If all involved parties had acted differently, could we have avoided losses and shared successes, which were never made?

In all the aforementioned cases, the investors were directly represented in the board of directors In the first cases, the chairman also represented the investors and their interest. In the last case, the chairman was independent. In all the cases, the chairman had casting vote. In the last case, his objective was catering to the interests of both parties (the entrepreneur and the investors).

---

[9]The software company PPU Maconomy, see Section 2.10, Chapter 2.

In the first case (the AEK case), the chairman of the board secured that everything "went according to the book" and he was requested to minimise the investors' risk. In short, he was the "investors' man" and operating with a limited mandate. His role was to secure realisation of the intention behind the business plan. His role was not to act as a mentor for the entrepreneur or the management. The board primarily based its decision on information from the management and was definitely "not involved" in the daily life of the company. The limited involvement was not caused by lack of interest, but simply lack of resources. A VC fund has limited resources, and by choice, this was one area where it was decided to save.

In the first case, when it became clear that the company could not meet its future obligations, if new funding was not allocated, the board would face severe liability issues if trading was continued. The investors' decision not to invest was, to a large extent, based on previous experiences (anchoring effect) from a number of similar disappointing diversions from original plans in other companies. In this case, the board members had limited direct understanding of the changes in technical, operational and market conditions, which had happened since the original investment was made. During the project period, there had been a veritable "changed in the rules of the game" in this particular market segment. The entrepreneur's trust in the investors was also limited. He considered them as providers of money only, and definitely not as partners in the venture. He had no inclination to involve the investors in his worries and concerns. The result was that the entrepreneur and the investors were "living on two different planets" with respect to knowledge and insight. Therefore, the investors felt they had no other choice than to limit both the loss and rescue their board members from potential future liability!

In the second case, the entrepreneur had become more and more convinced that the investors' objective was only "capital gain" and not "building an international company" with him as the CEO. This contrasted his objective, which had become more and more focused on "building an international company" with him at the helm. He found no understanding or recognition of his ambitions and interest from the side of the investors. The representatives of the investors had limited psychological insight, and in his mind they did not show that his performance and personal drive was appreciated. He, therefore, took the desperate decision to violate all agreements and "jump the ship". The sad outcome of this case was primarily caused by the investors mishandling of strong personal ambitions.

Had the investors been better in understanding the psychology and the mindset of the entrepreneur, they would probably have reacted in a different way and allowed him a more managerial role and invited him to constructive dialogue about his ambitions and their interest. However, we were more experienced in reading and understanding balance sheets than understanding mindsets.

In the last case, the chairman of the board acted as a mentor for the entrepreneur. He was more informed about the reason behind the shifts in business strategy than the other board members, who primarily criticised the deviations from the "original plans". The chairman took the role to build the "bridge" between the entrepreneur and the investors' representatives in the board. This pre-empted a number of drastic negative decisions.

The role of the chairman, particularly an independent one, can be an important factor in a crisis situation especially if he or she has gained good understanding of the business case, at least "at par" with the entrepreneur/management. The entrepreneur will almost always have a biased optimistic view on opportunities. The investors will most often have serious concerns when milestones are not met and plans keep changing. The chairman can balance the "optimistic view" against the investors' "scepticisms and concerns".

4.6 How and Why Decisions are Made?

One of the most critical board meetings is the one at the end of the month if a company is soon running out of money. This is the time when the members of the board are facing a personal liability issue if no further funding is provided. Under such pressure, often irrational behaviour is observed. The final decision often depends on the individual board members' subjective feelings, recollection of past broken promises and the parties' different attitude to "risk" and "opportunity". Theoretically, the board members directly representing the investors have (in most cases) funds available to secure future operations. Hence, their decision is either to "cut your losses" or "risk more money". The entrepreneurs will normally lose everything; hence they will push for more money and provide new sweet promises. If a closing decision is made, they know it is not often that they get a new start.

In a situation when the company cannot meet its obligations and no further funding is foreseen, the individual members of the board become personally liable if the company does not stop trading. Of course they can resign from the board, but then any minor influence is lost, and the alternative to stay on board implies the risk of liability. Therefore, investors have serious interest in how the voting rights in the board are distributed between the entrepreneurs and the investors. Prudent investors will often, via the shareholders agreement, secure a majority vote in such a situation. Therefore, in reality the "close the shop" decision is entirely up to the investors.

Daniel Kahneman has, in the book *Thinking Fast and Slow*, analysed decision situations which are analogous to the challenges investors are facing. If we borrow from his terminology, we can assume that a number of the previously mentioned typical underlying psychological factors play a determining part for the investors' final decision.

First of all, the "biased intuition" combined with the "anchoring effect" plays a role. If you have experienced losing money in previous and similar situations, your brains' "System 1" will focus on "similarities" rather than on "differences". The easy solution is to rationalise that similarities are dominant, and you will decide to minimise your losses. You will often disregard the potential differences between this case and the previous cases. You will also risk overlooking that this behaviour might have been the determining factor behind your previous losses in the other "similar" situations.

The second factor can be called "loss aversion", which can be explained in the following way.

Suppose a person who has already made a risky investment in a new company is confronted with the two options:

1. Lose all the money already invested with 100% certainty.

2. Invest more money and then have a fair chance of exiting in due time with a profit.

Most people who have been shown these options prefer the first option even if the theoretical value of the second option might be far higher. First, when the original investment was made, the investors knew that the total loss was an option; hence this option is now part of his "System 1" reference. Second, it is easy to have an opinion on a "sure thing" even if it is the unpleasant but foreseen outcome of the investment. It is more difficult to have an opinion about an uncertain upside potential which involves additional risk.

The third can be called "the reference error". We often overlook the flaws in Bernoulli's utility theory. The theory assumes that it is the utility of people's wealth which makes people more or less happy. However, if you have two investors, A and B, who can now exit from an investment with €5 million each in cash, will they be equally happy? Let us assume that A has invested €2 million and B has invested €9 million. They now both have €5 million in cash, but they will look upon the exit with very different eyes and will also behave in the board differently. Investor A will strongly support the chosen exit route, while Investor B will push for other solutions, eventually blocking this exit route because he or she will be facing a loss.

The fourth one can be called "framing". It involves mental accounting and the sunk-cost fallacy. If the investors look at a business case requiring follow-up funding without considering "sunk cost" and previous disappointments, the case would most probably have met their investment criteria, and they would have invested. The objective risk connected to the project has, in many cases, diminished since the original first investment was made. From a pure negotiation point of view, they could probably even have obtained an overall "better deal" if they decided to do the follow-up investment. But "framing" is distorting their normal rational judgement, and they look at sunk cost connected to this particular case and do not consider it as a potential new investment, which is to be compared to all other investment opportunities. If evaluated in this light, it might well pass all criteria and merit the investment, but because of "sunk cost" and "project history", the final verdict will be negative. *Ceteris paribus*, the only "rational" reason for not investing would have been, if the new investment would have brought their total engagement in one single project above the "single commitment ceiling" that many funds operate under.

Investors are only human beings, even though they are professional risk takers. When investment decisions are made by professional investors (VC funds as well as business angels), it is always done with the knowledge that the investment might turn sour. However, you still hope that this particular business will be the winner; otherwise, why not refrain from investing. Being professional investors, they also subconsciously upfront decide on an upper limit for their "gamble". However, in many cases, this upfront limitation does not take into account the changes in the objective risk between first-time investment and the objective risk associated with the venture at a later stage. From a portfolio risk, the principle of minimising strategy is a sound policy. However, when it comes to individual cases, the likelihood of "auto response" kicking in is high. This can easily prevent an unbiased evaluation.

The decision process is always influenced by a combination of "biased intuition", "loss aversion", "reference errors" and "framing". Often a too strong "System 1" prevents the investors from seeing that the individual cases might merit different decisions.

Statistics clearly show that early stage investments are associated with a high failure rate. Statistics, however, do not show to what extent this particular high failure rate is partially created by unwise decisions by the investors or, in other words, is partially self-inflicted!

In a number of investments in which I have been involved (as lead or co-investor or as an advisor), it was the decision by the investors which led to the financial loss, rather than decisions made by the entrepreneurs, but the investors were never in doubt!

In retrospect, the failure was often caused by the two parties' inability to communicate on the same wavelength. Often the investors' representatives in the board of the portfolio company failed fully to understand the business dynamics. Or they were unable to explain to the decision-makers on the investors' side (their partners or the more distant investment committee) the reason for a diversion from plans. Who is to most blame: the experienced investor or the young inexperienced entrepreneur? The latter might be a young "hot head" who does not behave as controlled and balanced as expected. Experienced investors should be able to cope; otherwise, they should not invest in these types of businesses.

Not all projects become a new Google or a Skype, and not all investors have the required wisdom to see that less can be a good business and make both the investors and the entrepreneurs comfortably wealthy. It is, therefore, important that the entrepreneurs do their own due diligence on potential investors and learn from what they find.

Due diligence is not only for investors!

4.7 Negotiations and the Process

Let us assume an entrepreneur has found an investor who is willing to invest in his or her project as it has been described in the business plan. Part of the background for the decision is, of course, the business plan, the budget, the team and a lot of other soft factors. But irrespective of how much soft factors has influenced the final decision, an agreement has to be reached now about how to share the "spoil" when an exit takes place and how to manage situations where deviations from the beautiful plans occur. Therefore, although all parties know that the budget is not "carved in rock", the numbers in the budget often become the cornerstone for hammering out the details regarding valuation, total funding requirements and milestones.

Unconnected to the budget is decisions about board composition, which also can be impacted if unexpected funding rounds are required.

4.7.1 Valuation

There are many ways to tackle the "valuation issue". None of them are "correct" in the sense that if a particular method is used, the true value of the business venture is found. The entrepreneurs will probably use the business plan as the basis for the valuation discussion. If the numbers in the business plan were taken at "face value", then the correct value of the company (for this scenario only) could, in principle, be calculated using the discounted cash flow method.

However, the budget numbers are not "carved in rock"; they are more likely "wishful thinking". Investors have a popular saying: "If you divide your revenue forecast with π^{10} and multiply your cost estimates with π and also multiply with π the numbers of months until you will make your first sale, then you will have a realistic budget. This may be an exaggeration, but the truth is that a budget will never materialise as written in the business plan.

Also what is the correct discount rate? Many industries use a discount rate of 30–40% for technology investments and similar risky investments. Investors are not different.

The investors will often be more inclined to look at the potential future exit value of their shares (fully diluted[11]) in the company, rather than on the "discounted cash flow". Their best guess might be influenced by the valuation of similar mature deals currently traded. They will try to imagine how the company will look if all goes well, when exit time is up. They will compare this picture of the company with the value of currently traded deals of similar type. They then use their own discount rate to convert this speculative future value to present time. Their discount rate will probably be not less than indicated above. The investors might also be using a different term, like "how many times do I get my money back" or ask for the return on investment (ROI).[12] Often investors will require that there is a realistic chance to get their money five times in 5 years.

If you add all the uncertainties together, neither the investors nor the entrepreneurs can claim to have the correct answer to the valuation question. Reaching an acceptable agreement on valuation depends, therefore, on negotiation skills and experience, but primarily on common sense. Behind all the fuzz about discounted

---

[10]$\Pi = 1.618$, also called the "golden number".

[11]Fully diluted means the expected ownership percentage at exit time, when taking into consideration the impact from new rounds of funding, eventual share option plans and other factors which might influence the investors' final ownership percentage in the company.

[12]ROI, multiples, IRR and discount rate are all related. For example, if you invest 100 and get 600 at exit time, the ROI is $[(600 - 100)/100] = 5$. If the exit time is 5 years after investment is made, the IRR is 38%, and if you use 38% as the discount rate, the net present value (NPV) is 0 (nil). Actually this is how the IRR is defined. Read more in Annexure 5.

cash flow, market risk, technology risk and dilution risk, the investors are often simply speculating on how "little" ownership will still make the entrepreneurs committed and happy, and how "much" ownership will satisfy the investors from the points of view of risk, value and influence. What the investors, in the end, feel sound and reasonable depends on their previous experiences, current situation and mood combined with the impact of "anchoring effects" and how System 1 and System 2 interact in their brain. When a conclusion on these elements has been reached, it is fairly easy to construct an elegant financial model, with built-in assumptions which give exactly this result. This could easily make it look as if it was the model which gave the positive or negative result!

It has often proven smart to de-couple "ownership" discussion from the "influence" discussion. In order to secure an acceptable potential IRR for the investors, it might be needed to offer the investors a larger ownership percentage than the entrepreneurs are willing to offer from an "influence" point of view. This disagreement can be easily solved by issuing a portion of "non-voting" shares to the investors. In this way, the investors can achieve the required "slice of the cake", while the entrepreneurs can retain a critical level of voting influence.

From a negotiation point of view, the entrepreneurs should really consider what they can "defend" as pre-money valuation with solid arguments and data. Even if they, after lengthy negotiations, are willing to accept a compromise far below their initial proposal, many investors will refrain from accepting this compromise. They will assume that the "original" valuation which was requested by the entrepreneurs was "what they expected". Any valuation compromise far below this valuation is assumed to have been obtained by "arm twisting" by the "rich investors". The investors will expect that this "pain in the arm" will never leave the mind of the entrepreneurs (subconscious depression). Hence, good relations will never be restored. Then better leave the deal. The valuation discussion should not, therefore, be like price haggling in a Turkish bazar!

Only valuation proposals which can be "defended" should be tabled for discussion. Furthermore, both the entrepreneurs and all professional investors should know that over time unexpected events will happen, as exemplified in the beginning of this chapter.

These events will require either additional funding or changes to the business concept and/or to the shareholders agreement. Hence, what you "lose" at the initial negotiation table can be easily redressed at a later event; alternatively, heavily fought gains are also easily lost. The entrepreneurs should understand that if they manage to push the valuation too high and still make the deal, the punishment for not delivering what is promised will also be proportionally more severe.

My best advice is to reach an agreement which recognises that both parties are facing an impossible task of defining the correct valuation, simply because of the inherent uncertainty. They should recognise with almost certainty that the budget used to structure the valuation discussion is never going to materialise as written in the excel sheet. In 2–3 years, the numbers will look different.

The initial compromise has to be—disregarding any mathematical calculation—acceptable to both parties. The entrepreneurs should feel the deal is fair, and the investors should be able to defend to themselves and their partners that the investment is made based on the best available data, e.g. the business plan, and that the valuation is fair.

Provisions in the shareholders agreement can prescribe ways of adjusting the ownership distribution (changes in valuation), if real life turns out to be different from the plan. For example, it could be agreed that the business plan is the common denominator for the valuation. If the company "underperforms" compared to the business plan, a share exchange would take place to compensate the investors, and vice versa, if the company exceeds expectation, then the share exchange in the opposite direction takes place to compensate the entrepreneurs. If the price for the shares to be exchanged is set to a small percentage of the original price, the share transfer does not have any liquidity implications for any of the parties involved.

If it is difficult to reach a mutually acceptable agreement on how to tackle the immense uncertainty connected to any business plan, my alarm clock would start ringing. How do you then think situations such as the cases previously described should be handled? Both the investors and the entrepreneurs should think twice: "Are they really meant for each other!"

4.7.2 Total Funding Requirements

In principle, the budgets associated to the business plan should outline both the short- and the long-term funding requirements. If the liquidity budget foresees temporary peaks in funding requirements, it is advisable, as discussed in an earlier section of the book, to seek such temporary peaks covered via a bank facility or a convertible loan, not by private equity.

However, it is prudent always to make budgets for the first 2 years on a monthly basis. A short-term peak in liquidity requirement during a year can easily exceed the liquidity requirement calculate on a yearly basis by a factor of 2 or more. Surprises regarding sales, liquidity and other nasty problems will occur.

My glider pilot training manual reads: "Precautions have to be taken **when** you make a crash landing – not **if** – You will make a crash landing at some point of time!" Unforeseen events will occur, and most likely such events will cause delays in revenue stream or add new cost. If not prepared, a "crash landing" may cause total wreckage, whereas only scratches at the fuselage, if you are well prepared!

Investors normally do not put aside a box of "contingency funds" filled with piles of cash to be drawn upon if need be. It is my personal experience that solutions for managing the unforeseen liquidity crisis or similar type of crisis are never described in the shareholders agreement. And it is the unforeseen events which create a crisis, not the foreseen. Therefore, before signing a funding agreement with investors, there is a need for an open discussion about the investors' experience and reaction to unforeseen situation with their other portfolio companies.

If it is difficult to have a constructive discussion on ways to tackle the immense uncertainty connected to budgets and liquidity issues, my alarm clock would start ringing. The entrepreneurs should again think twice: "Are they and the investors really meant for each other?"

4.7.3 Milestones

Many investors want to reduce the risk associated with an investment in a new venture. They want to limit their risk if promised results are not delivered. Hence, a milestone-based funding plan is often preferred by the investors. In other cases, the agreed funding might cover a long period. But the investors are probably better at securing a competitive return on excess capital than the entrepreneurs. Therefore, it is often in the interest of both the entrepreneurs and the investors to agree on a milestone-based funding.

A milestone-based funding, however, also has its drawbacks. Milestones are often defined as obligations for the investors to provide certain additional funding, when a specific milestone is met. Normally, the milestones are defined based on the business plan. But what happens if it is a sound business decision to divert from the plan and if, in the meantime, the investors have got second thought about their investment, may be not because there are problems, but because a better deal is taking all their attention.

The entrepreneurs then face a dilemma. The correct business decision would be to divert from the original plan, but then planned milestones will not be met, and the investors are "off the financial hook" with respect to planned funding. Alternatively, the activities can continue as planned, the money is coming, but in the long run, this move is not optimal from a business development point of view.

Dilemmas such as this should be high on the agenda at the board meetings of the company. However, board meetings are often held with too large intervals, while requirements for changes in the business strategy often appear out of sync with the schedule for regular board meetings. Young management teams are often hesitant to bring troubles and unforeseen events to the attention of their board. They fear its reaction, while hoping that the problem will go away or be solved by itself.

Therefore, it is important to align the timing of board meetings with deadlines of the milestones which have impact on liquidity. The timing must allow enough time to find solutions to the unforeseen events, like a diversion from the milestone plan. If a diversion is well explained and justified,[13] it becomes the responsibility of the board to secure that this diversion does not have an adverse impact

---

[13]In a number of cases, I have experienced and accepted dramatic diversion from the milestone plan as a means to secure the survival of the company, when unforeseen technology and market development required substantial diversions from the original milestone plans. Hence, it is important to leave room for flexible interpretation of these conditions.

on a milestone payment and on the liquidity and the survival of the company.

If it is difficult to have a constructive discussion on ways to tackle liquidity implications of potential diversion from milestone plans, my alarm clock would start ringing. The entrepreneurs should again think twice: "Are they and the investors really meant for each other?"

4.7.4 Investors' Success Criteria: The Profitable Exit

In general, financial investors want, at some time, to "exit" from the investment in order to regain liquidity and also to hopefully cash in a nice capital gain. If the company is so successful that a public listing is an option, the simple exit can take place via sales of shares in the open market after the IPO, and after the expiration of an eventual lock up period. Other less pleasant exits are involuntary and connected to bankruptcy of the company. If any value remains after creditors are paid off, normal shareholders agreements will allow for a preference position for the financial investors to get some of their investment back.

These are the "simple" exits.

More and more profitable exits take place as a so-called "trade sale" exits. In this situation, all or a majority of investors typically see an opportunity to sell their shares to a third party who is interested in the business or technology of the company via acquiring shares in the company. Trade sales conditions are often connected to a situation where the third party also gains management control of the company. This third party can be both an industrial and a financial entity. Trade sales conditions are often complex to exercise, partly because often a complicated due diligence prevails the actual transaction.

It is difficult to keep the process secret for the staff of the company, and if they feel uncertainty about their future positions, key staff members might decide to leave the company prior to the transaction. If these staff members are considered "essential" by the prospective buyer, the process might stop!

The sales price is often divided into two parts. The first part is paid at transaction time, and the second part can often be determined by the performance of the company during the first year of ownership by the new owner.

Other types of exit situations can be connected to management buy-out or buy-in situations, where the financing is established via financial investors combined with bank loans.

It is important that the shareholders agreement provides for easy implementable and transparent process, particularly the last types of exits, and that both the financial investors and the entrepreneurs fully understand and accept the implications of these sections of the shareholders agreement. Disputes on these share-selling processes have over time destroyed a lot of shareholder value.

4.8 Board Composition

Normally the composition of the board reflects the distribution of ownership in the company. However, "share of ownership" need not automatically reflect "voting rights", neither at the general shareholders meeting, nor in the board. As illustrated in the previous cases, no matter which way the board interacts with the management of the company, the entrepreneurs play a decisive role in how the crises are handled.

When a board decides against the interest or dreams of the entrepreneurs, it may still not win. The entrepreneurs can walk away. Experiences from many deals have demonstrated that if the driving force in a young company leaves, it often takes with it not only key knowledge but also key staff members, and the investors are left with an empty shell! Hence, strong financial muscles may not always be an efficient weapon to defend an investment against the interest of entrepreneurs.

There is no right way of composing the board and distributing voting rights. But from lessons learned, it is a good idea to give the chairperson casting votes and to secure his or her independence or neutrality. It is important that the chairperson has time and interest to interact with the management team/entrepreneurs on a regular (read: very frequent) basis. If the board wants to have unbiased information as a basis for the board meetings, an independent chairperson who represents both the investors and the entrepreneur is more likely to secure this, than if one of the parties have the right to elect the chairperson.

All board members should preferably have good industry and sector knowledge, and accept that their first role is to provide constructive input to the development of the business. Their second priority is to represent the interests of the parties who have elected them. The cases previously discussed indicate that it is also wise that psychological insight is present at the board level.

Sometimes members of the board forget that their role as board members is to support the development of the company. If they want to fight for their shareholders' interest, this fight should take place at a shareholders' meeting, not at the board meetings. A few years ago, a company was unfortunately hit by a combination of management health problems and postponed sales. In the board, we experienced a board member sending mails with the content below to the CEO in the midst of a difficult business survival situation:

> *"Stop trying to lay the blame on others. If the company has* **truly** *flopped (that still remains to be seen) that's because it was not in competent hands."*

It takes certain diplomacy to participate in board meetings when the tone is set like this. Some board members, even representing large companies, do not know how to behave. We managed to get things back in order but only after a lengthy fight with this particular board member.

I have experienced similar situations in many other boards, and the outcome was not always positive. As illustrated in previous sections, the personality and self-perception of the individual board members will heavily influence how the board reacts to challenges and unforeseen events. It is, therefore, a good idea that the chairperson or one of the other board members has a good understanding of how psychological factors also influence the behaviour of individual board members. It is definitely not always "greed" and "money" which is the determining factor behind a decision or the behaviour of an individual board member; it could be as simple as "lost pride".

As illustrated in the few cases, members of the board of entrepreneurial companies also need to understand that the management is fragile and have to cope with many challenges at the same time, and that it often stands alone without the traditional supporting staff of larger companies. The CEO's main objective is to "run the shop", not to cater to board members' interests and wishes, unless they directly support the business. The board can expect to be kept fully informed of all relevant matters connected to the business and its operation, but not necessarily in the same formal way as in larger organisations. This also goes for unexpected changes in plans, milestones and objectives. But to get the board to this level of understanding of business conditions requires a big effort from the entrepreneurs. However, on the priority scale of most entrepreneurs, this effort is placed very low, particularly if they do not feel they get solid advice and support from the individual board members. The interest of information sharing changes automatically, if the entrepreneurs experience that the individual board members are resource persons, upon whom they can draw support and information. If an appointed board member does not feel comfortable with this role, he or she should not take the board position in a young growth company.

It is, therefore, important early on in the investment negotiation process to have a constructive discussion on the criteria for election of the chairperson of the board, and of the composition of the board. Besides what is mentioned above, the individual board members should represent good industry and sector competence relevant for the business and secure a good balance between investors' interest and the interest of the entrepreneurs.

If the discussion about board composition becomes difficult, my alarm clock would also start ringing. Both the entrepreneurs and the investors should think twice: "Are they really meant for each other?"

4.9 The Exit: A Dream Scenario or Nightmare?

When an investor or an investment consortium agrees with the entrepreneurs to invest in an innovative company, the two parties' objectives are the same to some extent, namely, to secure funding for a potential growth which will make the company successful and valuable in the future. However, on other aspects, the objectives might differ considerably. The investors' prime focus is eventually to sell the shares (exit), experience a substantial capital gain and use the proceeds to reinvest in other ventures. Some entrepreneurs share this ambition and might become the US dream of a serial entrepreneur who again and again creates a successful company, sells it and starts all over again, or they turn their focus to become business angels or just enjoy the life and the money. These entrepreneurs have, to a large extent, their objectives aligned with the investors: aim at a quick and successful exit.

However, there are other entrepreneurs who dream to be part (e.g. CEO) of the continued success of the company, and for whom the exit situation poses real problems. If the entrepreneurs begin to doubt whether the objectives of the investors differ from their ambition, the investors might experience that the entrepreneurs will suddenly "walk out".

Therefore, it is important to understand the nature of an exit. Actually we have two separate entities: the company with its management and the shareholders. In principle, the company becomes unaffected if the ownership of the shares changes. However, the new owners of the shares may have different ideas or objectives behind the ownership, and this can have substantial impact on the company and the management.

Therefore, when the shareholders agreement is signed, it is so important to think through the exit situation, even if it might appear to be something of a blurred dream far out in the future.

The most typical exit scenarios are the following:

- **IPO** involves taking the company public at one of the many public stock exchanges. This is a very demanding and formal process which we will not go into details with. However, when successfully completed, the company suddenly becomes responsible for properly informing its "public" shareholders in a much more formal way than before, and shareholdings can shift like the wind blows. The IPO, in itself, is not an "exit" for the investors. It is not until the investors can sell their shares that an exit is realised. This might be a long time after the IPO took place, because there is often a lengthy "lock up" period imposed on the shareholders, which takes the company public.

- **Trade sale** is an alternative and an often-used exit route. A trade sale normally means that another company buys all the shares in the company or at least a controlling part of the shares. It is an exit route which can be pushed for by the external investors, or the offer might suddenly come from the clear sky from a business partner or large competitor. Trade sale is often a preferred exit route for the investors; you know the price for the shares and are not exposed to uncertainty during the IPO lock up period. However, it is not always the preferred exit route for the shareholding entrepreneurs. It also often has a direct impact on the company, its staff and management. In particular, in the trade sales negotiation period,[14] it creates uncertainty and the company risks that the best members of the staff take their leave if they are not directly incentivised to stay on board. For management and the entrepreneurs, it might also be a very problematic situation, particularly if the acquirer does not see any future for them in the new set-up. All trade sales are different, but it is, in particular, in the trade sales situation that the "drag along" and "take me along" and other of the share transfer clauses in the shareholders agreement become important. These are often clauses which were paid little attention to when the shareholders agreement was formulised many years back, and when the focus was to get the investors "on board", and the exit was only a vague dream.

  Share sale to financial investors is also an exit option, particularly for the investors. If the original investment was made by a seed fund or an early stage fund, and the continued growth depends on further investment with the purpose to take the company public in 5–10 years, the early investors will often eagerly seek to exit in connection to following rounds of funding. This can be a tricky negotiation or something which runs smoothly. This depends, to a large extent, on the wording of the shareholders agreement, which often, in these situations, is also amended or replaced with a new agreement. However, if not all shareholders have the same interest to contemplate the deal which is on the table, a very nasty play can begin. If, for example, the offer on the table is to pay €5 million in cash for each of the

---

[14]Remember that for practical reasons, it is almost impossible to keep secret for management and staff, even if they are not directly involved.

early investors' two blocks of shares, then the shareholder who has paid €2 million for his or her block of shares is happy and wants to sell, while the shareholder who paid, e.g. €9 million for his or her block of shares is far from happy and will try to block the deal or ask for a special ransom payment for releasing his shares for sale. Sometimes, we have situations where the "€9 million shareholder" even might hold a critical number of shares, which can tilt the voting at a shareholders meeting. His representative might also have a blocking voting right in the board of directors. This situation can block both trade sales and financial share sales. This is not a theoretical situation; I have lived through this type of trade sales situations, where one shareholder constantly found the terms unattractive, blocked the sale and in the end, the value of the company went down and all had to exit with a loss.

Share buyback is a solution which many entrepreneurs dream of. They want the investors to fund the growth of the company and eventually buy back the shares to restore the situation to be in full control of the company. For most, it will forever be a dream. The salary paid to the CEO will seldom, if ever, amount to a value which can pay the shareholders a decent price. However, if the CEO/entrepreneur is very good and he or she can find for himself or herself financial backers who will provide with the funds to buy back the shares from the investors, a "management buy-out" can be contemplated. This is seen and can be a perfect legitimate way to get control of the venture.

• **Liquidation** is such a sad exit scenario that it does not merit much attention, although unfortunately a large number of young companies are doomed to realise this as an exit route. It is an exit route which is often forced upon the management by the board and the investors, who want to avoid to be dragged into liability cases caused by accepting the continued operation of a company likely to fold.

To contemplate successful exit scenarios—and even the last sad one can be done in a more or less elegant way—it requires negotiation experience, good understanding of the motives and of even hidden agendas of all parties involved, combined with patience and flexibility. If all parties involved keep their cards hidden and play against each other, you can easily run into the "prisoner's dilemma".[15] In the end, all the parties can "bully" the others, and the investors can "pull" the liquidity plug or even refuse to comply with provisions in the shareholders agreement. The board can try to replace the management, and the entrepreneurs can threaten to walk out of the door with all their contacts and knowledge. And while the shareholders fight, the key staff members can take their leave, particularly if the outcome of the battle becomes too uncertain. Normally, it is the best members of the staff who leave first.

In many cases, it lies in the hands of the chairperson of the board to secure a peaceful settlement of this type of conflict around the exit process. One wise step to take, before it all blows up and the discussion becomes too heated, is to get an overview of who invested how much at what time and at what price per share. With a potential exit value at the table, the chairperson can easily get a quick overview of how the outcome of the planned exit operation will impact each of the shareholders, and with this information in hand, he or she can anticipate the individual shareholders' reaction to the offer.

If the investment situation is like the situation illustrated in Fig. 4.6 and the exit offer on the table is €6 million to be paid in cash

---

[15]The **prisoner's dilemma** is a standard example of a game analysed in game theory, which shows why two completely "rational" individuals might not cooperate, even if it appears that it is in their best interests to do so. It was originally framed by Merrill Flood and Melvin Dresher working at RAND in 1950. Albert W. Tucker formalised the game with prison sentence rewards and named it "prisoner's dilemma" (Poundstone, 1992), presenting it as follows: Two members of a criminal gang are arrested and imprisoned. Each prisoner is in solitary confinement with no means of communicating with the other. The prosecutors lack sufficient evidence to convict the pair on the principal charge. They hope to get both sentenced to a year in prison on a lesser charge. Simultaneously, the prosecutors offer each prisoner a bargain. Each prisoner is given the opportunity either to betray the other by testifying that the other committed the crime, or to cooperate with the other by remaining silent. The offer is:

- If each of A and B betrays the other, each of them serves 2 years in prison.
- If A betrays B but B remains silent, A will be set free and B will serve 3 years in prison (and vice versa).
- If both A and B remain silent, both of them will only serve 1 year in prison (on the lesser charge).

€1,000	Year 1	Year 2	Year 3	Year 4	Year 5	Year 6
Funding requirement: exit value after 6 years	1,000	1,000	500			6,000
Entrepreneur's investment % part of exit value						692
Founders' investment and part of exit value	-250					692
Investor 1 investment and part of exit value	-1,000	-500				2,538
Investor 2 investment and part of exit value		-500	-500			2,077
Price/share start year (€)	100	200	100			
Price/share end year (€)	150	200	100			
Total number of shares end year	11,667	16,667	21,667			

Figure 4.6 Investment case with exit value of €6 million.

for the entire shareholding, not all shareholders are happy, although they do not lose money directly.

Based on the aforementioned numbers and the knowledge of how the shares are distributed between the shareholders, the chairperson can create the table in Fig. 4.7, which gives an indication of the parties' relative "happiness".

Realized IRR and ownership at exit time	IRR	Ownership %
Entrepreneur	n.a.	12%
Founders (business angels)	23%	12%
Investor 1	12%	42%
Investor 2	23%	35%

Figure 4.7 Resulting IRR and ownership distribution.

The entrepreneurs had expected to get more out of all the efforts. The founding business angel can be satisfied with an ROI of well above 20% but probably far from what he or she had hoped. Investor 1 has obviously paid too much for his or her shares and is definitely not satisfied with the IRR of 12%, while Investor 2 is okay, not an

€1,000	Year 1	Year 2	Year 3	Year 4	Year 5	Year 6
Funding requirement: exit value after 6 years	1,000	1,000	500			6,000
Entrepreneur's investment % part of exit value						138
Founders' investment and part of exit value	-250					138
Investor 1 investment and part of exit value	-1,000	-500				3,646
Investor 2 investment and part of exit value		-500	-500			2,077
Price/share start year (€)	100	200	100			
Price/share end year (€)	150	200	100			
Total number of shares end year	11,667	16,667	21,667			

Figure 4.8 Impact of anti-dilution clause, with exit value of €6 million.

impressive result but still better than what could be obtained at risk-free investments. As can be seen from the numbers in Fig. 4.6, there is a drop in the share price from year 2 to year 3. This has benefited Investor 2, while Investor 1 got severely diluted. Had he or she been compensated via an anti-dilution clause, it would have been the entrepreneur and the funding business angel who should have transferred shares to Investor 1 at a low value.

Realized IRR and ownership at exit time	IRR	Ownership %
Entrepreneur	n.a.	2%
Founders (business angels)	-11%	2%
Investor 1	21%	61%
Investor 2	23%	35%

Figure 4.9 Resulting IRR and ownership distribution including "anti-dilution".

In the example, the entrepreneur and the founder investor each has 2500 shares. If via an anti-dilution clause, they had been forced to transfer, e.g. 75% of their shares to Investor 1, the situation would have looked like the table in Fig. 4.8.

Now the founding business angel will be "unhappy" as he or she has lost €112,000 on this investment. Investor 1 is still not overly happy, but the result is acceptable as the situation is taken into consideration.

There will most probably not be agreement among the shareholders to accept the offer as it stands, and the potential acquirer of all the shares will have to drop the case or increase his or her offer.

The aforementioned example illustrates a small fraction of all the complications, which often is associated to an exit situation. Therefore, the only advice if a chairperson is confronted with an exit opportunity: Get quickly a clear picture of how it will impact financially the individual shareholders and get a good feeling about the "happiness" or "sorrow" it will generate. Also get a good understanding about any alternatives to the offer on table, including doing nothing and continuing trading until a better offer appears. And last but not least, secure that the person at the end of the table, who takes the lead in finding a solution, is impartial, trustworthy and an experienced negotiator.

4.10 To Sum Up

Building of new and successful companies, both in the role as an entrepreneur and as investors, involves risks and opportunities. The best deals are made if "equal partners" join forces. Hence, it is important that the entrepreneurs have sufficient support to match the experience of the investors. If the investors are not experienced in this particular business, also they should seek advice from people with years of practical experience.

Remember that "Deals done when two blind persons have to agree on the colours are doomed to fail, so are deals when only one of the persons can see!"

The way to success, even when confronted with unexpected difficulties, is to create mutual trust and have a good understanding of the motives and interests of all involved parties. If we, the "experienced" investors, in the concrete cases illustrated in the book, had been better in creating good working relation with the two super entrepreneurs, whom we sacked or chased away many years back, we would probably have been part of their success. In the other case, which also turned out badly, if the entrepreneur had opened up for his worries and concerns about technical problems or market reaction, he might have triggered a "let us coach you" reaction rather than the "let us control you" reaction, which he was met with.

Investors are, besides being "money people", also human beings who often have a very tight time schedule. They are influenced in their decision behaviour by their personalities, System 1 and System 2 reaction pattern and the anchoring and other effects. Although they try to rationalise how they spend their limited time resources based on a "highest return on time spend" criteria, we have seen countless examples where they lend a helping hand to an entrepreneur who has gained their trust and with whom it is possible to engage in an constructive dialogue.

Coaching done in the right way does not require a lot of time spent from the coach if he or she knows his or her subject (which investors often do). My rule of thumb is: 1 hour coaching should lead to 8 hours of hard work from the coached. Never expect the investors to take the role of consultant. This is an entirely different role than the coach; the consultant also does the work and delivers the result.

If a relationship of mutual trust is not built, neither part in the business venture exploits properly the value of combining resources available. Too many investment cases do not exploit all the possibilities of a unique combination of skills in innovation, financial resources and practical business experience. There are countless examples which, in reality, look more like the famous "prisoner's dilemma" from the gaming theory than the happy "marriage" it should be. When you have fully understood the implication of the "prisoner's dilemma", it is clear that on the conditions given in most business cases, there is much to be gained by exchange of information. This is normally also the case when investors and entrepreneurs are working together. We are seldom facing a "zero-sum game",[16] but a game where cooperation could increase the sum.

The most fundamental condition for creating a sound and constructive basis for cooperation is to know and understand each other's concerns and ambitions: "What makes you happy or sad?" Whether you have investor ambitions or the inner drive of an entrepreneur, you do not need to lie down on Freud's coach and express your inner feelings, but I recommend that you really try to understand not only the preferences and concerns of your partners but also your own.

Entrepreneurs are very different but are often driven by a large ego and high personal ambitions. Do not ask them to be happy to do reporting in a way that would make an accountant proud. Neither should they be asked not to take risk; actually this is what drives them, but some risks are more foolish than other, which is fair to tell. Books are written about the psychology of entrepreneurs, and from the many biographies of successful entrepreneurs, a lot can be learned about the trait of their personality.

You should also be aware of what drives investors, what are their concerns and ambitions. It is important to understand that in the exit phases of an investment, the investors may react in a very different way to the same offer. Bernoulli's assumptions about the utility function do not apply without modification. This was clearly illustrated with the example of the outcome of an investment which leaves two investors both with €5 million. The happy one was the investor who had invested €2 million, while the sad investor was

---

[16]In game theory and e conomic theory, a **zero-sum game** is a mathematical representation of a situation in which each participant's gain (or loss) of utility is exactly balanced by the losses (or gains) of the utility of the other participant(s). If the total gains of the participants are added up and the total losses are subtracted, they will sum to zero. Thus, cutting a cake, where taking a larger piece reduces the amount of cake available for others, is a zero-sum game if all participants value each unit of cake equally (see marginal utility).

In contrast, **non-zero-sum** describes a situation in which the interacting parties' aggregate gains and losses can be less than or more than zero. A zero-sum game is also called a *strictly competitive* game, while non-zero-sum games can be either competitive or non-competitive.

the one who had seen the value of his investment dwindle from €9 million to €5 million.

It has been my ambition to provide a better understanding of the interest, ambition and concerns of investors. I have also tried to explain why there is a good reason behind the many questions they are posing before making an investment decision, or a decision to leave. The content and structure of the book are based on my own experiences. Others have had other experiences. The variation in the cases is enormous. Also in business, a "one size fits all" method does not work.

New investment cases will differ from the examples given. However, the structure provided in the book will hopefully help to navigate safely in the exiting but troublesome water of investors and funding opportunities.

In the end, besides excellent business ideas and technologies, mutual trust between the investors and the entrepreneurs and also between different investors is probably one of the most important factors behind the great successes. Unless you understand how psychological factors of the individual parties influence behaviour and decision-making, mutual trust is difficult to build.

Full Business Plan Checklist

It is always a good idea to double check the content and the assumptions behind a business plan, before it is presented to an investor. Try the simple checklist below.

It is also a good idea to ask a good friend or an advisor to do the same—and compare notes. Remember, investors will most probably ask most of questions below.

If you cannot say a clear "yes" to all the statements, it is recommended that you find a good excuse or an answer before being questioned by an investor.

Business plan evaluation questions	Yes	Not yet	May be	No	Forgot
Market & customers					
1 You have had positive feedback from actual or potential customers about the need/ interest for your product/solution.					
2 A thorough "market research" has confirmed that there is a demand/market (=customers willing to pay).					
3 The targeted users or user groups and their needs are well described.					
4 It is easy to understand why the customers will have an interest in buying the product/ solution?					
5 The business plan provides a realistic analysis of market conditions.					

6	It includes an assessment of all relevant market(s), their size and expected growth rates?					
7	The product(s)/solution(s) and the functionality is well described.					
8	The expected sales price is explained.					
	Technology and competition	Yes	Not yet	May be	No	Forgot
9	The business plan clearly demonstrate the functional or technical superiority of the products/solutions compared to competing products/solutions.					
10	It includes detailed development plans.					
11	There are well defined and realistic relevant milestones and time-lines.					
12	The elements in the expected cost price for the product/solution are justified.					
13	The company has the relevant resources and human skills available to realize the technical development and business strategy.					
14	The business plan includes a comprehensive analysis of the competitive "landscape".					
15	The relevant competitors, competing products or services including competing business models are described.					
	Knowledge protection & IPR	Yes	Not yet	May be	No	Forgot
16	The business plan includes a realistic strategy for knowledge protection?					
17	A comprehensive description of current IPR situation and history is included in the business plan.					

18	The results from a "freedom to operate analysis" is also included.					
19	Potential regulatory requirements are adequately addressed.					

Sales, marketing and business model	Yes	Not yet	May be	No	Forgot
20 The chosen business model and its elements are explained.					
21 It is explained why the chosen business strategy or business model is realistic.					
22 There is a good description of the sales and marketing strategy for each potential markets.					

Management & Team	Yes	Not yet	May be	No	Forgot
23 Both you and your team has sufficient commercial and technical experience to cope with all the business and technology challenges ahead.					
24 Combined you also have sufficient general management, financial and organizational experience to cope with all the funding and business challenges ahead.					
25 The business plan includes realistic initiatives to be taken to fill eventual gaps?					

Business realization	Yes	Not yet	May be	No	Forgot
26 The most recent company history and current stage of development is well described.					
27 The risks related to a successful market introduction of the product/solution are well described—if relevant, also from a regulatory point of view.					

		Yes	Not yet	May be	No	Forgot
28	The risks connected to product/solution development are described and well understood.					
29	The future financial and needed organizational challenges are well understood.					
30	The business strategy builds on a realistic time frame and implementation strategy.					
	Financials and funding	Yes	Not yet	May be	No	Forgot
31	The business plan includes yearly P & L budgets, balance sheets and a liquidity plan covering a relevant number of years.					
32	It is easy to extract a monthly P & L budget including liquidity budget for the upcoming 12–18 months.					
33	The budgets include an easy to understand overview of funding requirement and liquidity challenges.					
34	There is a realistic strategy for closing eventual liquidity gaps?					
35	If public funding or grants are foreseen, the business plan includes a convincing instrument selection and application strategy.					
36	There is a strategy for covering temporary liquidity gaps via bank loans/credit facilities.					
37	The investment opportunity and associated conditions offered to investors are attractive.					

Annexure 1b

Investor Search and Negotiation Checklist

Before embarking on an investor search process you should consider, if you are ready to invite investors to become co-owners of your company.

Are you ready for investors?	Yes	Not yet	No	May be	Do not know
A Willing to be diluted and share decision making with new co-owners?					
B Current co-owners are in agreement with the investment conditions to be offered.					

If you do not give two clear "yes" to the above statements, it might be too early to start the investor search process. May be it would be wise to consider building the business without external investors, look for a public grant or try your luck with the banks.

Even with two clear "yes" it is a good idea to double check the realism of the investor search process and investment strategy by using the simple checklist below. Try also to ask a good friend or an advisor to do the same—and compare notes.

If too many of the questions below are not answered with a clear "yes", you should consider postpone the process or invite an experienced advisor to assist in the investor search and negotiation process.

Investor search and negotiation	Yes	Not yet	No	May be	Do not know	Need help
1	A thorough analysis of investment preferences and past performance of each of the investors on your investor "to contact list" has been conducted.						
2	There is a good technology or business sector fit with investor's preferences.						
3	A comprehensive "investment summary" and an easy to read business plan is ready to be presented to investors.						
4	The pre-money valuation can be defended via company past performance and/or expected future business performance.						
5	The investment opportunity will meet the requirements of investors risk adjusted return of investment.						
6	The dilution risk/aspects connected to more rounds of investment have been thoroughly analyzed.						
7	The investment opportunity includes a clear and comprehensive exit plan/ strategy for the investor.						
8	If the investment plan foresees investments through investor syndication, the plan and timeline is realistic.						
9	It is ok that the current board composition will be changed when new investors/owners join the company.						
10	You have sufficient experience in investment /investor negotiations.						

Investor search and negotiation	Yes	Not yet	No	May be	Do not know	Need help
11 You are familiar with term-sheet and shareholder agreement terminology and other legal requirements.						
12 Ready to make "full disclosure of all relevant information" for an eventual upcoming due-diligence process.						
13 Your current co-owners are in full agreement with the proposed investment strategy.						
14 The company's administrative processes and various type of agreements can easily be adapted to the requirements of new investors.						

Annexure 2

References

Daniel Kahneman, *Thinking Fast and Slow*, Penguin Books, 2011

Daniel Kahneman is a senior scholar at Princeton University and Emeritus Professor of Public Affairs, Woodrow School of Public and International Affairs. He was awarded the Nobel Prize in economics in 2002. The book presents his current understanding of judgement and decision-making, which has been shaped by psychological discoveries of recent decades.

Alexander Osterwalder and Yves Pigneur, *Business Model Generation: A Handbook for Visionaries*, John Wiley & Sons, 2010

Dr. Osterwalder is an author, speaker and advisor on the topic of business model innovation. His practical approach to designing innovation business models has been developed together with Dr. Yves Pigneur, and is practiced in multiple industries throughout the world.

W. Chan Kim and Renée Mauborgne, *Blue Ocean Strategy: How to Create Uncontested Market Space and Make the Competition Irrelevant*, Harvard Business Review Press, 2005

W. Chan Kim is the Boston Consulting Group Bruce D. Henderson Chari Professor of Strategic and International Management at INSEAD, and Renée Mauborgne is the INSEAD distinguished fellow and professor of strategy and management. The book provides a systematic approach to making the competition irrelevant and presents a proven analytical framework and relevant tools.

Kai Hammerich and Richard D. Lewis, *Fish Can't See Water: How National Culture Can Make or Break Your Corporate Strategy*, Willey, 2013

Kai Hammerich is a Danish and international leadership and talent consultant with Korn Ferry. He has been nominated by *Business Week* as one of the most influential head hunters worldwide. Richard D. Lewis is a renowned British linguist who created Richard Lewis Communication and is an author of a number of books about how and when cultures collide. The book provides an interesting introduction to how cultures and nationalities differ in management and communication style.

Dan Ariely, *Predictably Irrational: The Hidden Forces That Shape Our Decisions*, HarperCollins, 2009

Dan Ariely is the Jame B. Duke professor of behavioural economics at Duke University, with appointments at the Fuqua School of Business, the Center for Cognitive Neuroscience and the Department of Economics. He is also founder of the Center for Advanced Hindsight and visiting professor at MIT Media Lab. Ariely explains how to break through systematic patterns of thoughts to make better, more financially sound decisions.

Malcolm Gladwell, *What the Dog Saw: And Other Adventures*, Little, Brown and Company, 2009

Malcolm Gladwell has been staff writer with *The New Yorker* magazine since 1996. In 2005, he was named one of *Time* magazine's 100 most influential people. In this book, he shows the intriguing story within everyone and everything, and provides a glimpse into someone else's head, and your own.

Manfred Kets de Vries, *Leaders, Fools, and Imposters: Essays on the Psychology of Leadership*, Jossey-Bass Publishers, 1993

Manfred Kets de Vries, *The Irrational Executive*, edited by Manfred Kets de Vries, International University Press, 1986

Manfred F.R. Kets de Vries is a practicing psychoanalyst and Raoul de Vitry d'Avaucourt Chair of Human Resource Management at the European Institute of Business Administration (INSEAD) in Fontainebleau, France. He is the author of a number of books on such topics as leadership, career dynamics and organisational diagnosis and intervention. He has been an executive development consultant to major corporations in the USA, Europe and Asia. Both books provide an insight into how decisions are being made, and how personalities, cultures, greed and sorrow influences decision-making in practice.

Goeffrey A. More, *The Gorilla Game,* **Harper Business, 1999**

Goeffrey A. More is the author of the two bestselling books on the development of high-tech markets: *Grossing the Chasm* and *Inside the Tornado.* He is chairman of the Chasm Group which provides marketing strategic consulting services to hundreds of high-tech companies. The Gorilla Game is an interesting introduction to the art of picking the winner.

William Isaacson, Steve Jobs, Simon & Schuster, 2011

William Isaacson is the CEO of the Aspen Institute and has been chairman of CNN and managing editor of *Time* magazine.

Mark van Osnabrugge, *Angel Investing: Matching Startup Funds with Startup Companies—The Guide for Entrepreneurs and Individual Investors,* **John Wiley & Sons, 2000**

Mark van Osnabrugge is a management consultant at Markon Associate and former Harvard Business School fellow.

William Kerr and Josh Lerner, *The consequence of Entrepreneurial Finance,* **HBS Working Knowledge, Hbswk.hbs.edu, 2012**

William Kerr is professor at Harvard Business School. Bill is the faculty chair of the Launching New Ventures program for executive education, and he has received Harvard's Distinction in Teaching Award.

Uffe Bundgaard-Jørgensen and Rune Bundgaard-Jørgensen, *Willingness to Take Risk,* **InvestorNet-Gate2Growth, 2009**

Rune Bundgaard-Jørgensen is a junior partner at the international consulting house McKinsey.

Michael E. Porter, Five competitive forces that shape strategy, *Harvard Business Review,* **Jan 2008.**

Michael Porter is an economist, researcher, author, advisor, speaker and teacher. Throughout his career at Harvard Business School, he has brought economic theory and strategy concepts to bear on many of the most challenging problems facing corporations, economies and societies, including market.

Annexure 3

Patenting and Other Forms of Intellectual Property Rights Protection[1]

As European patents are examined and published by the European Patent Office, rather than simply registered, patent rights are more certain than many other forms of legal protection available for inventions. For example, if a patent is infringed, the patent holder can sue for infringement or order customs to intercept imports of the patented products. On the other hand, it should be noted that patent enforcement costs can be substantial.

Patents are granted for technical solutions which solve only technical problems. They are disclosed to the public during the application process. A patent attorney must be used to file an application. Patent applications are examined in a process which can take between 3 and 8 years and can result in the patent being either granted or refused. Patents normally last for a maximum of 20 years from the date of filing, which means that if the patenting process takes 8 years, there will only be 12 years of protection remaining. As of 2013, the ownership of a patent belongs to the individual or organisation which is "first to file" the patent application.

In some countries, a special and less powerful kind of patent called a **utility model** (or petty patent) is also available. Utility models usually offer protection for a shorter period of time, often up to 10 years. In order to receive utility model protection, all countries require inventions to be new, although it is possible to apply for utility model protection under two procedures:

---

[1]Source of text for this section: extracts from EPO Patent Teaching kit, EPO, 2011.

1. Examination, where the novelty of the utility model is examined or

2. No examination

In the latter case, you run the risk that the protection could become void if it later arises that the invention was not new. However, this will only occur if the protection is challenged. As an invention's novelty is not examined under the No-Examination procedure, it is possible to register any utility model which complies with the formalities. Deciding whether or not the utility model meets its legal requirements is only carried out in the courts, if there is a legal dispute.

Copyright does not need to be registered as it automatically comes into being when the work is created. Any original, creative, intellectual or artistic expression is protected by copyright. Examples include novels, scientific literature, theatre plays, software, photographs and paintings, music, games, sculptures, television broadcasts, etc. In Europe as well as in the USA, copyright protection exists regardless of whether it is explicitly stated or not. The duration of a copyright is roughly the life of the author plus 70 years, but this depends on the specific case and country.

Trademarks are distinctive signs identifying and distinguishing the commercial source of goods or services. As long as trademarks are used and the fee is paid, the trademark protection is valid. It is also the trademark owner's own responsibility to police their trademark protection. Trademarks include words, logos, names and colours, as well as any other means of identifying commercial origin, such as the shape of a product, its packaging and possibly even sounds or smells. For instance, many Disney characters are registered as trademarks. Trademarks can be created simply through their use, or by explicitly registering the trademark at a national patent and trademark office or through international bodies such as the EU. This latter option is preferred by most companies as it is easier to prevent competitors from copying or damaging a trademark if it is registered. In the EU, trademarks are protected at the national level by trademark laws which have been harmonised on the basis of the EU Trade Mark Directive of 1988. In Europe, the trademark must be represented graphically in order to be registered, which is a challenge for trademarks based on, e.g. smell.

Infringement of trademark rights occurs if:

- An identical mark is used for identical goods or services, or
- An identical or similar mark for identical or similar goods or services gives rise to a likelihood of confusion, or
- The use of a mark takes unfair advantage of another with an identifiable reputation, or
- The use of a mark is detrimental to the reputation or the distinctive characteristic of the infringed trademark.

The proprietor of an earlier mark is also entitled to oppose the application for, or cancel the registration of, another mark which would be infringing. Where a trademark application is opposed by the proprietor of an earlier trademark, the new trademark application will not be registered if it is shown to be identical or similar to an earlier trademark and that the goods or services to which the new trademark applies are identical or similar to the goods or services for which the earlier trademark is registered. Registration will be refused if there is a likelihood of confusion on the part of the public in the territory where the earlier trademark is protected.

Registered designs protect the external appearance of a product. They do not provide any protection for its technical aspects. Registered designs include new patterns, ornaments and shapes. To be officially registered, designs need to be original and distinctive. The artistic aspects of a design may also be protected by copyright. Within the EU, protection period is 5 years and this can be extended for an additional 4–5 years.

Unregistered designs also enjoy some protection. An unregistered design is a free, automatic right which you get when you present a design to the public and gives you the right to stop anyone from copying your design. However, the protection provided by an unregistered design is typically of limited duration in comparison with that available for a registered design.

Trade secrets are an alternative to patents. Trade secrets cover information not known to the public. If the possessor of such information is careful in ensuring their information remains confidential, e.g. by signing non-disclosure agreements with employees/partners, they are able to sue anyone who copies it. However, trade secrets offer no protection against reverse-engineering or against competitors who independently make the same invention.

For information about rules and procedures to obtain IPR protection, contact your local patent lawyer or the EPO (www.epo.org).

Examples of Strategic Steps to be Considered in an Infringement Case

Let us assume that you hold a patent on a technology called NewTech, but there is a potential patent infringement issue with respect to your intellectual property (IP) and a competitor's IP. There may also be a risk that your competitor will transfer their IP to an even stronger competitor, or there might be a risk that one of your subcontractors will use experiences gathered in working with you to inform your competitor.

In such a case, it is important to consider alternative strategic options, such as the following:

1. Confront your competitor via your patent lawyer, and challenge the validity of their patent by claiming your patent dominates.

    ▪ This is costly and will divert attention from your core business
    ▪ A patent litigation can drag on for years

2. Confront your competitor via your patent lawyer by challenging the validity of their patent, but at the same time offer them a royalty (free) cross-licence.[1] If the offer is accepted, it would limit the possibility of them transferring their intellectual property rights (IPR) to a potentially more significant competitor.

---

[1] The term "cross-licence agreement" indicates that you offer another legal entity the right to produce and sell a technology protected via your patent, while the other legal entity is giving you the right to produce and sell a technology protected by their patent. A cross-licence agreement can be royalty free or be connected to full or discounted royalty depending on the two parties' strength and strategic value of the patent protection.

- Only do this when you have established a good understanding of the business strategy and intentions of your competitor.
  - In many instances, it is better to start in a confrontational manner and then show that you can also be reasonable. However, if your true intention is to find a compromise, this approach can sometimes backfire.
- If the market is big enough for two suppliers, and if you are able to exclude others from entering the market with cross-licences, it could be in the interest of both parties to find a compromise.
  - However, not all business managers favour pragmatic solutions.

3. Contact your competitor and explain the situation and offer them a royalty (free) cross-licence. This would limit the possibility of them transferring their IPR to a potentially more significant competitor.
   - Detailed intelligence on your competitor is first required, including their management and business style, and financial strength.
   - Follow arguments in option 2.

4. Disregard your competitor's patent infringement threat and hope for the best.
   - This option could create a risk that your competitor will chose to challenge and raise a patent infringement case against you.
   - Even if they have little chance of winning the litigation, it will create uncertainty for your business operations.

5. Limit your sales effort to markets where no infringement is at risk.
   - Is this a real option available to your product?

6. Other items to consider.

It can be beneficial to conduct a structured analysis of both parties' positions before deciding which route to take. This requires an understanding of the "hot buttons", or most relevant issues and decisions that confront each business. These will vary from company to company and from situation to situation. The table on next page is an example from a structured analysis.

	Patent strategy consideration					
	Your Company	Competitor		What is your interest ?		
	Comments	Comments	Confront	Cross licence in your interest	Limit your sales to where no infringe-ment	Disregard only if you are stronger
International market experience	Strong	Weak	👍			
Company's financial strength	Strong	Weak	👍			
Industrial production experience	Strong	Strong		👍		
Patent claim strong and easy to police	Yes	Yes		👍		
Patent coverage only useful combined with process "knowledge"	Yes	No	👍			
Patent protection of solutions essential for business case	Yes	Yes		👍		
Can the solution be defended by additional patents?	Probably not	Yes			👍	👎
Can the solution be ringfenced by third party hostile patents?	Yes	No		👍		
Will cross licence strategy limit new parties to enter the market?	Yes	No		👍		
Can current and/or new patents limit your business strategy?	Yes	?				
Can current and/or new patent limit your competitor's business strategy?	Yes	No				
Willingness and strength to start a patent litigation	No	?				
Impact on sales if customers fear that injunction for chosen solution might occur	Big	?				
Advantages connected to a cross licence strategy—Royalty based/Royalty free	Big	?				
Disadvantages connected to a cross licence strategy—Royalty based/Royalty free	Small	?				
How important is it that a patent litigation does not create uncertainty on your right to produce and sell?	Important	?		👍		
Other issues	?	?				👍

Annexure 5

The "Rosetta" Term Sheet

[COMPANY]

SUMMARY OF TERMS FOR SALE OF SERIES SEED SHARES

Company	[Company]
Founders	[Founder 1], [Founder 2], & [Founder 3]
Investors	[Lead Investor] (the "Lead Investor") in conjunction with other investors (the "Investors") mutually agreeable to the Lead Investor and the Company.
Structure of Financing	The financing will be up to an aggregate of [__] at a fully diluted pre-money valuation of [__], including an unallocated employee share option plan ("ESOP") of [ ]%. The Lead Investor will invest up to [__] and would hold no less than [__]% of the Company on a fully diluted basis.
Conditions to Close	(i) Completion of confirmatory due diligence and anti-money laundering checks (ii) all employees having entered into service agreements containing IP assignment provisions and (iii) receipt of all necessary consents.
Estimated Closing Date	[Closing Date].
Type of Security	Newly issued series seed convertible preferred shares ("Seed Shares"), which shall rank senior to all other shares of the

Company in all respects [and be provided with the same rights as the next series of preferred stock (with the exception of anti-dilution rights).]

Liquidation Preference	Upon a liquidation, dissolution, winding up, merger, acquisition, sale, exclusive licence or other disposal of substantially all of the assets or a majority of the shares of the Company (a "Change of Control"), *Option 1*: [the holders of the Seed Shares shall receive the higher of: (a) one times the original purchase price for the Seed Shares; or (b) the amount they would receive if all shareholders received their pro rata share of such assets or proceeds.] *Option 2*: [(a) the holders of the Seed Shares shall receive the one times the original purchase price for the Seed Shares; and (b) all shareholders shall receive their pro rata share of any remaining assets or proceeds.]
[Anti-Dilution Provisions]	[In the event that the Company issues additional securities at a purchase price less than the current Series Seed Preferred conversion price, such conversion price shall be adjusted on a [ ] basis. The following issuances shall not trigger an anti-dilution adjustment: (i) securities issuable upon conversion of any of the Series Seed Preferred, or as a dividend or distribution on the Series Seed Preferred; (ii) securities issued upon the conversion of any debenture, warrant, option, or other convertible security; or (iii) Common Stock issuable upon a stock split, stock dividend, or any subdivision of shares of Common Stock; and (iv) shares of Common Stock (or options to purchase such shares of Common Stock) issued or issuable to

employees or directors of, or consultants
to, the Company pursuant to any plan
approved by the Company's Board of
Directors.]

Important Decisions

Option 1: [Certain important actions of the
Company shall require the consent of the
holders of a majority of the Seed Shares
(a "Seed Majority") or the Seed Director,
to include amongst others, actions to: (i)
alter the rights, preferences or privileges
of the Seed Shares; (ii) allot any new
shares beyond those anticipated by this
investment; (iii) create any new class or
series of shares having rights, preferences
or privileges senior to or on a parity with
the Seed Shares; (iv) increase the number of
shares reserved for issuance to employees
and consultants, whether under the ESOP
or otherwise; (v) redeem or the selling of
any shares; (vi) pay or declare dividends or
distributions to shareholders; (vii) change
the number of board members; (viii) take
any action which results in a Change of
Control; (ix) amend the constitutional
documents; (x) effect any material change
to the nature of the business or the agreed
business plan; (xi) subscribe or otherwise
acquire, or dispose of any shares in the
capital of any other company.]

Option 2: [The consent of the holders of
a majority of the Seed Shares held by the
Investors (an "Investor Majority" shall
be required for the important decisions,
substantially in the form listed in Appendix
[__]

Conversion

Each holder of Seed Shares shall have the
right to convert its shares at any time into
ordinary shares of the Company ("Ordinary

Shares") at an initial conversion rate of 1:1, subject to proportional adjustment for share splits, dividends or recapitalisations [and any anti-dilution adjustments]. The Seed Shares shall automatically convert into Ordinary Shares if (a) a Seed Majority consents to such conversion or (b) upon the closing of a firmly underwritten public offering of shares of the Company.

Pre-emption

All shareholders will have a pro rata right, but not an obligation, based on their ownership of issued capital, to participate in subsequent financings of the Company (subject to customary exceptions). Any shares not subscribed for may be reallocated among the other shareholders. The Investors may assign this right to another member of their fund group.

Right of First Refusal and Co-Sale

The holders of the Seed Shares shall have a pro rata right, but not an obligation, based on their ownership of Seed Shares, to participate on identical terms in transfers of any shares of the Company, and a right of first refusal on such transfers (subject to customary permitted transfers, including transfers by Investors to affiliated funds). Any shares not subscribed for by the holders of Seed Shares would then be offered to the holders of Ordinary Shares.

Drag Along

In the event that a Seed Majority and the holders of a majority of the Ordinary Shares wish to accept an offer to sell all of their shares to a third party, or enter into a Change of Control event of the Company, then subject to the approval of the Board, all other shareholders shall be required to sell their shares or to consent to the transaction on the same terms and conditions, subject to the liquidation preferences of the Seed Shares.

Restrictive Covenants and Founders Undertakings

Each Founder will enter into a non-competition and non-solicitation agreement, and an employment agreement in a form reasonably acceptable to the Investors, and shall agree to devote their entire business time and attention to the Company and to not undertake additional activities without the consent of the Investors. A breach of any of the foregoing restrictive covenants or undertakings by a Founder shall result in immediate dismissal for cause of such Founder

Founder Shares

Shares held by the Founders will be subject to reverse vesting provisions over three years as follows: [25% to vest one year after Closing and the remaining 75% to vest in equal monthly instalments over the next following two years.] If a Founder leaves the Company voluntarily or is dismissed for cause, they shall offer for sale to the Company (with a secondary purchase option for the holders of Seed Shares) any unvested shares at the lower of nominal value or subscription price. There shall be acceleration upon double trigger provisions so that if a Founder leaves after a Change of Control, unvested shares may become vested.

Board of Directors

[The board of directors of the Company (the "Board") shall consist of a maximum of three members: the holders of Ordinary Shares may appoint two directors and the holders of Seed Shares may appoint one director.]

	The Lead Investor may appoint a non-voting observer to attend meetings of the Board.
Information and Management Rights	The Lead Investor shall receive weekly reporting and monthly financial information [and a management rights letter to satisfy its venture capital operating company requirements.]
Documentation and Warranties	Definitive agreements shall be drafted by counsel to the Lead Investor and shall include customary covenants, representations and warranties of the Company (which shall be liable up to a maximum of the investment amount) reflecting the provisions set forth herein and other provisions typical to venture capital transactions. The Founders will also complete a personal questionnaire.
Expenses	*Option 1* [The Company shall pay the Lead Investor's fees and expenses in the transaction at Closing, anticipated not to exceed [£XX,000].] *Option 2* [Each party shall pay their own legal and other fees and expenses in the transaction. If the financing does not complete within 60 days or because the Company withdraws from negotiations (except as a result of the Lead Investor making a material change in the terms), the Company shall bear the Lead Investor's legal costs incurred to that date.]
Exclusivity	In consideration of the Lead Investor committing time and expense to put in place this financing, the Company and Founders agree not to discuss, negotiate or accept any proposals regarding the sale or other disposition of debt or equity

securities, or a sale of material assets of the Company for 45 days from the date of the Company's signature below.

Confidentiality	The Company and Founders agree to treat this term sheet confidentially and will not distribute or disclose its existence or contents outside the Company without the consent of the Lead Investor, except as required to its shareholders and professional advisors.
Non-binding Effect	This Summary of Terms is not intended to be legally binding, with the exception of this paragraph and the paragraphs entitled Expenses, Exclusivity and Confidentiality, which are binding upon the parties hereto and shall be governed and construed in accordance with the laws of England and Wales.

Acknowledged and agreed .... Signatures from investors and entrepreneurs

Appendix A: Capitalisation Table

Shareholder	Class of Shares	Number of Shares	Ownership (%)
[FOUNDER 1]	[Ordinary Shares]	•	•%
[FOUNDER 2]	[Ordinary Shares]	•	•%
Lead Investor	[Ordinary Shares]	•	•%
Additional Investor	[Ordinary Shares]	•	•%
Option Pool	[Ordinary Shares]	•	•%
Total		•	**100%**

Investment Theory for "Dummies"

1. Introduction

In this annexure, we look at the logical reason behind the formal economical criteria responsible for economical dispositions.

From a simple assumption about people's impatience (time preference) and rational behaviour, it is possible to deduce the well-known interest calculation formulas.

2. Interest

Everyone knows the term "interest". It is the price of borrowing money, or the payment for lending money out. Financial institutions' prerequisite for paying interest on the money deposited in an account is that they lend the money out at a higher interest.

The nature of the term interest and the size of the interest have, throughout history, been the cause of heated political, moral and religious discussions.

However, you can give a simple economical explanation of the term. Throughout history, there have been many, and today famous, examples on why it is possible to pay a debt back with interests' interest, and why it is not, in particular, amoral to be required to pay these costs.

One well-known example is about the person who borrows money from another person to purchase (or invest in) a batch of freshly pressed wine. As time goes on, the fermentation process will enrich the wine, meaning that potential buyers will pay an increased price for the product. Our investor will, after a few years, be able to sell the wine at a higher price than the person purchased it for. The profit he makes will allow him to pay back his loan with interest.

The moral–philosophical discussion can, therefore, only be about how much he has to pay the loan giver, not if it is fair that he has to pay interest at all.

That a loan giver will demand an interest is logical. The loan giver could have used the money to buy the wine himself or make another investment. Therefore, the loan giver will demand an interest on the loan, which is, at least, equal to the return he could have got by investing the money himself. (This is also known as an "offer" cost.)

3. Impatience as an Explanation of Interest

The deduction of the traditional interest formula is based on what is commonly known as the "impatience axiom".

A rational person will always, if he can choose, prefer a payment of p euros today, instead of a payment of p euros in the future.

This can also be expressed as (the symbol > stands for prefer):

Payment I > Payment II

Where Payment I is a pay-out on p euros at time t and 0 euros at time $t + 1$, while Payment II is a pay-out of p euros at time $t + 1$ and 0 euros at time t.

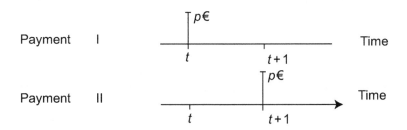

Figure 1 Payment in different time periods.

There are several reasons for this general known phenomenon:

- Consumption opportunities today are more attractive than consumption opportunities in the future.
- It is possible that during period $t \rightarrow t + 1$ to invest the p euros and earn an interest (i.e. the payment for making the money available, e.g. for production for that period: the wine example), so that you, in the end of the first period, not just have the p euros but also the interest.

Let us disregard uncertainty and only consider impatience, i.e. the fact that the present-day usage is preferred for the future consumption, anything else being equal (*ceteris paribus*).

4. Determining the Time Preferences for Tests/Trial

To find a person's time preference, one can imagine the following example/test.

Let us assume a person A is facing the following options: The outcome of a coin toss can be *x* or *y*, faced with a variety of payment plans: plan 1, 2, 3, 4. Person A must pre-select the payment plan to which he is indifferent (does not care) whether the actual outcome of the cast would be *x* or *y*.

Table 1 Various payment plans

Payment plan	If the outcome is X, the following amount is paid today and € 0 in 1 year.	If the outcome is Y, the following amount paid in 1 year and € 0 today
Plan 1	1000	1000
Plan 2	952	1000
Plan 3	909	1000
Plan 4	714	1000

Let us assume that A has the following preferences for the payment plans as shown in Table 2.

Table 2 A's evaluation of the payment plans

For the payment plan 1, the outcome of X is preferred to the outcome of Y
For the payment plan 2, the outcome of X is preferred to the outcome of Y
For the payment plan 3, the outcome of X is similar to the outcome of Y
For the payment plan 4, the outcome of Y is preferred to the outcome of X

If A prefers the payment plan 3, he has indicated that the present value of €1000 paid for 1 year has a value of €909 for him. (He is, in other words, indifferent to whether he gets €1000 for 1 year or €909 today).

One could also put it this way:

The value today (the present value) of a payment in the future of €1000 is for A = €909. Which can also be written as follows:

$$U_1 \times €1000 = €909 \tag{1}$$

where U_1 is the impatience factor or time preference, U_t is deemed to be within the range 0 to 1 for all positive values of t. U_t is often called the discounting factor.

One could also reverse the problem and ask what would A be willing to borrow today if the payback options look like Table 3.

Again several alternative payment plans can be set.

Table 3 Payment plans

	Euros borrowed today	**Euros paid back in 1 year**
Plan 1	1000	1000
Plan 2	1000	1050
Plan 3	1000	1100
Plan 4	1000	1200
Plan 5	1000	1400

Assume that A indicates that the repayment plan 3 fit his preferences. He has now indicated that he is indifferent to having €1000 at his disposal today or €1100 available in 1 year.

This can be written as follows:

The future (for 1 year) payment which is required for A to refrain from disposing of €1000 today is:

$$1000 \times V_1 = €1100 \tag{2}$$

where V_1 expresses the compensation factor or return factor.

It is assumed that V_1 is greater than or equal to 1 for all times in the future.

5. More Time Periods

(A) Discounting

The first line of reasoning can be extended to multiple time periods. Let A be presented with a payment plan which will guarantee him a regular income (P_t euros) over a period of 5 years. What is this payment plan worth for A this year?

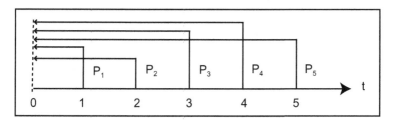

Figure 2 Payments in year t are attributable to time zero.

Each payment must, therefore, be assessed by the principle in the first example (Tables 1 and 2). Using the same reasoning as set forth in (1) will give the total present value (Y_0) of the five payments:

$$Y_0 = P_1U_1 + P_2U_2 + P_3U_3 + P_4U_4 + P_5U_5 \tag{3}$$

where U_t is the impatience factor for the year (t).

U_t can be derived from the following expression (4):

$$U_t = (1 + r)^{-t} \tag{4}$$

where r is the time preference rate, and if we use the symbol $\sum$ for the addition of n elements, (3) can be rewritten by means of (4) as:

$$Y_0 = \sum_{(t=1)}^{5} P_t(1+r)^{-t} \tag{5}$$

and in general:

$$Y_0 = \sum_{(t=1)}^{T} P_t(1+r)^{-t} \tag{6}$$

where Y_0 is the present value (or capital value) of a payment row, which runs in time $t = 1 \to T$.

(B) Interest Expense

The term in equation (2) shows how much A must be paid in 1 year for lending someone €1000 for 1 year. This term can be generalised assuming that the repayment to A not only can happen next year, but also in 2, 3, 4, 5, ..., n years. We can then, e.g. measure the amount A will require to receive in about 4 years to lend €1000 today:

$$V_4 * €1000 = €1464 \tag{7}$$

Or to borrow €1000 today, one should:

In 1 year, payback = €1000 × V_1
Or in 2 years, payback = €1000 × V_2
Or in 3 years, payback = €1000 × V_3
Or in t years, payback = €1000 × V_t

V_t can be developed into the general interest rate formula (8):

$$V_t = (1 + r)^t \quad \text{where } r \text{ is time preference rate.} \tag{8}$$

6. Example of Using Net Present Value Criteria

One can illustrate the present value criteria used by looking at an investment decision. We can assume that person A is in possession of €7000, which he wishes to place/invest in such a way that he gains a return. We may assume that there exist only the following five investment projects that he can place his money in allowed, except for keeping them in his pocket. Each project guarantees a certain payment as showed in Table 4, and there is full security, no inflation, no tax reasons or other circumstances to take into account.

Tabel 4 Investment projects

Investment	Year	Project 1 (€7000)	Project 2 (€7000)	Project 3 (€7000)	Project 4 (€7000)	Project 5 (€7000)
The project	1	1000	1000	4000	4000	0
pays out	2	1000	0	1000	1000	0
each year.	3	1000	3000	1000	1000	0
	4	1000	2000	0	0	0
	5	1000	4000	0	0	10,000
	6	1000	0	0	0	0
	7	1000	0	0	0	0
	8	1000	0	0	4000	0
	9	1000	0	4000	0	0
	10	1000	0	0	0	0
Total		**10,000**	**10,000**	**10,000**	**10,000**	**10,000**

In this example, we also assume that the investment is the same (€7000) for all projects, and each project pays out €10,000 during the 10 years. The payments just fall differently depending on the project.

In the first examples (Table 1), the person A revealed a time preference rate, corresponding to 10%. Let us consider the projects through this time preference rate.

We must, therefore, evaluate expression (9):

$$Y_0 = \sum_{(t=1)}^{10} P_t (1+r)^{-t}, \text{ where } r = 0, 10 \qquad (9)$$

and P_t is the payment each year as indicated in Table 4 to obtain the following present values for the five projects:

Table 5 Present values at 10% discount rate of the projects shown in Table 4

	Project				
	1	**2**	**3**	**4**	**5**
Y€	6.145	7.013	6.911	7.080	6.209

We see that project 4 provides the greatest net present value (NPV), and as this value is higher than the purchase price, it will be advantageous for A to "replace" his €7000 with project 4's payment row, if his time preference rate is equivalent to 10%.

Had A's impatience been less, e.g. corresponding to a time preference rate of 5%, we would have got the following picture:

Table 6 Present values at 5% discount rate of those shown in Table 4 projects

Project					
	1	**2**	**3**	**4**	**5**
Y€	7.722	8.323	8.159	8.288	7.835

We now see that the present value of the payment streams has increased, and what is also interesting is that now it is project 2 which is to be preferred, while project 4 was preferred when the discount rate was 10%. If, however, the discount rate or time preference rate is increased to 15%, the present value of all of the payment streams is less than €7000.

Table 7 Present values at 15% discount rate of those shown in Table 4 projects

Project					
	1	**2**	**3**	**4**	**5**
Y€	5.019	5.973	6.029	6.200	4.972

From these examples, we can see that the "best" project is very dependent on the discount rate used:

Table 8 Ranking of Table 4 projects as a function of discount rate

	Project 1	**Project 2**	**Project 3**	**Project 4**	**Project 5**
r = 0%	I	I	I	I	I
r = 5%	V	I	III	II	IV
r = 10%	V	II	III	I	IV
r = 15%	IV	III	II	I	V

The ranking of the alternatives related to a 15% discount rate indicate "where the loss is minimized, which is also an important information.

The present value of a payment stream/project revenue is very dependent on the discount rate used for the calculation. This also means that payment streams with different payment profiles will be ranked differently if the discount rate changes.

7. Net Present Value

In most investment cases, we talk about NPV. In principle, it is the same reasoning as explained above; we now only introduce two payment streams: income/revenue and cost/investments. The NPV is calculated by combining cost and revenues in one calculation. The discount rate to be used is the "time preference rate", and often risk factors are added to reflect the uncertainty about future cost and earnings. Often this is very simply done by applying a high discount rate.

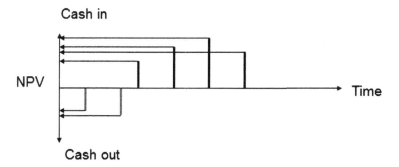

Figure 3 NPV calculation.

By using a high discount rate, future cost and earnings will get a constantly smaller influence on the calculation the further out in the future they materialise. Hence, this is another way of addressing the uncertainty about the future. This is also clearly illustrated if you revisit Table 4–7.

8. Internal Rate of Return

An alternative way of comparing investment opportunities is using the internal rate of return (IRR) method. This method is very simple. The IRR is simply defined as the discount rate which makes the present value of a payment stream equal to 0.

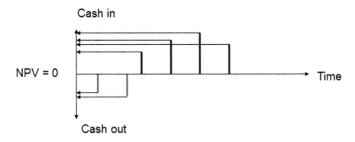

Figure 4 Internal rate of return.

9. Money Times Back

Many investors use the "money times back" method. Some investors will request their money five times back; others require money 10 times back. But often they do not say over how long a period.

Some investors even argue that the IRR method and the money times back method are very different ways of looking upon investments.

But if the time element is introduced, the IRR and money times back method are two sides of the same coin.

- Money 5 times back in 5 years corresponds to an IRR of 38%.
- Money 5 times back in 4 years corresponds to an IRR of 50%.
- Money 10 times back in 5 years corresponds to an IRR of 59%.
- Money 10 times back in 4 years corresponds to an IRR of 78%.

Therefore, both methods are practical methods for quick comparison. However, without taking into account the money involved and the time dimension, it is, strictly speaking, not possible to compare either IRR or money times back from two different projects.

Money times back in 5 years equals a very different IRR than money times back in 10 years. And an IRR of 15% from an investment of €10,000 has a completely different significance with respect to value, compared to the return from an investment of €1,000,000. But investors know this well and use both terms as synonyms when they speak about successful or less successful investments.

10. Return on Investments

This expression is also often used and misused. In the "undiscounted" example in Table 9, we have an investment case of €1 million and estimated cost and revenues over the next 5 years.

Table 9 Undiscounted investment case

	Year 1	Year 2	Year 3	Year 4	Year 5	Sum
Investment	−1000					**−1000**
Cost	−500	−500	−1000	−1000	−1500	
Revenues	50	100	1000	2500	4000	
Profit	−450	−400	0	1500	2500	**3150**
"ROI"						**2150**

It could also look like Fig. 5.

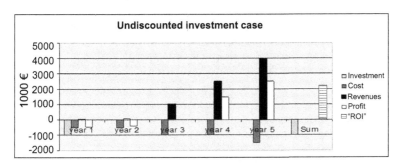

Figure 5 Undiscounted investment case.

However, this case looks different, if you look at it as a pure investment case. In Table 10, the investor invests in year 1 and gets a return in both year 4 and year 5. This would correspond to an IRR of 47%. But if he had to wait until year 5 to get his money, the IRR would drop to 41%.

Table 10 Looked upon as an investment case

€ 1,000	Year 1	Year 2	Year 3	Year 4	Year 5
Investment	−1,000	0	0	1,500	2,500

The cases illustrate that it is important to be sure how a case is described and the assumptions behind before you can judge how financially interesting the case will look in the eyes of an investor.

Annexure 7

Further Readings and Few Abstracts

Dr. Aistë Dirzytë from the Psychological Well Being Research Laboratory, Vilnius, Litauenia, has kindly provided the following relevant abstracts addressing the same issue and with more or less the same conclusions as presented in this book.

'I like how you think': Similarity as an interaction bias in the investor–entrepreneur dyad.

Murnieks, Charles Y.; Haynie, J. Michael; Wiltbank, Robert E.; Harting, Troy. *Journal of Management Studies*, 48(7), 2011, 1533–1561. http://dx.doi.org/10.1111/j.1467-6486.2010.00992.x

ABSTRACT

Investigating the factors that influence venture capital decision-making has a long tradition in the management and entrepreneurship literatures. However, few studies have considered the factors that might bias an investment decision in a way that is *idiosyncratic* to a given investor–entrepreneur dyad. We do so in this study. Specifically, we build from the literature on the 'similarity effect' to investigate the extent to which decision-making process similarity (shared between the investor and the entrepreneur) might bias or otherwise impact the investor's evaluation of a new venture investment opportunity. Our findings suggest venture capitalists evaluate more favourably opportunities represented by entrepreneurs who 'think' in ways similar to their own. Moreover, in the presence of decision-making process similarity, the impacts of other factors that inform the investment decision actually change in counter-intuitive ways.

Investor behavior: The psychology of financial planning and investing.

Baker, H. Kent (Ed); Ricciardi, Victor (Ed). Hoboken, NJ, USA: John Wiley & Sons Inc, 623 pp. http://dx.doi.org/10.1002/9781118813454

ABSTRACT

Why do investors behave as they do? Investor behaviour often deviates from logic and reason. Emotional processes, mental mistakes, and individual personality traits complicate investment decisions and increase the difficulty of comprehending clients' judgements. Behavioural decision-making can also have a detrimental influence if investment professionals ignore or fail to grasp this aspect of decision-making. *Investor Behavior: The Psychology of Financial Planning and Investing* is a collection of must-read chapters by leading scholars and practitioners. This book edited by H. Kent Baker and Victor Ricciardi, two leading experts in the psychology of investing, is indispensable for anyone who works with individual clients and needs to manage those difficult-to-predict investment decisions. This comprehensive volume provides essential contributions to the field of behavioural finance and economics including mental mistakes (heuristics), emotional issues, bounded rationality, biases, and risk perception. *Investor Behavior* also goes beyond the basics, introducing new and cutting-edge research on individual behaviour in areas including financial therapy, motivation and satisfaction, transpersonal economics, personality traits, financial coaching, money and happiness, retirement planning, neurofinance, and evidence-based financial planning. The book concludes with an authoritative selection of developments in such behavioural topics as ethical and socially responsible investing, real estate investing, and mutual funds. Each chapter in *Investor Behavior* focuses on real-world examples that can be easily understood and applied. Readers learn how practitioners are converting new research on human psychology into measurable performance gains. Current best practices and concrete applications for understanding and managing client behaviour are presented alongside clear, scholarly explanations of theoretical principles.

How to trust a perfect stranger: Predicting initial trust behavior from resting-state brain-electrical connectivity.

Hahn, Tim; Notebaert, Karolien; Anderl, Christine; Teckentrup, Vanessa; Kaßecker, Anja; Windmann, Sabine. *Social Cognitive and Affective Neuroscience*, 10(6), 2015, 809–813. http://dx.doi. org/10.1093/scan/nsu122

ABSTRACT

Reciprocal exchanges can be understood as the updating of an initial belief about a partner. This initial level of trust is essential when it comes to establishing cooperation with an unknown partner, as cooperation cannot arise without a minimum of trust not justified by previous successful exchanges with this partner. Here we demonstrate the existence of a representation of the initial trust level before an exchange with a partner has occurred. Specifically, we can predict the Investor's initial investment—i.e. his initial level of trust towards the unknown trustee in Round 1 of a standard 10-round Trust Game—from resting-state functional connectivity data acquired several minutes before the start of the Trust Game. Resting-state functional connectivity is, however, not significantly associated with the level of trust in later rounds, potentially mirroring the updating of the initial belief about the partner. Our results shed light on how the initial level of trust is represented. In particular, we show that a person's initial level of trust is, at least in part, determined by brain electrical activity acquired well before the beginning of an exchange.

Investor perceptions of financial misconduct: The heterogeneous contamination of bystander firms.

Paruchuri, Srikanth; Misangyi, Vilmos F. *Academy of Management Journal*, 58(1), 2015, 169–194. http://dx.doi.org/10.5465/amj. 2012.0704

ABSTRACT

We suggest that, when one firm reveals financial misconduct, others in the industry suffer lower valuations, but do so heterogeneously. To understand this heterogeneity, we conceptualize such contamination as a generalization–instantiation process: investors generalize the culpability to the industry category and perceive the instantiation of generalized culpability within the industry bystander firms. This theoretical separation allows us to hypothesize the factors that affect the degree to which both of these elements of the contamination process occurs. Specifically, we predict that characteristics of the misconduct firm or event—factors that lend to investors' familiarity with the misconduct firms, or that prompt attributions of blame for the misconduct—affect the potency of the generalization of culpability to the industry, while characteristics of the industry bystander firms—investors' familiarity with such firms, or factors that lend to investors' perceptions that they have strong governance—affect the firms' vulnerability to being perceived as instantiating the generalized culpability. We tested our hypotheses on a sample of 725 firms across 84 financial misconduct events, and the results of our event analyses broadly support our predictions. Our study thus has implications for future research on the social view of financial markets, organizational misconduct, and corporate governance.

Are entrepreneurial venture's innovation rates sensitive to investor complementary assets? Comparing biotech ventures backed by corporate and independent VCs.

Alvarez-Garrido, Elisa; Dushnitsky, Gary. *Strategic Management Journal*, 2015, No Pagination Specified. http://dx.doi.org/10.1002/smj.2359

ABSTRACT

Entrepreneurial ventures are a key source of innovation. Nowadays, ventures are backed by a wide array of investors whose complementary asset profiles differ significantly. We therefore assert that entrepreneurial ventures can no longer be studied as a homogeneous group. Rather, we harness the inherent dichotomy in the profiles of independent VCs and corporate investors to study ventures' innovation outcomes. Our sample consists of 545 U.S. biotechnology ventures founded between 1990 and 2003 and backed by independent venture capitalists (VCs) or corporate VCs (CVC). We find CVCs' investees exhibit higher rates of innovation output, compared to independent VC-backed peers. Moreover, the performance of CVC-backed ventures is sensitive to their ability to leverage corporate assets, underscoring the role of CVC accessibility and FDA approval requirements as the mechanisms associated with CVC contribution. Copyright © 2014 John Wiley & Sons, Ltd.

The influence of angel investor characteristics on venture capitalist decision making.

Drover, Andrew William. *Dissertation Abstracts International Section A: Humanities and Social Sciences*, 76(2-A(E)), 2015, No Pagination Specified.

ABSTRACT

It is well established that the social relations of an organization can serve as an important signal of perceived quality (Reuber and Fischer, 2005; Suchman, 1995). Here, an organization's patterns of affiliations are often used by third parties to make inferences about intrinsic quality, which can assist in shaping the perception of that venture (Gulati and Higgins, 2003; Pollock et al., 2010). By extension, this dissertation focuses on how organizational affiliations influence the process of venture capital investment decision making. Specifically, given that angel investors often invest prior to venture capitalist involvement, I draw on signaling theory to explore whether certain characteristics of affiliated angel investors can influence the judgement of venture capitalists. Taking a multi-study approach, I explore this effect through the sequential evaluative process. In study one, I leverage conjoint analysis to investigate the influence of affiliated angel characteristics within the initial screening stage— i.e. whether awareness of certain distinguishing characteristics of vested angels increases the probability that a venture reaches the formal due diligence stage. Study two focuses on the final investment decision; I utilize logistic regression on a secondary dataset of angel-backed ventures in an attempt to understand whether ventures backed by certain angels stand a higher probability of securing venture capital financing than ventures absent such affiliations. Significant effects from both studies support the idea that angels do indeed influence the evaluation and investment activity of formal venture capital investors.

Investor biases in financial decisions.

Sahi, Shalini Kalra, Copur, Zeynep (Ed), 2015. *Handbook of Research on Behavioral Finance and Investment Strategies: Decision Making in the Financial Industry*. Advances in finance, accounting, and economics (AFAE) book series, pp. 147–169. Hershey, PA, USA: Business Science Reference/IGI Global, xxxii, 525 pp. http://dx.doi. org/10.4018/978-1-4666-7484-4.ch009

ABSTRACT

Financial Decisions involve making choices between various investment alternatives, with the aim of increasing the individual's net worth. The investor today is exposed to various investment options, but does not have the knowledge and capability of evaluating all the options and making a rational decision. Due to the limitation in the information processing capacities of the individuals, their beliefs and preferences, the investment decision-making process, gets biased. This chapter highlights ten such biases and throws light on how they impact investment behaviour, both positively and negatively. This understanding of investor psychology will generate insights that will benefit the financial advisory relationship. Further for Individuals, recognizing how the biases impact their financial decisions, can help create self-awareness and an understanding that would help them in better financial management, in case these tendencies are leading them to make unsatisfactory investments

Investor regret: The role of expectation in comparing what is to what might have been.

Huang, Wen-Hsien; Zeelenberg, Marcel. *Judgment and Decision Making*, 7(4), 2012, 441–451.

ABSTRACT

Investors, like any decision maker, feel regret when they compare the outcome of an investment with what the outcome would have been had they invested differently. We argue and show that this counterfactual comparison process is most likely to take place when the decision maker's expectations are violated. Across five scenario experiments we found that decision makers were influenced only by forgone investment outcomes when the realized investment fell short of the expected result. However, when their investments exceeded prior expectations, the effect of foregone investment on regret disappeared. In addition, Experiment 4 found that individual differences in the need to maximize further moderated the effects of their expectations, such that maximizers always take into account the forgone investment. The final experiment found that when probed to make counterfactual comparisons, also investments that exceed expectations may lead to regret. Together these experiments reveal insights into the comparative processes leading to decision regret.

Trust between entrepreneurs and angel investors: Exploring positive and negative implications for venture performance assessments.

Bammens, Yannick. *Journal of Management*, 40(7), 2014, 1980–2008. http://dx.doi.org/10.1177/0149206312463937

ABSTRACT

The study of trust-related outcomes has had a long tradition in the organizational literature. However, few have considered potential darker sides of trust or have explored its effects in the setting of entrepreneurial ventures. This study does so by examining how perceptions of entrepreneurs and angel investors concerning the degree of trust in their relationship impact the latter's assessments of venture performance. Hypotheses are tested using survey data from the lead entrepreneur and angel investor of 54 ventures. Results indicate that angel investors evaluate portfolio company performance more positively when they perceive high trust, whereas entrepreneurs' trust perceptions are negatively associated with angel investors' assessments of venture performance. Further, these effects are partially mediated by the quality of information exchanges between both parties. Together, these findings point to the benefits as well as threats that come with the presence of strong trust in entrepreneur–angel investor relationships.

Do investor capabilities influence the interpretation of entrepreneur signals? Theory and testing in the private equity setting.

Gera, Azi. *Dissertation Abstracts International Section A: Humanities and Social Sciences*, 70(9-A), 2010, 3532.

ABSTRACT

Informing outsiders of the potential and quality of the organization in a way that will benefit the organization and avoid putting it at risk is a challenging task in competitive settings. Under conditions of uncertainty, in which external entities are imperfectly informed about the organization, outsiders will seek for signals of quality. Current research of interfirm signaling has focused on the sender's ability to generate signals. In this dissertation, I propose that receivers of signals are heterogeneous in their ability to interpret signals and that this heterogeneity significantly influences the outcome of the interaction between signaler and interpreter. I apply this insight in an entrepreneurial setting to explain differences in signaling to venture capitalist and informal private equity investors (business angels) over the early stages of a firm's lifecycle. The findings have strong implications for entrepreneurial firms' strategy and, generally, to signaling theory. I argue that signals are multifaceted. Outsiders may base their decisions on two aspects of signal: the informative aspect, which relays direct information on the capabilities of the organization; and, the legitimizing aspect, which conveys legitimacy through actions of third-party entities. The use of each aspect is determined by the abilities of the sender to generate the signal and the receiver to interpret it. I posit that the informative aspect of the signal will be prominent when both the sender's and the receiver's abilities are high. When either the sender's ability to generate a signal, or the receiver's ability to interpret it, is limited, the legitimizing aspect of the signal will be prominent. When both the sender and the receiver possess low signaling abilities, the interpretation will be based on idiosyncratic data. This dissertation explores the differences between these two facets of signals, and the usefulness of each signal aspect when considering the organization's target audience. The first essay explains the purpose of the two signal aspects for stakeholders and the recursive nature of interpretation. The two following essays test the theory by utilising two large datasets of private equity investment solicitations. The second essay evaluates the effectiveness of the legitimizing aspect of the signal as a mechanism for screening startups' funding solicitations. The third essay compares the informative and legitimizing aspects of signals as decision making mechanisms for both angel and venture capital investors.

Index

Printed in the United States
by Baker & Taylor Publisher Services